Vocabulary Instruction for Struggling Students

WHAT WORKS FOR SPECIAL-NEEDS LEARNERS

Karen R. Harris and Steve Graham
Editors

Strategy Instruction for Students with Learning Disabilities
Robert Reid and Torri Ortiz Lienemann

Teaching Mathematics to Middle School Students with Learning Difficulties
Marjorie Montague and Asha K. Jitendra, Editors

Teaching Word Recognition: Effective Strategies for Students with Learning Difficulties
Rollanda E. O'Connor

Teaching Reading Comprehension to Students with Learning Difficulties
Janette K. Klingner, Sharon Vaughn, and Alison Boardman

Promoting Self-Determination in Students with Developmental Disabilities
Michael L. Wehmeyer with Martin Agran, Carolyn Hughes, James E. Martin, Dennis E. Mithaug, and Susan B. Palmer

Instructional Practices for Students with Behavioral Disorders: Strategies for Reading, Writing, and Math
J. Ron Nelson, Gregory J. Benner, and Paul Mooney

Working with Families of Young Children with Special Needs
R. A. McWilliam, Editor

Promoting Executive Function in the Classroom
Lynn Meltzer

Managing Challenging Behaviors in Schools: Research-Based Strategies That Work
Kathleen Lynne Lane, Holly Mariah Menzies, Allison L. Bruhn, and Mary Crnobori

Explicit Instruction: Effective and Efficient Teaching
Anita L. Archer and Charles A. Hughes

Teacher's Guide to ADHD
Robert Reid and Joseph Johnson

Vocabulary Instruction for Struggling Students
Patricia F. Vadasy and J. Ron Nelson

Vocabulary Instruction for Struggling Students

Patricia F. Vadasy
J. Ron Nelson

THE GUILFORD PRESS
New York   London

© 2012 The Guilford Press
A Division of Guilford Publications, Inc.
72 Spring Street, New York, NY 10012
www.guilford.com

All rights reserved

No part of this book may be reproduced, translated, stored in a retrieval system, or transmitted, in any form or by any means, electronic, mechanical, photocopying, microfilming, recording, or otherwise, without written permission from the publisher.

Printed in the United States of America

This book is printed on acid-free paper.

Last digit is print number: 9 8 7 6 5 4 3 2 1

The authors have checked with sources believed to be reliable in their efforts to provide information that is complete and generally in accord with the standards of practice that are accepted at the time of publication. However, in view of the possibility of human error or changes in behavioral, mental health, or medical sciences, neither the authors, nor the editor and publisher, nor any other party who has been involved in the preparation or publication of this work warrants that the information contained herein is in every respect accurate or complete, and they are not responsible for any errors or omissions or the results obtained from the use of such information. Readers are encouraged to confirm the information contained in this book with other sources.

Library of Congress Cataloging-in-Publication Data
Vadasy, Patricia F.
  Vocabulary instruction for struggling students / Patricia F. Vadasy, J. Ron Nelson.
    p. cm. — (What works for special-needs learners)
  Includes bibliographical references and index.
  ISBN 978-1-4625-0282-0 (pbk.) — ISBN 978-1-4625-0289-9 (hardcover)
  1. Vocabulary—Study and teaching. 2. Learning disabled children—Education—Language arts. 3. Reading—Remedial teaching. I. Nelson, J. Ron. II. Title.
  LB1574.5.V64 2012
  372.44—dc23
                                                            2011044147

About the Authors

Patricia F. Vadasy, PhD, is Senior Research Scientist at the Oregon Research Institute in Seattle. Her background is in early reading acquisition and instruction, instructional design, and intervention research. Dr. Vadasy oversees a research team investigating effective school-based literacy interventions for at-risk and struggling students. Findings from her grant-funded intervention research have been published widely in peer-reviewed journals. She is the first author of the Sound Partners code-oriented supplemental tutoring program and coauthor of the Ladders to Literacy preschool and kindergarten programs.

J. Ron Nelson, PhD, is Professor in the Department of Special Education and Communication Disorders at the University of Nebraska–Lincoln. He has extensive training and experience in professional development, child development, explicit and intentional instructional design principles, scientifically based early literacy and reading, randomized field trial research methodologies, and risk factor developmental pathways for learning and mental health problems. Dr. Nelson has written more than 150 articles, book chapters, and books that focus on serving children at risk for school failure and other research issues. He has developed a number of behavior and literacy interventions that have been recognized by the U.S. Department of Education, including the registered behavioral strategy Think Time®, Stepping Stones to Literacy, Early Vocabulary Connections, and the Multiple Meaning Vocabulary program. In 2000, he received the Distinguished Early Career Research Award from the Council for Exceptional Children.

Preface

Teachers across grade levels and content areas endeavor to help students access a wide and useful vocabulary. Vocabulary is key to understanding written and spoken language from preschool through adulthood. The relationship between vocabulary and understanding what we read is well established. A large vocabulary is a pleasure to use in our speaking and writing, and, as Steven Pinker (1994) notes, it uniquely equips human beings to exercise our remarkable ability "to shape events in each other's brains with exquisite precision" (p. 15). The more well developed a vocabulary a person has, the more easily the person can achieve that degree of precision in reading, writing, and speaking.

Students learn an impressive number of words during their school years. Researchers estimate that the typical high school graduate knows between 45,000 and 60,000 word forms, which translates to learning roughly 10 new words per day between the ages of 1 and 17 (Nagy & Anderson, 1984; Pinker, 1994). It might appear that, because students acquire vocabulary at this impressive rate, learning new words must be an easy task. But there are substantial differences in students' vocabulary knowledge, beginning in preschool, and, as with other reading skills, these early differences widen appreciably as they progress through school.

How can teachers help students who have reading and language difficulties acquire new vocabulary? In this book we set out to synthesize research on vocabulary learning and vocabulary instruction. We draw from research that has been conducted across several distinct disciplines, incorporating studies that teachers can use to make informed decisions about their pedagogical practices. We summarize research on vocabulary acquisition and instruction in order to offer teachers useful and practical guiding principles for vocabulary instruction in typical school settings, including instruction for students who need more intensive, nuanced, and responsive vocabulary approaches. The nature of where this information resides and how the research was conducted has led to three important features of our approach.

First, our synthesis reflects an awareness of the diversity of discipline perspectives on vocabulary instruction. There is often limited interchange of research and practice across these disciplines. For example, research in the field of linguistics has informed our understanding of how children learn the meanings of words. Cognitive psychologists have tested theories of word learning, often in laboratory and small-scale studies. Another branch of linguistics has generated research on the features of words that influence learning and instruction. More recent efficacy studies utilizing randomized field trials add information on teacher and classroom influences on vocabulary learning. In writing this book, we drew from all of these sources. The challenge in synthesizing the research from these diverse disciplines is that the principles and practices do not necessarily correspond among them. For example, linguists use relatively precise statistical analyses of the frequency and coverage (i.e., dispersion or distribution) of words in oral and written language to identify important words to consider teaching, while educational researchers use a more conceptual approach to identify these words. Nonetheless, we try to honor these various disciplinary perspectives in our presentation of how vocabulary is learned and how it can best be taught.

Second, we intended our research synthesis to suggest instructional approaches helpful in typical school settings, including those using multi-tiered or response-to-intervention (RTI) models, specific frameworks for assessment and intervention that have been fostered by the Individuals with Disabilities Education Improvement Act of 2004 (IDEIA; Public Law 108-446). Most RTI models feature three tiers of reading intervention and use a problem-solving approach for prevention and intervention. Typically, Tier 1 is primary intervention, the core curriculum provided to all students in the classroom. Tier 2, or secondary, intervention is often provided to students identified through screening or progress monitoring who are not responding adequately to the core curriculum and therefore need supplemental interventions. Tier 3, or tertiary, intervention is reserved for those students who fail to respond to the primary or secondary intervention. However, most of the interventions we describe in this volume were not conducted within RTI models, and most were not recommended for specific multi-tiered applications. Thoroughgoing research on vocabulary instruction within the RTI model, in fact, remains to be done. In the meantime, we properly assume that effective approaches tested in general classrooms are also beneficial to students who require more intensive instruction. This assumption is especially defensible because much of the research has been conducted with populations of students with, or at risk for, vocabulary difficulties. Therefore, the chapters that follow describe vocabulary instructional techniques designed to ensure that all students make adequate vocabulary progress, including both students at risk for school failure and those with high-incidence disabilities, including linguistically and culturally diverse students for whom effective Tier 1 vocabulary instruction is particularly crucial.

Finally, most of the vocabulary approaches we describe as promising and viable were not tested specifically with special education students. As noted above, many were tested in general education classrooms, and some were tested with students with, or at risk for, language difficulties (and therefore used at the Tier 2 or 3 level). The populations included in many of these studies include bilingual learners and English as second language (ESL) learners, and a small number of studies were conducted with special education populations and other at-risk student samples. Our assumption is that many of the small-group and individual approaches are appropriate for use in Tier 2 or 3 interventions with students with disabilities or those with, or at risk for, vocabulary difficulties. Vocabulary skills, unlike more constrained reading skills like letter knowledge or phonological awareness, are more difficult for at-risk students and students with learning disabilities to learn, and therefore require more opportunities for practice.

Given these realities of the research to date in vocabulary skills, this is our approach. We extracted information from the various disciplines that we judged would be of greatest value to teachers. Our objective was practical information on how vocabulary is learned and how it can be most effectively taught.

Because vocabulary knowledge strongly influences reading comprehension, a wide variety of interventions have been studied to increase school-age students' vocabulary knowledge. These interventions in fact begin at preschool. In keeping with a developmental perspective, some of the research we reviewed is from the early childhood field. Young children learn words from spoken contexts and interactions. One widely studied group of related early childhood interventions includes the storybook reading interventions, in which vocabulary is taught in the context of reading aloud and talking about books. Speaking, reading, and written vocabulary vary considerably. These differences call for different teaching techniques for expanding a young child's speaking vocabulary, versus directly teaching older students new vocabulary words and/or strategies to use independently to maximize their incidental learning from reading contexts. At the other end of school-based interventions, we summarize comprehension and word-learning strategies taught to help middle school and older students learn new vocabulary in their independent reading. Many of the principles and practices we highlight characterize effective vocabulary interventions across the preschool through middle school grades. Careful consideration of these principles and practices reveals the key elements that teachers can use to inform their vocabulary instruction.

Included in this book is research from the fields of linguistics and second-language learning, some of which is informed by cognitive processing models as well as by training studies. This work has raised awareness of the importance of vocabulary in language learning, in particular for older students. For example, the work of linguists on word features seems important to consider initially in deciding upon a starting point for instruction—that is, a principled set of key words for inclusion—as well as to review the complexity of words often overlooked in vocabulary instruction. Research on second-language learning likewise targets word corpora that are a high priority for new English language users, including a focus on the types of words that are most important to teach, identified in specialized groups of written word corpora. Linguists have contributed practical information on word features that influence how to teach vocabulary.

Across the developmental span and across these disciplines, we include the teaching strategies that are most promising, based on the research evidence and design features. We elaborate on several prominent approaches and further direct our readers to original studies and published handbooks that include complete information on teaching procedures. Across the fields and teaching approaches, however, we highlight instructional principles that teachers can apply regardless of the reading content they use in their classroom. Teachers have shifting instructional priorities, and the time they can allocate to vocabulary will vary greatly. In some cases, teachers have the opportunity to implement a very intensive vocabulary program. For example, a teacher may be in a school that has adopted a schoolwide approach to vocabulary like the Word Generation program (Snow, Lawrence, & White, 2009). At other times, however, vocabulary instruction may take a "back seat" in a school's teaching agenda. Regardless of the amount of time and energy available for a full-scale vocabulary effort, the instructional principles we spotlight may be applied across the breadth of instructional programs and goals.

Chapters in this book summarize the range of vocabulary topics informed by this cross-disciplinary synthesis that emphasizes practical relevance for teachers. In Chapter 1 we present a developmental perspective on vocabulary acquisition, including a review of the chief metalinguistic influences on vocabulary development; the reciprocal relationship between phonemic awareness and vocabulary; the contributions of morphological awareness to vocabulary and comprehension; the multiple meanings of words; and the contributions of syntactic awareness to reading vocabulary and comprehension. We summarize research on the influence of early language experiences as well as individual differences in children's early vocabulary growth, and we assess their implications for later learning.

In Chapters 2 and 3 we "unpack" aspects of vocabulary knowledge that influence reading and understanding texts. Many words have multiple meanings that are often overlooked in teaching vocabulary, and good readers and writers are sensitive to this aspect of words. Properly understanding morphology contributes to both vocabulary instruction and growth. Word frequency may inform the sequence and choice of vocabulary that is directly taught. Collocations, or words that occur frequently together, may also be useful in planning instruction and in building word patterns and phrases. When teachers plan explicit instruction in individual words, they often draw from word lists. The most widely used word lists, or corpora of words, draw together high-frequency, root, and academic words. We elaborate on the major word collections and their usefulness during particular stages of instruction.

Finally, we review the most widely recommended approaches for vocabulary instruction. Chapters 4 to 6 provide a developmental overview of vocabulary instruction from preschool to middle school. In these chapters we summarize instructional approaches that are either "scientifically based" or "research based." We review their empirical bases and describe the instructional strategies. Because many of these approaches are embedded in research studies, we attempt, to the extent possible, to operationalize them and describe the explicit learning activities. Early preschool and kindergarten approaches include the extensively researched dialogic reading strategy, other storybook reading approaches, and the Early Vocabulary Connections (Nelson & Vadasy, 2008) scripted instruction. School-based approaches include the robust Tier Two vocabulary approach (Beck, McKeown, & Kucan, 2008) and the academic word-learning program Word Generation (Snow et al., 2009). Finally, we review independent learning approaches based on specific word-learning strategies, such as context use, the keyword method, semantic analysis, morphological analysis, and dictionary use.

The two remaining chapters address areas for which there are at present only limited research and resources available. Chapter 7 addresses the current state of the art of vocabulary assessment. In this chapter we review norm-referenced and standardized vocabulary assessments as well as alternative vocabulary assessment approaches. Chapter 8 summarizes the state of our knowledge regarding vocabulary instruction for language-minority students, and we suggest specific ways in which schools can provide comprehensive prevention and intervention approaches for increasing numbers of students from culturally and linguistically diverse backgrounds.

Contents

1. Origins of Vocabulary Knowledge and Its Role in Reading Comprehension ... 1

Chapter Vocabulary 1
Introduction 2
Early Vocabulary Development 2
Vocabulary and the Simple View of Reading Comprehension 4
Acquiring Vocabulary Knowledge 5
Sources of Vocabulary Growth in School-Age Children 10
Instructional Principles 14

2. Word Properties That Affect Vocabulary Instruction ... 16

Chapter Vocabulary 16
Introduction 17
Word Form 18
Word Structure 20
Word Grammar 24
Word Meanings 26
Multiple Meanings 28
Collocations and Idioms 29
Word Frequency 31
Tiers 32
Academic Vocabulary 32
Dictionaries 33
Instructional Points for Language-Minority Students 36

3. Making Principled Decisions about Vocabulary Instruction ... 38

Chapter Vocabulary 38
Introduction 39
Principled Decisions about Teaching and Learning Vocabulary 40
The Sequence in Which Words Are Acquired 43
The Development of Word Lists 44
Word Lists 46
Instructional Implications 60

4. Early Approaches to Vocabulary Instruction — 62

Chapter Vocabulary 62
Introduction 63
Picture Book or Storybook Read-Aloud Interventions 63
Summary 82

5. Evidence-Based Instructional Approaches for School-Age Children: Specific Important Word Meanings — 86

Chapter Vocabulary 86
Introduction 86
Rich and Robust Vocabulary Instruction 88
The Word Generation Program 94
Summary 100
Instructional Implications 101

6. Independent Vocabulary Learning Approaches — 102

Chapter Vocabulary 102
Introduction 103
Semantic Approaches to Vocabulary Instruction 104
Using Context to Learn Word Meanings 107
Using the Dictionary and Other References 113
Remembering the Meanings of Words: Mnemonic Techniques 116

7. Vocabulary Assessment — 120

Chapter Vocabulary 120
Introduction 121
Differences in Conceptions of Vocabulary Knowledge 123
Locating Diagnostic and Outcome Measures 130
Examples of Vocabulary and Language Skills Measures 131
Summary 144

8. Teaching Vocabulary to English Language Learners — 146

Chapter Vocabulary 146
Introduction 146
Effective Vocabulary Instruction for Preschool Language-Minority Learners 148
Effective Vocabulary Instruction for School-Age Language-Minority Students 151
Research Informing Vocabulary Instruction for School-Age English Language Learners 154
Conclusion 166

References — 167

Index — 185

Vocabulary Instruction for Struggling Students

CHAPTER 1

Origins of Vocabulary Knowledge and Its Role in Reading Comprehension

CHAPTER VOCABULARY

Language-minority	In this book we use the term *language-minority* to refer to "individuals from homes where a language other than a societal language is actively used. . . . A language-minority student may be of limited second-language proficiency, bilingual, or essentially monolingual in the second language" (August & Shanahan, 2006, p. 2).
Lexicon	A person's knowledge of words stored in long-term memory.
Metalinguistic awareness	Ability to reflect on and manipulate the features of language, including the subunits of words.
Morphological awareness	Awareness of the structure and parts of words at the level of the *morpheme*, the smallest part of the word with meaning.
Phonological awareness	Awareness of the sounds in oral language and ability to manipulate the sounds in words.
Root word	The *root* is the basic part of the word that carries meaning (like *port* in *transport*), and a *root word* is a root that can stand alone as a word (like *yellow*).
Semantic awareness	Knowledge of word meanings and the relations among words and concepts.

Syntactic awareness   Knowledge of word relations and word usage.

Word family   A base word and its inflected and derived forms (e.g., *love, loves, loving, loved, lover, unlovable, lovingly*).

INTRODUCTION

Across the period of infancy through high school, during which children develop both language and reading skills, vocabulary plays a central role in literacy development. In early childhood and preschool, children rapidly develop their oral vocabulary through interactions with parents, family, and other adults. These early language experiences play a major role in literacy development. During the school years when children are learning to read, their oral language skills interact with emerging code-related skills that underlie skilled reading and writing. Phonological awareness, which plays an important role in early reading development, is closely related to early oral language skills, including vocabulary development. Phonological awareness in turn becomes a prerequisite for decoding skills, which play a prominent role in early reading. Vocabulary, which supports the development of these critical early reading skills, becomes a strong predictor of reading comprehension in the later stages of reading development. These early language skills—including phonological awareness and vocabulary knowledge—are closely interrelated and change roles across time in the development of literacy skills.

Vocabulary knowledge builds up incrementally over time. In this chapter, we describe the development of vocabulary during the preschool period, the factors that influence vocabulary development, and the influence of early vocabulary knowledge on early reading skills. We review the role of vocabulary in reading comprehension and how its role changes as word reading skills develop. We then examine the research on influences on vocabulary learning and describe the primary sources of vocabulary growth in school-age children, incidental word learning, and explicit vocabulary instruction. Finally, we explore the interactions between language and literacy skills that account for the observable differences in students' rate of vocabulary acquisition.

EARLY VOCABULARY DEVELOPMENT

Vocabulary, or knowledge of the meanings of words, is perhaps the most obvious language skill that influences reading development. This is quite clear if you try to understand a sentence in which you don't know the meaning of most of the words—perhaps a page from an advanced physics text. Vocabulary knowledge plays an important role in reading, beginning in the early grades when it influences the development of word reading skills (Jean & Geva, 2009). Vocabulary knowledge is essential for comprehending oral and written language, and as the reading texts become more difficult, it plays an increasingly important role in reading comprehension in both older monolingual (Biemiller, 2003) and language-minority students (August & Shanahan, 2006; Laufer, 1997; Nation, 2001).

Differences among children in their levels of vocabulary knowledge emerge early. In their well-known study of children's early language experiences, Hart and Risley (1995) found large differences between the vocabulary words heard by children in disadvantaged versus more affluent families during the first 3 years of life. Children from families of low socioeconomic status were exposed to dramatically less spoken language and to language much less rich in vocabulary than language used in advantaged families (see Table 1.1).

Early oral language development plays a pivotal role in reading development: the size of children's expressive vocabulary at age 2 predicts a wide range of literacy outcomes through grade 5 (Lee, 2011). Early vocabulary differences create a language gap that is difficult to close, and by the end of second grade students already possess very different levels of vocabulary knowledge (Biemiller, 2005). Students who enter school with comparatively small vocabularies continue to lag behind peers with average vocabularies in their rates of vocabulary acquisition (Biemiller & Slonim, 2001). The native- and second-language vocabulary knowledge of primary school language-minority children both contribute to their English reading comprehension (Carlisle, Beeman, Davis, & Spharim, 1999). Language-minority children who hear less English spoken in the home also know less English vocabulary than their native English language peers, and they also continue to lag behind peers in vocabulary development through middle school (Jean & Geva, 2009; Umbel, Pearson, Fernandez, & Oller, 1992). Even when language-minority students develop their basic English conversational skills, they still need to make up a large gap in their academic vocabulary (Cummins, 1979; Nation, 1990; Scarcella, 2003).

Research on language and vocabulary development in the preschool and early grades suggests how these early language and literacy skills, including vocabulary, are intertwined. One hypothesis (lexical restructuring) is that early vocabulary growth fosters the development of phonological awareness (Fowler, 1991; Goswami, 1999; Metsala, 1999; Metsala & Walley, 1998). According to this *lexical restructuring hypothesis*, vocabulary growth stimulates the child's awareness of the smallest

TABLE 1.1. Differences in the Amount of Talk and Vocabulary Size and Variety in Professional, Working-Class, and Welfare Parents and Children

	Professional		Working-class		Welfare	
	Parent	Child	Parent	Child	Parent	Child
Vocabulary size	2,176	1,116	1,498	749	974	525
Avg. utterances/hr	487	310	301	223	176	168
Avg. different words/hr	382	297	251	216	167	149

Note. From Hart and Risley (2003). Reprinted with permission from the Spring 2003 issue of *American Educator*, the quarterly journal of the American Federation of Teachers, AFL-CIO.

speech sounds in words, called *phonemes*. As the child's vocabulary expands, the young child progresses from recognizing words as whole units, which is sufficient when the vocabulary size is small (e.g., when the child knows only the word *dog*), to recognizing the features that differentiate similar words. As the child's vocabulary size increases, the child develops increasing awareness of these smaller word features. These phonemes differentiate very similar words that are added as the child's vocabulary expands. Through this type of analysis, the child learns to differentiate among such different but similar words as *dog, dot,* and *dock* (Nagy, 2005).

> **Steps in Learning New Vocabulary from Context**
>
> 1. The student pronounces the new word or decodes the word (matches the sounds to letters and blends the sounds).
> 2. The student processes the letter–sound relationship to retain the word's spelling in memory.
> 3. The student works out the syntactic role and the meaning of the word from context.
> 4. The student bonds these phonological, orthographic, syntactic, and semantic identities in memory. Strongly bonded connections enable the student to accurately and efficiently retrieve the word pronunciation and meaning in later word encounters.

Thus, a rich background of language experiences leads young children to discover the constituent parts of words, including phonemes (Dickinson, McCabe, Anastasopoulos, Peisner-Feinberg, & Poe, 2003). These phonemes are later matched to printed letters when the child learns to read words. During the early phase of learning to read words, the child's knowledge of word meanings bootstraps word identification. Finally, the child's expanding knowledge of the meanings of words and their associated networks of concepts incrementally builds the cognitive context for reading comprehension. This process of vocabulary acquisition is described in Ehri's connectionist theory of word learning (Ehri, 1992, 1998, 2005). The sidebar outlines the steps in this process and indicates the points at which a student may need additional help.

VOCABULARY AND THE SIMPLE VIEW OF READING COMPREHENSION

One way of understanding the reading process and its components is the "simple view" model of reading (Gough & Tunmer, 1986; Hoover & Gough, 1990). According to the simple view, reading comprehension is the product of decoding and language comprehension: $R = D \times LC$. During early reading development, reading comprehension (R) and listening or language comprehension (LC) are closely correlated. As the words and structures in texts become more complex, the child encounters words and syntax not used in spoken language. In this simple view, as children develop accurate and fluent decoding and word reading skills in the early elementary grades, decoding has a lesser influence on reading comprehension in the upper elementary grades. At that point, language comprehension including vocabulary knowledge plays a greater role in reading comprehension.

Vocabulary knowledge and the network of word and knowledge connections are, not surprisingly, the strongest predictors of reading comprehension. Children's vocabulary knowledge at school entry predicts word reading ability at the end of first grade (Sénéchal & Cornell, 1993). Vocabulary knowledge continues to predict reading comprehension up through the 11th grade (Cunningham & Stanovich, 1998; Muter, Hulme, Snowling, & Stevenson, 2004).

Although the effects of vocabulary on reading comprehension are more direct in the upper grades, it is important to keep in mind that this relationship is evident even early in reading development (Tabors, Roach, & Snow, 2001). The oral language experiences of early childhood provide the foundation for emergent literacy development, and during early childhood most vocabulary growth occurs through oral language experiences (Nagy & Anderson, 1984; Sternberg, 1985). For young readers through grade 3, reading comprehension and oral language comprehension are very closely intertwined, as their reading vocabulary and speaking vocabulary are similar in difficulty (Sticht, Beck, Hauke, Kleiman, & James, 1974).

Vocabulary knowledge begins to play a larger role in reading comprehension as children begin to read more difficult books in grades 3 and 4 (Chall, Jacobs, & Baldwin, 1990; Scarborough, 2001; Storch & Whitehurst, 2002) and as reading materials feature increasingly more difficult vocabulary in the upper grades. Many students need to build their vocabulary in order to comprehend these more challenging school texts, particularly children who enter school with lower language and vocabulary skills, children with high incidence disabilities, and children from homes in which English is not the primary language.

Steps from Theory to Practice

- Use early language experiences to stimulate phonemic awareness, syntactic awareness, and the acquisition of word meanings.
- Stop to point out new words—act them out or illustrate them.
- Provide definitions of new words in reading contexts.
- Draw attention to the letters and spellings of the words.
- Have students pronounce the new words, and repeat them aloud several times to create an accurate memory and pronunciation–meaning link (Rosenthal & Ehri, 2008, 2011; Silverman, 2007a; Silverman & Crandell, 2010).

ACQUIRING VOCABULARY KNOWLEDGE

What exactly do we mean when we talk about "learning a word"? Linguists have diverse notions of what a word is. In some cases, the same word may have two very different meanings—like the word *loaf*, which means both "a shaped mass of bread" and "to idle." These are two distinct meanings that the student needs to know, and for the purposes of instruction both meanings need to be learned (at some point).

Then there is the question of whether the inflected forms of a root word are separate words—like the forms *sing, singing,* and *sings.* For the purposes of instruction, these inflected forms do not need to be taught as separate words because children also learn the morphological rules for adding inflections to use the word forms correctly in a sentence. For the purpose of vocabulary instruction, it makes sense to consider meanings as most relevant but also to pay attention to student knowledge of the morphological rules (i.e., how to add inflections and affixes) and grammar that support correct word usage.

What does it mean to know a word well enough to understand its meaning in text? Recent research confirms that both the breadth and depth of vocabulary knowledge matter. Vocabulary *breadth* describes the number of word meanings known. Some words are stored in the student's *lexicon*, or mental dictionary of word knowledge, just well enough to be recognized again but not necessarily well enough to be fully understood or used correctly. Vocabulary *depth* describes how well each word is known, which develops through repeated encounters with the word in varied contexts. Vocabulary breadth is often assessed with receptive measures that require pointing out or marking the correct word in a multiple-choice test or exercise. Vocabulary depth is measured through tasks that require the student to produce a written or spoken definition or response or to identify correct usage of the word in context. Research suggests that the depth of vocabulary knowledge contributes to reading comprehension beginning in the early grades and continues to influence comprehension for older students (Nation & Snowling, 2004; Oullette, 2006; Snow, Tabors, Nicholson, & Kurland, 1995).

Vocabulary knowledge includes knowledge of word meanings as well as the web of knowledge or semantic associations that develop around words. Students draw upon this background knowledge in comprehending text. For example, a student whose parents have read aloud to him or her many books about animals and have discussed them at length with the child are able to draw upon this oral and written knowledge when he or she independently reads other books about animals. Language-minority students also draw upon their knowledge of words and concepts acquired in their first language as they are learning to read in English (Ordonez, Carlo, Snow, & McLaughlin, 2002).

Students learn words both incidentally and incrementally through their oral language and reading experiences. These language experiences vary, depending on their family's social, economic, and educational characteristics (Hart & Risley, 1995; White, Graves, & Slater, 1990). By school age, vocabulary expands increasingly through encounters with new words in reading. School-age children's word-learning opportunities afforded by listening, talking to others, and reading books continue to vary widely. Less skilled students read much less than average readers and skilled readers and therefore may encounter fewer unknown words (Allington, 1984; Nagy & Anderson, 1984). This *reciprocal* relationship between vocabulary and comprehension is thought to boost the development of reading skills through increased amounts of reading (Fielding, Wilson, & Anderson, 1986; Nagy, Anderson, & Herman, 1985). As students develop skills in word reading, vocabulary, and

The Matthew Effect and the Role of Vocabulary Instruction	
Children's early experiences create differences in vocabulary knowledge.	Early childhood and preschool programs should offer high-quality literacy experiences and parent involvement and education.
Students with higher vocabulary levels have better comprehension.	Teachers should select books and novels to match the student's independent reading level and preteach difficult vocabulary.
Students who know more words and have better comprehension enjoy reading more and therefore read more.	Teachers should provide explicit vocabulary instruction to foster interest in words and to "catch up" students with lower levels of vocabulary.
Students who enjoy and read more learn more vocabulary through incidental word exposures.	Teachers should continue explicit vocabulary instruction in oral read-alouds while focusing on word spelling and pronunciation.

content knowledge, they read more, are exposed to more words, learn some of these new words through incidental exposures, and apply their expanding vocabulary and domain knowledge to better comprehend what they read (Anderson, Reynolds, Schallert, & Goetz, 1977; Anderson, Spiro, & Anderson, 1978). This process is described as the "Matthew effect" (i.e., that early differences in literacy skills have far-reaching consequences on later literacy; Stanovich, 1986; Walberg & Tsai, 1983, 1984). Vocabulary knowledge thus confers an advantage in developing early reading skills as well a broader knowledge base that bolsters comprehension (Sternberg, 1985).

Reading experience is a powerful influence on vocabulary development (Cunningham & Stanovich, 1998). The importance of reading as a source of higher-level vocabulary is illustrated in research on the number of rare words (those not likely to be in the spoken vocabulary of a typical student) that students encounter in television programs, children's books, and adult conversation (Hayes & Ahrens, 1988). Students encounter 50% more rare words in children's books than in television or adult conversations. Moreover, print information provides a richness and depth of knowledge that are not provided in electronic information sources or personal experiences (Hayes & Ahrens, 1988). Put simply, children who read little will have fewer opportunities to learn new words or to expand their knowledge base, skills that enhance reading comprehension.

This reading experience is important to develop vocabulary breadth. But recall that word learning is an incremental process—and often more extended and intensive for students with language and learning difficulties. It often begins when a student indicates a shallow level of knowledge of a word. This initial word knowledge may be adequate for the student to recognize the word in context but not necessarily sufficient for him or her to use the word in writing. During the early stages of word learning, the student may have a fuzzy knowledge of a word, as reflected in Dale and O'Rourke's (1986) levels of word knowledge.

1. "I never saw the word before."
2. "I've heard of the word, but I don't know what it means."
3. "I recognize this word in contexts, and it has something to do with . . ."
4. "I know the word!"

As the student gains more experience with the word, learns to recognize and produce its written form, sees it used in different contexts, discovers how it is related to other words, and practices using it in speech and writing, his or her knowledge of the word sharpens and becomes more precise.

The way that word meanings are often initially acquired in an incidental fashion is called "fast mapping," that is, laying out the knowledge of partial meaning. This partial meaning is reinforced with more word encounters and with the acquisition of related words (Gershkoff-Stowe & Hahn, 2007). This process eventually becomes "extended mapping" (Carey, 1978), which describes the period of time—often years—taken to fully learn a word.

Other commentators have outlined the various dimensions that describe vocabulary depth. One outline (Cronbach, 1942) postulates five dimensions:

1. Defining the word.
2. Choosing situations in which to appropriately use the word.
3. Knowing different meanings of the word.
4. Knowing exactly how to apply the word in different situations.
5. Using the word in discourse.

Another framework (Russell & Saadeh, 1962) used to describe vocabulary depth elaborates the following features:

1. Precision of knowledge to discriminate between words similar in meaning (e.g., *compose* and *comprise*).
2. Breadth in the number of different words and the number of different meanings of words (e.g., several meanings for the word *vessel*: a ship, a bowl, a tube carrying blood).
3. Ability to use the word in reading, speech, and writing.

These frameworks for incremental word learning illustrate the importance of providing multiple exposures to a word in varied contexts as well as opportunities to use the word in spoken and written contexts in order to know and "own" many words. As children build their world knowledge and deepen their knowledge of words and their appropriate uses and multiple meanings, their knowledge of words and concepts deepens. Children who know more words and develop rich networks of vocabulary knowledge are able to utilize this knowledge in their reading comprehension (Verhoeven & Van Leeuwe, 2008). Finally, the child builds knowledge of a specific word to the depth that "I know it, I can define it, and I can use it correctly" (Dale, 1965).

This brief overview returns us to the question of what it means to know a word. We learn some words to an adequate level for use in *receptive* functions—in listening or reading. Other words must be learned more deeply for *productive* functions—in speaking, reading, and writing. Each of the nine aspects of knowing a word outlined by Nation (2001, p. 21) has both a receptive aspect and a productive aspect:

Form	Spoken	R	What the word sounds like.
		P	How the word is pronounced.
	Written	R	What the word looks like.
		P	How the word is written and spelled.
	Word parts	R	What parts are recognizable.
		P	What parts are needed to express meaning.
Meaning	Form and meaning	R	What meaning the word form signals.
		P	What word form is used to express this meaning.
	Concept and referents	R	What is included in the concept.
		P	What items the concept can refer to.
	Associations	R	What other words this word calls to mind.
		P	What words can be used instead of this one.
Use	Grammar	R	In what patterns the word occurs.
		P	In what patterns the word must be used.
	Collocations	R	What words or types occur with this word.
		P	What words or types must be used with the word.
	Use constraints	R	Where, when, how often we encounter the word.
		P	Where, when, how often we can use the word.

We most often think of teaching vocabulary as word centered; yet, words often appear in the company of other significant groups of words. Such *collocations* embrace the other words commonly encountered with the target word. For example, the vocabulary word *search* has a collocation that might include *rescue, engine, seizure, party, light,* and *warrant.* As you learn progressively more about any new vocabulary word, you come to know the other words often encountered with the target word, and you learn the other words that you must use with the target word; for example, repeated encounters with the word *toxic* may lead the learner to its associations with the words *substance* and *levels*. Experience with a word also builds knowledge of collocations that better enable correct and productive use of the word—for example, to know that the word *urge* is associated with *to* rather than *for*. New English learners often have difficulty in knowing which words go together (e.g., we say "afraid of the dark," not "afraid from the dark"). Teaching word collocations adds depth of knowledge, including knowledge about common word usage.

SOURCES OF VOCABULARY GROWTH IN SCHOOL-AGE CHILDREN

Readers who have been motivated to expand their reading vocabulary may have tried listing unfamiliar words they encounter in their reading. They may look up the definitions, write them down, and review their lists, with good intentions, until they have learned the words. Readers may often find this is only a moderately successful strategy. Why it may fail to result in learning words well enough to use them in varied contexts has something to do with how words are normally learned through incidental encounters in text and direct instruction.

Incidental Word Learning

There is general agreement that incidental word learning is the major source of vocabulary learning. Recall that the average size of the typical undergraduate student's vocabulary is 20,000 words, meaning that native English speakers learn some 1,000–2,000 root words per year, or 3–7 words per day (Anglin, 1993; Nagy & Anderson, 1984; Nation, 1990). It would be impossible to directly teach enough vocabulary to ensure that students create this knowledge base, and therefore it is fortunate that vocabulary learning also occurs automatically while reading (Jenkins, Stein, & Wysocki, 1984; Nagy et al., 1985; Stanovich, West, Cunningham, Cipielski, & Siddiqui, 1996).

Incidental word learning occurs through word exposures during independent reading, oral discussions, and reading aloud (Brabham & Lynch-Brown, 2002; Bus, van IJzendoorn, & Pellegrini, 1995; Elley, 1989; Nagy, Anderson, & Herman, 1987; Penno, Wilkinson, & Moore, 2002; Schwanenflugel, Stahl, & McFalls, 1997; Swanborn & de Glopper, 1999). Young children who are exposed to low levels of oral language and older students who engage in little reading learn less vocabulary through context. Most vocabulary growth in school-age students occurs with wide reading. Even 20 minutes of daily reading is estimated to result in learning 1,000 new words each year (Nagy et al., 1987). Students are more likely to acquire new vocabulary through independent reading if they have strong reading skills and read books well matched to their reading level that are rich in vocabulary. Wide reading is a less useful source of extensive vocabulary growth for younger readers, struggling readers, students with high incidence disabilities, and language-minority students. These students will continue to benefit from oral language experiences that expose them to new words and engage them in conversations about texts that feature richly diverse (often academic) vocabulary. Reading aloud to students in books just above their independent reading level provides a source of vocabulary exposure for less skilled readers.

Acquiring word meanings incidentally in context is—not surprisingly—an incremental process. When Swanborn and de Glopper (1999) reviewed studies of incidental word learning through typical reading, they found that students learn about 15% of unfamiliar words they encounter in texts. The likelihood of word learning was greater for students in higher grade levels and with superior reading abilities. Success in inferring word meanings from the context also depends upon the proportion of unknown words in the text and the types of words (e.g., verbs appear to be easier to correctly assess than nouns; Liu & Nation, 1985). The depth of knowing that students take away from incidental exposures is quite varied. The likelihood of partial word learning from context is higher than the likelihood for more complete word knowledge. Incidental word learning is influenced by two processes. First, the student needs to be able to *derive* the meaning of a word from the context. Successfully deriving a word's meaning from the surrounding context generally depends upon what proportion of words in the text the student already knows. Some estimate this figure needs to be as high as 90–95% (Laufer, 1988). Second, the student must be able to *remember* the meaning of the word. Instruction in how to use context to derive word meanings may improve word learning from context. Instruction that improves memory for words, such as the keyword method (discussed in detail in Chapter 6), may also increase the depth and retention of incidental word learning. Finally, the contribution of incidental word learning to vocabulary growth depends upon how much a student reads. While incidental word learning may add significantly to the vocabulary of a student who is a voracious reader, it may add little to the vocabulary of a student who rarely engages in independent reading. Students who do little free reading may be disproportionately those students who struggle with reading skills. They may choose reading materials that are easy, and they therefore encounter few new and unknown words. They may have a more limited basic reading vocabulary, including knowledge of academic and function words, which limits their skills in learning new words. They may lack the skills to notice or to use context to derive the meanings of unfamiliar words. Incidental vocabulary learning through reading will be more limited for these students—another example of the "rich get richer" pattern described as the Matthew effect (Stanovich, 1986).

Maximizing Incidental Word Learning

- Encourage students to engage in wide reading daily.
- Match students to books at their independent reading level.
- Read aloud to students in books just above their independent reading level.
- Teach the skills used in deriving word meanings from context.
- Teach appropriate academic vocabulary that supports students' ready access to grade-level texts.

Teaching Word Meanings

The important role of vocabulary knowledge in advancing one's reading comprehension has led researchers to study the most effective methods of teaching word meanings. We devote Chapters 4 and 5 to reviewing the studies on research-based approaches for both preschool and school-age children. When the National Reading Panel (2000) reviewed the research on vocabulary approaches, it considered 50 studies that met its review criteria, most of them relating to students in grades 3–8. The panel's instructional conclusions included:

1. Vocabulary should be taught both directly and indirectly.
2. Repetition and multiple exposures are important.
3. Learning in rich contexts is valuable.
4. Students should be actively engaged in learning tasks. [A recent meta-analysis of vocabulary instruction studies found that higher levels of vocabulary outcomes were associated with interventions that used higher levels of discussion (Elleman, Lindo, Morphy, & Compton, 2009).]
5. Dependence on a single instructional method will not result in optimal learning. (National Reading Panel, 2000, pp. 4–27)

The panel's conclusions echoed three principles of instruction that Stahl (1986) had derived from earlier research:

1. Teach context and definitions—through multiple activities and multiple contexts.
2. Encourage "deep" processing of words through connections to different contexts, related words, and background knowledge; and stimulate deeper mental effort and deep reasoning about words.
3. Provide multiple exposures to words in different contexts, and assure that students are given adequate time per new word learned.

The key importance of an adequate vocabulary in reading development argues for our devoting time to formal vocabulary instruction. Students clearly learn much vocabulary from context—progressively more if they read more—and they learn some vocabulary as well from explicit teaching.

Because teachers must be parsimonious in choosing vocabulary for explicit instruction in Tier 1 settings, it is important to choose carefully the words that offer the greatest benefits for teaching intensively. In Chapter 3 we describe the features of widely used word lists that teachers may use to guide their word selection. Word selection leads to a question often pondered by linguists, namely, What do we *count as a word* in estimating vocabulary size, constructing a vocabulary test, or selecting vocabulary targets? Linguists must deal with this problem of related word forms (e.g., *run, runs, running, runner; habit, habits, habitation, habitable*) by identifying a *base* form (e.g., *run*) and inflected and derived forms. Together, these word forms constitute a *word family*—related words that share an underlying common meaning. Most estimates of vocabulary size reflect the number of word forms rather than word families.

Researchers have suggested word targets for explicit vocabulary instruction. One priority is *high-frequency* words that appear in grade-level texts. Several lists are often used as resources for teaching high-frequency words (see Chapter 3) or word families (e.g., the *Living Word Vocabulary*, Dale & O'Rourke, 1981; the *University Word List*, Nation, 1990; the *Academic Word List*, Coxhead, 2000). High-frequency *root word* meanings (e.g., *admire*) are a particularly worthwhile target for instruction because students can often independently figure out the meaning of derived words (e.g., *admirer, admiration*). Biemiller (2009) has identified the sequence in which new root word meanings are learned between grades 2 and 6 to guide this instruction.

There is considerable support for vocabulary instruction that is "rich," "deep," and "extended." These terms are often used together or interchangeably, referring to approaches that emphasize extended instruction and student interactions with new words. *Depth* and *richness* of instruction are features of many research-based vocabulary approaches. *Depth* is characterized by elaborated instruction as well as multiple exposures and opportunities to use words in speaking and writing, including manipulating the word and its various forms, relating it to associated words and experiences, and employing it in speaking and writing on occasions that present opportunities for feedback, particularly outside of the classroom (Coxhead, 2006; McKeown, Beck, Omanson, & Perfetti, 1983; Nation, 2001; Stahl & Nagy, 2006). Comprehensive instruction is direct, situated in the context of wide language experiences, and includes instruction in word learning strategies (Stahl & Nagy, 2006). This rich and deep instruction builds word consciousness intended to lead to independent word learning.

Deep vocabulary instruction approaches are based in part on *the depth of processing hypothesis* (Craik & Lockhart, 1972a; Craik & Tulving, 1975) that suggests students learn better when they are required to use the words, relate the words to other words, concepts, and experiences, and provide reasons for their word choices. This deep processing requires both attention and effort that affect whether or not the word is remembered. When students are required to discriminate among similar words, for example, or to discuss the use of the word, they learn about correct usage that is more difficult to teach explicitly, and they may also reveal their misunderstandings about the word, enabling these to be corrected.

Experts in teaching vocabulary and cognitive psychologists who study language learning agree that effective vocabulary instruction involves both *deep processing* of words and *repetition* (Baddeley, 1990; Coxhead, 2006; Craik & Lockhart, 1972a; Craik & Tulvig, 1975; Nation, 1990; Sokmen, 1997; Stahl & Nagy, 2006). *Repetition* seems to be most effective when there is some time between repetitions, but not too much time. Spaced retrieval of words and their meanings (Baddeley, 1990) means that the word is not simply repeated eight times when it is first introduced. Rather, the research suggests that when the word is initially introduced the repetitions should be spaced closely together in time. These repetitions should require the student to retrieve and recall the word—to bring either the word or the meaning forward in memory. Later repetitions of the word should be spaced further apart. However, there is no exact formula for spacing these reviews because so many variables typically influence instruction and the student's memory (e.g., the time of year when the word instruction is initiated, the difficulty of the word). A general principle might be to cluster the early repetitions, exposures, and practice opportunities for a word and then continue to review the word, but spacing out the later repetitions. Some 16 repetitions may be needed to properly establish one's memory of a new vocabulary word. These repetitions also build the student's fluency in recognizing new related vocabulary that permits greater understanding of the text (Schmitt, 2008). Finally, effective instruction avoids introducing interference between similar words. This recommendation entails spacing out instruction in words that look the same, sound the same, and/or are similar or opposite in meaning (e.g., do not introduce *disperse* and *dispense* together).

Direct vocabulary instruction is effective in helping students learn target words and may also transfer to gains in comprehension (Beck, Perfetti, & McKeown, 1982; McKeown et al., 1983; see review by Elleman et al., 2009). Use of the rich vocabulary instruction approach appears to also benefit language-minority students (Shanahan & Beck, 2006) and students with little initial vocabulary knowledge (Silverman & Crandell, 2010), often with supplemental support through pictures or illustrations, added oral language activities, and scaffolded practice in using the words. Vocabulary learning by students with learning disabilities is often constrained by their relatively inefficient learning strategies and lower levels of word knowledge. Learning words from independent reading is much more difficult for these students as well, making direct instruction of vocabulary even more crucial for them than for students with stronger learning and language skills. Research supports the added benefits of direct approaches to vocabulary instruction for students with learning disabilities, and these benefits apply across all grade levels (Jitendra, Edwards, Sacks, & Jacobson, 2004). This research suggests that repeated instructional encounters and extended practice in using words is critical to longer-term learning and generalization, especially for this population of learners.

INSTRUCTIONAL PRINCIPLES

This body of research on the origins of vocabulary knowledge suggests the following instructional principles. These principles underscore the important role of the child's early language environment and the significant influence of early adult–child language interactions on vocabulary and language learning. The principles summarize effective ways in which teachers can both foster vocabulary learning for all students and even help those children who arrive at school with limited language and vocabulary skills to improve their skills.

1. The oral language environment that children experience *before* they enter kindergarten develops a vocabulary base and background knowledge that support skilled reading.
2. Early vocabulary knowledge supports the development of phonological and decoding skills that are needed for word recognition.
3. Children entering school with impoverished vocabulary knowledge normally do not catch up with their peers under a typical classroom instruction regimen alone unless a strong vocabulary intervention or emphasis is added.
4. Vocabulary knowledge plays an increasingly important role in reading comprehension in the higher grade levels.
5. Knowledge of many word meanings is acquired incidentally through wide-ranging reading.
6. Incidental word learning is more likely to occur with repeated word encounters and for students with stronger reading skills and disproportionately in the higher grades.
7. A greater depth of vocabulary knowledge results from repeated and varied interactions that require active processing of new words. Students at risk for reading problems and with learning difficulties generally need more intensive and varied opportunities to interact with words to acquire new vocabulary.
8. Directly teaching word meanings has a positive effect on vocabulary learning and benefits students' overall reading comprehension.

CHAPTER 2

Word Properties That Affect Vocabulary Instruction

Chapter Vocabulary

Affix A prefix or suffix (e.g., *pre-*, *-ful*).

Collocation A word grouping that commonly occurs associated with a particular word (e.g., for *event*: *main event, current events, in the event of*).

Concordance An alphabetical index of all the words in a text or corpus of texts, showing every contextual occurrence of a word.

Derivations Related words formed by adding an affix to a root, often changing both the meaning and the part of speech (e.g., *intense, intensive, intensify, intensely*).

Grammar A term having several meanings, the most immediately relevant being (1) the structural patterns observed in putting words together in sentences and (2) the rules that people agree to follow in constructing sentences.

Homonym A term that includes homophones, words that sound the same but have different meanings (e.g., *rain, reign, rein*), and homographs, words spelled the same but have different meanings (e.g., *wind* in the trees, *wind* the clock).

Idiom A multiword unit. There are core idioms and figurative idioms. Core idioms consist of words often grouped together (e.g., *for the most part*). Figurative idioms are often colorful phrases whose meaning is different from the ordinary meaning of the individual words (e.g., *a can of worms, raining cats and dogs*).

Inflections	Words formed by adding an ending that indicates number or tense (e.g., *-s, -es, -ed*).
Lexicon	A person's mental dictionary of words and meanings.
Morpheme	The smallest meaningful part of a word. Morphemes may be free or bound. In the word *shoeboxes, shoe* and *box* are free morphemes, and *-es* is a bound morpheme that indicates number.
Polyseme	A word or phrase that has multiple related meanings (e.g., *flat* as in thin, *flat* as in a deflated tire, *flat* as in a place to live, *flat* as in a type of shoe).
Prefix	A morpheme added to the beginning of a base word (e.g., *re-, mis-*).
Root	The basic morpheme in a word or word family.
Suffix	A morpheme added to the end of a base word (e.g., *-est, -ity*).
Synonyms	Words that are similar in meaning (e.g., *big, large*).
Syntax	Patterns of arranging words in phrases or sentences.

INTRODUCTION

Teachers face numerous decisions in planning how best to teach vocabulary. Students in a typical classroom have a range of vocabulary skills and gaps. Yet, if as a general goal we expect that students should learn about 1,000 additional word families a year to adequately build their vocabulary, most of them will need purposeful instruction to acquire words at this rate. Children who enter school already far behind in vocabulary knowledge will need even more intensive instruction to help them catch up. Second-language learners will need instruction to close the gap in their English word knowledge. Students at risk and with learning disabilities normally need supplemental vocabulary instruction; since their less developed word learning skills, lower levels of independent reading, and often shallower levels of word knowledge serve as obstacles to efficient independent vocabulary learning. Students with strong language skills also benefit from instruction that expands their core vocabulary. All students learn some new word meanings through incidental exposure, but they nonetheless benefit from explicit instruction intended to build up their vocabulary. There is a continuum along which words are known—some known less well, less automatically, and others known more deeply in ways that

> **Word Examples**
>
> Throughout this chapter we use two different kinds of words as examples of how to consider these word features when teaching vocabulary. The first word is a high-frequency academic word often encountered in school texts, namely, *interpret*. The second word is a lower frequency "interesting" word, *magnanimity*.

enable them to be productively used in reading and writing almost automatically. Word features influence the depth of knowledge a student accumulates for each particular word.

How do word properties influence word learning and vocabulary instruction? In this chapter, we discuss the specific features of words that affect how they are learned, which primarily relate to each word's form and meaning. We also address word frequency, an aspect that teachers often use to categorize words and make decisions about which ones to teach.

WORD FORM

A word's *form* includes the phonological and orthographic features that affect its pronunciation and spelling. Students learn the phonological identity of a word when they can map the individual phonemes onto the letters to successfully pronounce the word. Students have knowledge of the word's orthographic identity when they know how the word is spelled and can recognize it by its spelling pattern. And although teachers often do not give much thought to pronunciation and spelling when they plan vocabulary instruction, careful attention to both of these word features deepens the student's knowledge in terms of vocabulary learning. Students' multiple exposures to word spellings develop their knowledge of the written word form, helping them remember new vocabulary pronunciations and definitions (Rosenthal & Ehri, 2008, 2011).

Word forms, or spellings, are often acquired by L1 (primary-language) students through repeated exposures to the words and are learned more easily because they gradually have become familiar with the regularities and features of English spellings. For example, native English-speaking students learn to recognize the spelling patterns that represent the sounds in English words. English language learners (ELLs), however, are generally not as familiar with the regularities (or irregularities) of English spellings, and for these students it is especially helpful to make the link explicit between the word form and the meaning (Ryan, 1997; Schmitt, 2008; Sparks et al., 1997).

A set of related word forms makes up a *word family*, including the inflected and derived forms of the *base* word. Students need rules for creating and spelling each word form, for its pronunciation, and of course for its specific meaning (e.g., as with *create, creator, creationist, creation, creative, re-create*).

Pronunciation

Correctly identifying the constituent phonemes that make up the letters of a word is necessary for correct pronunciation, word learning, and using the word correctly in speech with confidence. A word's pronunciation becomes closely connected in one's memory to its spelling and meaning, and its correct spelling helps form a more complete mental representation of the word in one's mind. Students who cannot pronounce a word correctly normally have greater difficulty retrieving its meaning, its spelling, and/or using the word properly in speech or writing. Students with speech and articulation problems generally have greater difficulty in pronouncing a new word correctly. Words that are difficult to pronounce are more difficult to learn and remember (Ellis & Beaton, 1993). For language-minority students, in particular, words that are difficult to pronounce correctly may be more difficult to learn, and pronounceability may be influenced by the differences in language features between the students' native language and English (i.e., language-minority students may experience special difficulties in differentiating English vowel sounds and the related spelling).

When a word is first introduced to students, it is important that they understand and pronounce it correctly. Teachers should present the written word form clearly and provide a model of the correct pronunciation. Teachers should also provide opportunities for students to repeat the word several times and use it in simple sentences, with immediate feedback given on pronunciation and syllable stress. The following interaction illustrates one step in the sequence for teaching the word *devastate*:

> **Introduce Word Spelling and Pronunciation**
>
> Our first word example, *interpret*, is a root word. Present the written form when teaching the word to help students pronounce this root correctly. Likewise, many of its derivations may be challenging to pronounce, and their pronunciation should be modeled to help students adjust to the stressed syllable in each word form: *interpretive*, *interpretation*, *misinterpretation*.
>
> The word *magnanimity* with its series of *m*'s and *n*'s is a tongue twister for many adults who are familiar with the word. Provide exposure to the spelling to help students learn and remember the pronunciation. This is a word that calls for explicit pronunciation modeling and practice.

TEACHER: (*Refers to the word written on the board while talking.*) Look at this word—it's one of our new words—*devastate*. It means "to destroy or damage something badly." Everyone say the word with me—*devastate*.

STUDENTS: (*Respond while looking at the spelling of the word.*) Devastate.

Spelling

Spelling is often overlooked in vocabulary instruction, given the natural tendency to focus on word meanings. Vocabulary knowledge, however, includes learning to recognize the written word form. Spelling the word correctly helps students remember both how to pronounce it correctly and also its meaning (Rosenthal & Ehri, 2008, 2011). Word spellings become stored in memory. The associations between word spellings and pronunciations support word reading, and the spelling also activates the word's meaning. Research by Rosenthal and Ehri (2008) suggests that teachers should present the written word forms and have the students take note of the

> **Don't Forget to Show Word Spellings**
>
> Taking our two word examples, instruction would begin by introducing each word and indicating its respective spelling. Then model correct pronunciation, having students repeat the word until they can pronounce it correctly. If students still cannot say the word correctly, more deliberately demonstrate how the pronunciations specifically map onto the spelled-out morphemes and affixes.

spelling when teaching word meanings. Such a procedure helps students form the strong orthographic–phonological–semantic connections that characterize depth of word knowledge. Knowledge of its correct spelling also enables the student to use the word productively in writing. Language-minority students whose first, or native language (L1) has a different writing system generally experience greater difficulty in learning English word spellings and pronunciations. Naturally, English words with *irregular* spellings or verbal forms are especially difficult for them to spell correctly.

WORD STRUCTURE

Features of word structure that affect word learning include *morphology, derivations,* and *inflections*. Morphology describes the structure of words, as they are made up of small pieces called *morphemes*. *Derivation* has to do with the process of making related words out of root words—for example, by adding affixes. *Inflection* describes the process of changing a word to reflect its proper use in a sentence—so that, for example, it indicates the appropriate number or verb tense. Students usually master knowledge of inflections first (in the primary grades), and then they begin to develop their knowledge of derivations (Carlisle, 1995, 2000; Nagy, Diakidoy, & Anderson, 1993).

Morphology

A *morpheme* is the smallest unit of meaning in language. A *root* is the most basic morpheme in a word or word family. A *root word* (e.g., *dance, bird, home*) is the simplest kind of word and contains the core meaning for understanding related (e.g., derived and inflected) words (e.g., *dancing, dances, birds, birder, homes, homeless*). The root is the part of the word to which *inflections* and *affixes* are added (e.g., the root of *alacrity* is *alacr-* and the affix is *-ity*). An inflection can indicate verb tense, number, and degree. An affix indicates function (i.e., whether the word is a noun, adjective, or adverb—as with the word family for the verb *create* that includes *creator, creative,* and *creatively*). Affixes can also radically modify the meaning of the base word (e.g., changing the root word *form* to *reform*) and include both prefixes and suffixes (e.g., *pre-, de-, -able, -tion*).

Although the pronunciation of morphemes may vary across word forms, as these examples illustrate, their spelling is more fixed and is often helpful in figuring out the meaning of derivations. Students who learn to pay attention to the spelling of word roots are better able to use this orthographic knowledge to acquire new vocabulary words that are derivations. For example, students who notice the spelling regularity in the root word *plastic* (a word the student already knows) and *plasticity* (a word derivation the student has not encountered before) will be able to use this information to derive the meaning of the new word. Research shows that this knowledge of morphemes is related to word recognition as well as to reading comprehension (Nagy, Berninger, & Abbott, 2006; Nunes & Bryant, 2006).

Derivations

Derived words are made up of a *root* and an *affix*, which may be a *prefix* (before the root) or a *suffix* (after the root). Derived words are semantic variations on the root word. A derivational affix may often change the part of speech of the root (e.g., *polite, politeness*). Consider that derived words make up most of the vocabulary growth in children between grades 1 and 5 (Anglin, 1993). By grade 5, students know five times as many derived words and idioms as root words. By this time, they are also able to figure out the meanings of inflected or derived words through morphological analysis—that is, when they know the root word and the meanings of the affixes (Anglin, 1993). Table 2.1 lists the most common affixes and their meanings.

> **Don't Forget to Model and Practice Correct Word Pronunciation**
>
> In our word examples, the word *magnanimity*, a noun, may be taught with its adjectival form *magnanimous*. Again, teach the meanings of these words with the written forms of the words clearly present, specifically pointing out the spellings of the word base (*magnanim-*) and affixes. Note that the placement of the syllable stress in the base changes in these two affixed forms, and be sure to model this pronunciation correctly and to have students practice the correct pronunciations.
>
> The second example word, *interpret*, is the root word (and also the root) and can be altered with affixes to produce many words, including *interpret-er, interpret-ive, interpret-ation, mis-interpret*, and *re-interpret*. Model the specific pronunciations to show how the stressed syllable may change in the derived forms.

Given how important derived words are in promoting vocabulary learning, researchers generally recommend explicit vocabulary instruction in morphological awareness (Nunes & Bryant, 2011). Such instruction may include discriminating the correct spelling of derived and inflected forms and teaching the meanings and grammatical functions of morphemes. Some derived words are more difficult to analyze than others. For example, in some cases a derived word changes the pronunciation of the base or root word, as in, for example, *inhibit* and *inhibition*. Yet, a student who knows the word *inhibit* and its spelling will normally be able to deduce the meaning of the derived word *inhibition*, particularly in a clue-rich context. While the knowledge of word parts (morphemes, prefixes, suffixes) and parts of speech (nouns, verbs, adjectives) will not assure that students figure out the meaning of every morphologically complex word, certain word parts are well worth knowing and being taught.

TABLE 2.1. Common Affixes and Their Associated Meanings

Prefixes		Suffixes	
Prefix	Meaning	Suffix	Meaning
ab-	from	*-able, -ible*	is, can be, able
ad-	to	*-age*	action, process, belonging to
anti-	against	*-al, -ial*	relating to
com-	with	*-ance*	state, quality of
contra-	against, opposite	*-ar, -er, -or*	one who
de-	from, away, down	*-ary*	place for
dis-	not, opposite	*-ed, -t, -d*	past tense
en-	in, into	*-en*	to make
equi-	equal	*-ent*	one who, that which
ex-	out of, former	*-er*	more, one who
for-	prohibit	*-ess*	female who
hemi-	half	*-est*	most
hyper-	excessive	*-ful*	full
im-, in-	not, into	*-ic*	relating to
inter-	among, between	*-ion, -tion, -ation*	condition of
intra-	within	*-ing*	happening now
mal-	bad	*-ish*	relating to
mega-	large	*-ism*	state, quality of, doctrine of
meta-	change, beyond	*-ist*	one who
micro-	small, short	*-ity*	state, quality of
mid-	middle	*-ive, -tive, -ative*	inclined to
mis-	wrong, not	*-less*	without
multi-	many, much	*-ly*	resembling, like
neo-	new	*-ment*	state of
non-	not	*-most*	most
over-	too much, beyond	*-ness*	being
poly-	many	*-or*	one who
post-	after	*-ous, -eous, -ious*	full of, having
pre-	before	*-s, -es*	plural
pro-	Before, forward, favor	*-ship*	state, quality of
pseudo-	false	*-some*	having, like, inclined to
re-	back, again	*-ward*	direction
semi-	half	*-y*	being, having
sub-	under, beneath		
super-	above, beyond		
trans-	across		
ultra-	beyond		
un-	not, opposite of		
under-	below, less than		

In fact, some 20 prefixes account for fully 97% of the prefixed words that appear in school reading materials (White, Sowell, & Yanagihara, 1989), suggesting a definite benefit to teaching these affixes. Further, the majority of words student encounter in school texts are affixed and/or compound words that are morphologically transparent (Nagy & Anderson, 1984), making them comparatively easy for students to figure out by using their knowledge of word roots and word parts.

Research suggests that teaching the most common prefixes (e.g., *re-*, *un-*) should begin around the fourth grade (Stahl & Nagy, 2006). Since suffixes (e.g., *-ity*, *-ious*) have meanings that are more difficult to explain, instruction is often targeted at the secondary level, but they can be introduced earlier whenever there are opportunities to teach them in a supportive reading context.

> **Introducing Word Derivations**
>
> When derivations of *interpret* and *magnanimity* are introduced, their pronunciations and spellings may require added instruction. If the related words *interpretive* or *interpretation* are taught, spelling and stress changes that influence pronunciation should be noted. These derivations may be difficult to pronounce: *misinterpretation, reinterpretation*.
>
> Students may have more difficulty correctly pronouncing derivations of *magnanimity* and the word relative *magnanimous*. It will be worthwhile to compare the two word forms, compare the spellings, and model and note the consistent spelling of the word base (*magnanim-*), and also note changes in stress and pronunciation when the affix is added.
>
> Both of these root words provide strong meaning clues to their various derived forms.

> **Teaching Spelling Patterns That Underlie Spelling Rules**
>
> - Present a group of one-syllable words that illustrate the spellings of two groups of words with short vowels and long vowels that end in *-ing*.
> - Present the words *skip, trot, stop, shop, cram, leap, plow, wait, float, shout*.
> - Add the suffix *-ing* to each word in these two groups.
> - Have students look for the patterns for adding the suffix to each type of word.
> - Help students state the rule for adding *-ing* to one-syllable words that have a short vowel; then do the same for words with a long vowel or vowel team.
> - Dictate a set of new one-syllable words (e.g., *trap, plan, drag, skim, knit, grow, reach, faint, fail, gloat*), and have students generate the spellings of the words with the *-ing* inflection by using the rules that were just derived.

Inflections

An *inflection* is a word ending that creates a syntactic variation of the root word (e.g., *write, writing*). Inflections may express that a noun is plural or that a verb is in the past tense, or they may express degree in comparative forms (e.g., *happy, happier, happiest*). Inflections may change the grammatical role of a word and/or the spelling of a word. Students usually master knowledge about inflections by the second grade, generally being able to use this knowledge to produce the correct forms of the words (Carlisle, 1995). Most native English-speaking students understand how to use the different inflected forms of words and do not need explicit instruction in grammatical functions (although English language learners may require more instruction on these inflected forms).

Knowledge of inflections enables young students to increase their vocabulary by more readily absorbing whole word families—which include all of the inflected and affixed forms of a root word. For example, the word family of inflections for the word *document* includes the additional forms *documents*, *documented*, and *documenting*. Students who struggle with the spelling rules for adding inflections can be instructed in how to use dictionaries or spell check to confirm the correct spelling of the forms. While certain generic rules apply to most verb tense formations, teachers should urge students to notice and become familiar with the spelling patterns for different types of words (Graham, Harris, & Chorzempa, 2002).

WORD GRAMMAR

A word's syntactic role, or part of speech, is a feature that influences vocabulary instruction and learning. In order for students to use new vocabulary words correctly, they need either an explicit or implicit understanding of grammar. Grammar is the set of rules that specifies how words are used in sentences. For example, nouns and verbs and some adjectives are used to refer to concepts. Words that are prepositions and articles, on the other hand, have meanings that depend on their role in a sentence. The word's part of speech will determine how it can be used, and rules of syntax allow us to build correct phrases and sentences that we all can understand. To know that a word is a noun or a verb helps the student to use a new word correctly. For example, a student who does not understand that the new word *innovate* is a verb and know how verbs are used may use the word incorrectly, as in the following sentence:

> **Student incorrect sentence:** Edison was an *innovate* who gave us many useful things.

A student who knows that *innovate* is a verb and knows the rules for using verbs in a sentence is able to use the word correctly in a sentence like this one:

> **Student correct sentence:** We had to *innovate* in our cooking class because we ran out of an ingredient.

Teaching grammar is, of course, a subject unto itself (often a hotly debated one), and instruction in grammar is conducted throughout the elementary school grades. When teaching vocabulary, however, grammar can be included as part of teaching a word's meaning, its part of speech, and how it is used in the structure of a sentence. Grammar can also be emphasized when students are taught how to use a dictionary. Point out the dictionary notation for part of speech, grammatical patterns such as plurals and inflections, and dictionary usage examples—information that students can use when they independently look up new vocabulary words and attempt to use the new words correctly.

Vocabulary activities should be structured to provide opportunities for students to practice using new vocabulary under conditions in which they receive immediate feedback on correct usage. For example, an initial exercise in usage might have students fill in the blanks with the target word, using sentences that illustrate correct usage, and having students choose from a group of words that differ in their parts of speech.

> **Example fill-in-the-blank practice sentence for the new vocabulary word (the verb *conduct*):** The scientist decided to _____ an experiment to test his theory. (subject, *conduct*, concept)

Later practice would have students use the word in speech or in writing and receive feedback on its usage, including why the word was used properly or not.

> **Example of an incorrect student-constructed sentence using a newly introduced vocabulary word (the verb *conduct*):** The scientist did a *conduct* to test the chemical.

This exercise allows the teacher an opportunity to review the meaning of the word and to emphasize that *conduct* (in the meaning being taught) is a verb and therefore cannot be used as a noun. To *conduct* is to do something, and it requires an object, as in this sentence:

> **Student-corrected sentence:** Our science class *conducted* a small test on the melting point of ice.

The teacher then confirms that this is the correct use of the word *conduct* as a verb in the sentence.

Scaffolded Introduction of New Vocabulary

Taking our first chapter vocabulary example, *interpret*, instruction may be scaffolded to offer students practice in using the word correctly. An early activity may require students to choose the correct word form to complete a sentence:

He offered an _____ of the statistical analysis. (interpreted, *interpretation*, interpretive)

The zoo has a new _____ exhibit on African elephants. (interpretation, *interpretive*, interpreter)

After practice with a scaffolded multiple-choice sentence, create sentences that require students to fill in the correct related word form on their own, without suggested choices. Provide corrective support for subject–verb agreement and syntax.

The team of UN _____ assisted in delivering medical care to the refugees. (*interpreters*)

WORD MEANINGS

The word feature we most often consider when planning vocabulary instruction is the word's meaning. We often think of the meaning as constituting a one-to-one match with the word. Yet, word meaning is quite a complex feature, primarily because many words have multiple meanings. The more frequently a word appears, the more meanings it is likely to have. High-frequency words get heavy use. People begin to use these words in slightly different ways, and often over time a word may take on new shades of meaning that gradually evolve into new distinct meanings. While a relatively rare word like *sprocket* often has only one meaning, a high-frequency word like *check* (e.g., to write a *check*, to *check* up on Grandma, to mark a *check* in a box, to have a medical *check*-up, a *check*ered pattern on a scarf) may have many meanings. The common words *cold, cool,* and *hot* that originally indicated temperature have come to have very different meanings—as in a really *cool* movie, a *hot* ticket item, the *cold* war, a *cold* shoulder. For words with multiple meanings, teachers must often choose the meaning most useful to teach. Words with multiple meanings may be more difficult for students to learn, and English language learners may be particularly confused by multiple meanings. Teachers often need to decide whether to teach these multiple meanings as separate or as related and nuanced shades of one meaning. If a word has several meanings that are very closely related, for example, often the closely related meanings won't need to be taught explicitly and separately.

> **Word Meaning Facts**
>
> High-frequency English words often have multiple meanings.
>
> - Choose the most useful meaning to teach for a multiple-meaning word.
> - Word meanings can be taught with definitions, pictures, examples, and related words.
> - The construction of dictionary definitions makes them difficult for many students to understand.
> - For a multiple-meaning word, find and teach a core meaning that extends across several meanings.

We most often think of teaching a word meaning as providing a definition. Yet, there are many ways to teach word meanings. With younger children or students with limited English skills, we may teach a word meaning with the help of pictures or gestures. This approach is most useful in teaching words (particularly nouns) whose meanings can be readily illustrated or acted out. It is difficult to teach a word meaning that is highly complex or abstract solely with pictures or gestures (e.g., a picture of a child *pouting,* or modeling a *solemn* face). Some words can be taught by providing examples that either illustrate or help the student deduce the meaning (e.g., eating the same food over and over again might illustrate *tedious*). Some words might be introduced by providing a more familiar synonym for the word (e.g., "*Recompense* is like a *reward*") or in some cases by providing an antonym that contrasts the new word with its opposite (e.g., "*Seldom* is the opposite of *often*"). Knowledge of a word's synonyms and antonyms adds to one's depth of word knowledge.

We most often teach and learn new vocabulary through *definitions*. Explicit vocabulary instruction usually means providing the definition of the word to explain the word's meaning. Teachers and students consult dictionary definitions as sources of word meanings. While dictionary definitions may seem to be the most accurate source for word meanings, as Stahl and Nagy (2006) have warned, there can be problems with dictionary definitions. First, the meaning of a word depends upon the context in which it is used (e.g., a student who chooses the meaning for *posture* that refers to the position of the body may not necessarily understand a sentence in which *posture* is used to mean an attitude toward something). Second, definitions don't tell us how to correctly use a word (e.g., a student may take away an understanding of the word *precedent* that leads to using it as a noun, but incorrectly, as in "My Halloween costume was a *precedent*, and I wore it again this year"). And third, the language of dictionaries is often opaque and circular (e.g., *convergence*: "the act, condition, or quality of converging").

A common vocabulary activity is to have students look up a list of new words in the dictionary and write down their definitions. Yet, dictionary definitions are often a dead end for students—for the reasons just noted. Fortunately, there are several ways to help students better understand dictionary definitions. First, consider that publishers of dictionaries must include so many words that they have developed conventions intended to save space. Most dictionary definitions are constructed in phrases that save space but that are sometimes cryptic (e.g., "melodramatic—having the emotional appeal of melodrama"). Second, many dictionary definitions take the Aristotelian approach of describing the word in terms of a larger class or group to which the word belongs and then providing information on how the word *differs* from other words in that main class (see Stahl & Nagy, 2006, pp. 182–194, for an extended discussion). For example, *The American Heritage Dictionary* (1985) defines *pincers* as "a grasping tool having a pair of jaws and handles pivoted together to work in opposition." As Stahl and Nagy (2006) point out, this is an unnatural language form, and many students need instruction to understand this convention. Definitions often include academic language and require knowledge of related words and subcategory concepts that the student may not know. When students are asked to provide a formal definition, the task therefore reflects both a certain breadth and depth of word knowledge (see Vermeer, 2001). Constructing a definition often requires the use of academic vocabulary and the knowledge of the words used to construct the definition (e.g., a *forest* is a *dense growth* of trees that covers a large *area*).

Familiarizing students with this definition structure helps them make better sense of dictionary definitions. Students also need to know what to do when the dictionary provides several definitions for a word (see below). Because so many words have more than one meaning, it is useful to teach students how to determine whether there is a common or core meaning that is shared across various the definitions. Begin instruction with this central meaning, and gradually develop depth of knowledge by adding information on the secondary meanings.

MULTIPLE MEANINGS

Polysemes are words that have multiple related meanings, such as the *road* to recovery and the *road* to town, or a *grave* in a cemetery and a *grave* offense. Textual analyses reveal that about 40% of dictionary entries contain more than one meaning, with each entry averaging about 2.3 meanings and high-frequency words particularly prone to multiple meanings (Nagy, 1997). Some words with multiple meanings may confuse students who know only one common meaning (Bensoussan & Laufer, 1984) (e.g., for the word *command*, "to give an order" is often the first meaning learned, and the student may not know the less common meaning "to deserve and receive," as in "to *command* authority").

One type of word with multiple meanings is a *homograph*, a word that has two identical forms with different meanings. For example, the word *tear* has a noun form (a *tear* in the fabric) and a verb form (to *tear* the page). Words can also have different nuances of meanings, depending upon their use in context. For example, the word *whiff* in the phrase *a whiff of prominence* may be understood in a text by the reader's past encounters with the word (e.g., "a whiff of lilac," "a whiff of smoke") and its use in the newly encountered phrase and context.

Teachers often need to decide which meanings to target for instruction. For some words, the meanings are so similar that it is most useful to teach a core meaning. For example, when teaching the word *meet*, the dictionary may feature several meanings that are very closely related, For example "(1) to come face to face with, (2) to come into contact with, (3) to come together to deal with." It makes sense to introduce the core meaning and to help students analyze these related meanings to identify what they have in common—perhaps for this word, the common meaning is "to contact."

Other words with multiple meanings may have one meaning that is much less commonly used. For example, unless this is a meaning that needs to be taught in relation to a text that is being read, it would make sense to teach a more common meaning for the word *cry* "a loud sound or shout" before teaching its meaning "to declare publicly or proclaim."

Introducing Multiple Meanings

The first word example, *interpret*, may have several meanings: "to find the intended meaning of something; to express your own ideas about what something means; to translate between languages." One way to help students differentiate these meanings is to use the word in a sentence that illustrates these different meanings:

It is difficult to *interpret* this legal document.

I *interpret* the music to express sadness and loss.

The translator *interpreted* the senator's speech.

Discuss each sentence and ask students to identify the particular meaning ilustrated in each sentence. Ask students to generate a sentence that illustrates each meaning.

COLLOCATIONS AND IDIOMS

The basis for teaching some word chunks—including idioms and collocations—is the research on language processing that shows that learners seek to identify the patterns observable in language (for example, the clusters of letters) that occur most frequently. These patterns get recognized more easily because they are processed as chunks or units rather than on a letter-by-letter or word-by-word basis. These patterns include words that occur together and are meaningful units (idioms like "make no bones," "pony up," "mint condition") and words that native speakers frequently group together (collocations like the word phrases "make a point," "a tight budget," "a heinous crime," "safe and sound"). Depth of word knowledge in part reflects the networks of word relations for a particular word that students build over time with use and repeated exposures to a word in reading contexts. This model describes word knowledge as the number and type of connections between words rather than knowledge of isolated words (see Meara, 1997).

Collocations are words that are often used together, that is, common word pairings or groupings. Because these words predictably co-occur in text with each other, they become mentally linked in our personal lexicon. Teaching collocations can help students use words properly and learn words that are often and best used together, and many words are more effectively taught in examples that feature commonly occurring collocations. For example, collocations for these following words include:

Point	*make a point, point out, case in point, key point*
Resource	*natural resource, limited resource, water resource, limited resource, resource dependent*
Significant	*significant finding, significant problem, significant change, significant factor, significant role, significant difference*
Green	*green grass, green bean, green energy, green with envy, green thumb*

Some vocabulary experts recommend teaching word phrases as an efficient way to help students use vocabulary correctly. Widely available concordance dictionaries, software, and search engines can provide lists of specific word pairings and their frequency for teachers' use in planning instruction. When a word has many collocations that students are likely to encounter (and this will vary greatly, depending upon the specific word and the student's grade level), it is useful to include these in the instruction. A useful learning exercise may be to have students find or recall the collocations for a new word. Familiar collocations also facilitate learning some word meanings because they create complete units of meaning and do not require the student to work out the meaning and relation of each word in the phrase (Ellis, 1997). Teaching collocations is often an aspect of instruction for college-level students who are not native English speakers. It may also be especially helpful for younger language-minority students who are not familiar with English word usage. For example, general knowledge of collocations may help students avoid these errors in word usage:

Usage Errors	Correct Usage
Quick food	Fast food
Make a crime	Commit a crime
Slice the grass	Cut the grass
Make action	Take action

Introducing an Academic Vocabulary Word

Our vocabulary example word, *interpret*, is a high-frequency academic word with several collocations that may be useful to include for instruction:

Interpret the results.
Interpret the graph, figure, chart, map.
Interpret accurately, literally, easily.

To develop depth of knowledge about the word *interpret*, compare and contrast the word with other types of mental operations (e.g., *criticize, examine, summarize*).

Some collocations or common phrases will have a meaning distinct from the meaning of the individual words, as in these collocations: *key point, raw deal*.

Word learning reflects not only the knowledge of meanings and co-occurring words but also some familiarity with meaning relationships. As students learn and organize new word items, they also devise categories that begin to characterize their lexical knowledge. These hierarchical relations help to deepen students' vocabulary knowledge. For example, students may first learn the meaning of the words *water* and *wood* and then later learn that these are types of *resources*. Even later they can draw upon these semantic networks to construct greater understanding of the texts they read about such concepts as conservation and the environment.

Idioms are groups of words that we use together in a standard phrase, the correct meaning of which cannot necessarily be figured out solely by knowing the meaning of the individual words. Some idioms and expressions act like high-frequency words, and their meaning is based on the entire phrase rather than on individual words (e.g., we cannot interpret the

---

Teaching Points for Idioms and Collocations

- Idioms are word phrases that have a unique meaning different from the literal meaning of their individual words.
- Teach common idioms to help students understand these phrases, to use them correctly, and to foster a greater love of and interest in language.
- Collocations are words that often appear together. Teach collocations that help students use words correctly.

meaning of the idioms *go bananas* or *can of worms* on a word-by-word level; Nation & Waring, 1997). The words in an idiom are grouped in a familiar phrase, have meaning as a unit, and therefore cannot be separated without losing their unique meaning. They often have interesting origins. Many word meanings are more easily learned because the words occur in idioms or phrases that support their comprehension (e.g., *murky* waters, *rudderless* ship, even-*keel*).

WORD FREQUENCY

A word's frequency of appearance is a feature that importantly affects word learning and instruction. About 80% of the running words (i.e., the main body of words) in academic texts are *high-frequency* words (Nation, 2001); that is, ones that appear over and over again in texts. When it comes to choosing which words warrant the instructional time and effort needed to teach individual words explicitly, high-frequency words are most often considered the logical choices (Biemiller, 2009; Coxhead, 2006; Nation & Waring, 1997). A number of word-frequency lists compile how often words appear in certain types of texts, with some of these lists focusing on specific word types. The most popular word-frequency lists include:

- The Most Common 100 Words in English (Fry, Kress, & Fountoukidis, 1993). These 100 words, which collectively make up about half of all the text words encountered, include such words as *the, of, and, I* and *at*.
- The Dolch List (Buckingham & Dolch, 1936) includes 220 high-frequency sight words that account for some 50–75% of all words read by students.
- The *Living Word Vocabulary* (LWV; Dale & O'Rourke, 1981) is a list of 44,000 root words and derived forms tested with students in grades 4–12 to identify the order of word learning. The LWV is ordered by age groups. Biemiller (2009) has taken a subset of LWV root word meanings (chiefly those known by 40–80% of students at the end of grades 2 and 6) as a guide for words worth teaching in the primary and upper elementary period.

When using a frequency list to guide instruction, it is important to consider when the list was developed. Older lists may be based on a corpus of words from written texts that may be dated, as word usage changes over time. Some lists are based on running words in text rather than word families and collocations that may not be counted but may merit separate instruction (e.g., *identity theft, flip-flop, regime change*).

Because most words have multiple meanings, lists that focus on word meanings and their frequency are very useful. Dale and O'Rourke's (1981) *Living Word Vocabulary* list, for example, describes word meanings that are acquired by given grade levels and the proportion of students who know each word by that level. This list has been updated by Biemiller (2009) to describe root word meanings, including LWV meanings, known by students in grades 2–10. While older lists were often compiled by hand, the newer electronic lists of words that teachers and researchers have compiled enable users to readily access specialized lists and keep them updated.

TIERS

Researchers have tried to categorize words to help guide a sequence for explicit vocabulary instruction. Frequency is one useful way to organize words. The researchers Beck and McKeown (1985) categorized words in three tiers to identify word targets for instruction. Tier One includes basic words that most native English-speaking children know and understand. These are often high-frequency words. Tier Three includes words that are low-frequency and that often appear in specialized texts. Tier Two includes high-frequency words used by skilled language users. These are words that add a level of precision and richness to written and verbal language use and that often occur across domains. Beck, McKeown, and Kucan (2002) identified Tier Two words as productive targets for vocabulary instruction. Chapter 3 describes in greater detail Beck et al.'s (2002) rich vocabulary approach, in which Tier Two words are made the focus of vocabulary instruction.

> ### Introducing a Tier Two Word
>
> Our chapter vocabulary example *magnanimity* (and its derivation *magnanimous*) is a Tier Two word. Because it is unfamiliar to many students upon introduction, it is very important to provide student-friendly sentence examples in which the word is used.
>
> The winning team was *magnanimous* in sharing the prize.
>
> Then the teacher can show how the word *magnanimous* gives more precision to the sentence than these Tier One words:
>
> The winning team was *great* to share their prize.
>
> The winning team was *kind* to share their prize.
>
> Point out how the word *magnanimous* carries the meanings of generosity, unselfishness, high-mindedness—meanings that the words *great* and *kind* do not convey.

ACADEMIC VOCABULARY

One particular type of high-frequency word list specifically identifies academic words, the words that play an especially important role in academic learning. These are the words that occur most frequently in school texts and that become increasingly important as students move through school—such words as *establish, principle, relevant, minor, interact, justify, context,* and *assess*. Perhaps the most widely used source of this type is the *Academic Word List* developed by Coxhead (2000), which identifies some 570 word families frequently appearing in written academic texts. These words, 80% of which have Greek or Latin origins, account for about 10% of the words in these texts. The list is divided into 10 sublists based on frequency, enabling teachers to target the word families that occur most often. Although the list was originally developed for use by teachers in preparing students for university-level study, it includes many words that middle school students commonly encounter in texts and use and that are therefore valuable for earlier instruction. The list is included as an appendix in the Coxhead (2006) volume and is also available online (*nottingham.ac.uk/~alzsh3/acvocab/index.htm*). In Chapter 5, we describe the Word Generation program (Snow et al., 2009) for teaching academic words to middle school learners.

DICTIONARIES

Dictionaries are an important independent learning tool. Lifelong vocabulary learning requires the effective use of dictionaries. There are many kinds of dictionaries, including dictionaries of slang and word phrases as well the more familiar dictionaries of word meanings. There are also many differences among dictionaries of word meanings that make them more or less useful for young users. Dictionaries differ in the clarity of their definitions and in their comprehensiveness (how many words are included). They also differ in whether or how well they describe word features like pronunciation, grammar, word origins, word phrases, and derivatives. Dictionaries differ in their conventions; for example, some list multiple meanings for a word in chronological order, while others list the most current widespread use first. An important consideration for young users is how well the dictionary illustrates usage and whether the emphasis is on correct versus common and widespread usage.

Providing students with a functionally useful dictionary is extremely important (Graves, 2006)—one that (especially crucial to lower-skilled and language-minority students) has clear and well-written definitions. A study by Miller and Gildea (1987) revealed that students who looked up words in the dictionary and then wrote sentences using those words often took away a limited understanding of the words and their correct usage (as revealed by numerous inapposite sentences). This shortcoming might be attributable to the way the definitions are written or how the meanings are organized. Thus, for example, given a weekly list of vocabulary words to look up and learn, a student might unwittingly choose to write and learn a less commonly used meaning for a word with multiple meanings. If the student chooses *"to make amiable and agreeable"* as the meaning to learn for the adjective *supple*, she may not be able to understand the word's use in the sentence on the weekly vocabulary test: "The ballet dancer did regular exercises to keep her joints *supple*." Again, teachers are best advised to begin by teaching a word's most common meaning and then later expanding instruction to teach the finer discriminations in multiple meanings (Coxhead, 2006).

Some dictionaries are more helpful than others in learning word meanings. The COBUILD (Collins Birmingham University International Language Database) dictionaries that originated in the United Kingdom provide word definitions in the form of complete sentences rather than phrases; these sentences, in turn, closely reflect actual usage in the corpus of words upon which the dictionaries are based. British and American newspapers, books, television programs, and spoken conversations (about 25% of texts are American, and 5% from other English-speaking countries; Collins Birmingham University, 2003) are the chief sources of the corpus. The dictionaries include phonetic transcriptions of words, some collocations and synonyms, and, most important for students, an example sentence for nearly every word entry. The COBUILD dictionaries were originally created for a British audience and now have American English versions; one small drawback is that there are still some differences in meanings for American English.

It can be instructive to compare a less helpful to a more helpful definition (one from a traditional dictionary and the other from a COBUILD dictionary) and the type of understanding a student may take away from each. In the case of the word *politic*, two definitions are:

- *Politic*—"artful and shrewd"; the first definition listed in *The American Heritage Dictionary* (1985).
- *Politic*—"if it seems *politic* to do a particular thing, that seems to be the most sensible thing to do in the circumstances"; the definition provided in the *COBUILD Advanced Learner's English Dictionary* (2006).

It would not be surprising if a student read and studied the first definition for the word *politic* and used the word as follows:

> The *politic* thief stole the gems from the museum.

On the other hand, it seems less likely the student would take away this understanding from the COBUILD definition.

Most COBUILD word entries include a sentence that illustrates the meaning and correct usage. For example:

> Malleable—1. If you say that someone is **malleable**, you mean that they are easily influenced or controlled by other people. 2. A substance that is **malleable** is soft and can easily be made into different shapes. *Silver is the most malleable of all metals.*

Comparing Dictionary Definitions

Taking our word example *magnanimous*, we can contrast the *Webster* and COBUILD definitions:

Webster—Noble of mind and heart.

COBUILD—if you are *magnanimous*, you behave well and generously towards other people, especially people who are weaker than you or who have been opposed to you in some way. (Collins Birmingham University, 2003).

For a more difficult Tier Two word like *magnanimous*, the COBUILD definition is more likely to help the student understand the precise meaning and prepare the student to use the word correctly.

Electronic Dictionaries

Many dictionaries are now available in both a print version and an electronic version, with subscriptions to websites and with CD-ROMs also commonly available. These dictionaries offer users the opportunity to locate every occurrence of a word item in the dictionary, including derived and compound forms, idioms, and collocations, as well as links to online sources. Online dictionaries allow users to search by word or meaning and to study word histories and word families. Unlike printed dictionaries, online dictionaries can be rapidly updated. For example, every 3 months the online version of the *Oxford English Dictionary* adds 1,800 new or revised words to its corpus. In December 2010, for example, the noun *blogosphere* was added.

The website One Look (*www.onelook.com*) allows the user to search hundreds of online dictionaries simultaneously. A search for the word *interpret* yielded 39 dictionaries with definitions, and a similar search for *magnanimous* yielded definitions from 35 dictionaries. Many of these dictionaries provide audio pronunciations and translations into other languages.

Conclusion

As the overview of word properties presented in this chapter attests, words have a complex anatomy, and their diverse formations and occurrences significantly affect how they are learned and taught. The implications for instruction are summarized by the following principles.

Instructional Principles

1. Instruction in the word's *form* includes close attention to correct pronunciation and spelling. Students are naturally more likely to be able to use and practice a new word in their speaking and writing if they can confidently pronounce and spell it. Students with language problems and from linguistically diverse backgrounds may experience disproportionately greater difficulties in pronouncing new vocabulary words.
2. Instruction in word *structure* includes teaching all about word roots, high-frequency affixes, and inflections, including how affixed and inflected words are formed and their meanings.
3. Instruction in word *grammar* is provided by means of practicing reading sample sentences and completing and producing sentences in which the target word is used correctly.
4. With younger students, word meanings can be taught with pictures or examples as well as with definitions. Students need guidance and background on the structure of dictionary definitions in order to use them independently and productively.
5. Many words have multiple meanings. Teachers should keep this in mind in choosing the core or most useful meanings for instruction.

6. As noted, all students should understand the conventions of traditional dictionaries, in which definitions are often written in a form that first identifies the category to which the word belongs and then differentiates it from other members of the category. COBUILD dictionaries offer an attractive alternative, providing particularly clear explanations of word items and featuring a sample sentence showing how the target word is used.
7. It is often helpful to know the company a word keeps. Some words are frequently used with other words, their collocations. Teaching collocations is one way to develop knowledge of word relationships.
8. Teaching idioms fosters an interest in word usage and origins and can be particularly helpful for language-minority students, as the meaning of idioms cannot be figured out based on the meanings of the individual words alone.
9. Teachers must be judicious in choosing the words for explicit vocabulary instruction. The selection of words is often based on word frequency, tier, or importance in academic school texts.

INSTRUCTIONAL POINTS FOR LANGUAGE-MINORITY STUDENTS

Word features may influence vocabulary learning for language-minority students, in particular, and other students with lower language skills. Instructional considerations include:

1. The student's native language knowledge will influence English vocabulary learning. Students who already have a strong native language vocabulary and language skills will have knowledge of words and concepts that they can draw upon in learning English vocabulary. For example, a student who knows the meaning of the word *river* in his native language can draw upon his knowledge of that concept in learning the English word. This makes learning the word *river* easier than learning a word such as *parapet*, for which the student has no knowledge to draw upon from his native language.

2. The English word form will also influence the learning burden for vocabulary. If the phonemes and letters in the English word are similar to those in the student's native language, the word will be easier to learn than if the word form does not share the orthographic or phonological features of the student's counterpart native term. Further, words in some languages do not indicate number or tense, making these English word properties more difficult for language-minority students to learn.

3. Language-minority students may find the English word grammar confusing. Structural patterns differ between languages. For example, some languages do not have subject–verb structures, and nouns in some languages do not have singu-

lar and plural forms. Learning these word features becomes an added burden in acquiring knowledge of English vocabulary.

4. Researchers estimate that a language-minority learner must know a minimum of 3,000–5,000 English words to read nontechnical English texts competently (Nation & Waring, 1997) and even more vocabulary knowledge to successfully read specialized texts. One recommended starting point for teaching students who are non-native English speakers is the 2,000 most frequently occurring word families that form a foundation for language learning (Coxhead, 2006).

5. Idioms and figures of speech may be particularly difficult for language-minority students to understand, as the students are often not familiar with these phrases and it is often not possible to work out their meaning on a word-by-word basis (e.g., *piece of cake*).

6. Differences in the language system and sounds in the student's primary language may make it difficult for the student to discriminate the sounds in English words and to pronounce the words correctly. Words that are difficult to pronounce are more difficult to learn (Ellis, 1997).

7. Differences in the student's native language writing system may also create confusion in learning how to pronounce and spell English words. For example, some languages have clear rules for spelling vowel sounds, whereas there are multiple options for spelling many English vowels (e.g., the long *-a* sound in English, which may be spelled *ay, ai, eigh*, or with an acute-accented *e*, as in *café*).

8. Polysemes—or related word meanings—and homonyms—words that sound the same but have different meanings—may be especially confusing for language-minority students.

9. Words that have irregular plurals (*goose, geese*), irregular inflected forms (*fight, fought*), and less phonologically predictable derivations (*decide–decision, type–typical*) are more difficult to learn, as the student must also learn the proper use of the word forms as well as the meaning. These words often lead to student errors in usage (*fighted, stealed, goed*) and pronunciation.

CHAPTER 3

Making Principled Decisions about Vocabulary Instruction

CHAPTER VOCABULARY

Academic words	Words (e.g., *substitute, establish, inherent, analyze*) that appear in a broad range of academic texts and that serve a supportive role to more specialized technical vocabulary in all fields of study.
Base word	The form of the word after all affixes are removed. Thus, base words are the primary lexical unit, which carries the most significant semantic content and cannot be reduced into smaller constituents. Base words (sometimes referred to as *root words*) can be independent, such as *mount* in *dismount*, or may be dependent, such as *liter* in *illiterate*.
Corpus	A defined set of texts used to derive word lists that can be used to guide vocabulary instruction. The corpus is typically used to identify the frequency and coverage of words within a given subject area. On a broader level, corpora (currently electronically stored and processed) are used to conduct linguistic research through statistical analysis, hypothesis testing, and/or validating rules on a defined universe of texts. Plural is *corpora*.
Coverage	How widely a word is used across different text types within a corpus. Words that appear in one of a few text types have limited coverage, whereas those that appear in multiple text types have high coverage. There are different statistical processes used by linguists to determine the coverage of words within a corpus. Sometimes referred to as *dispersion*.

Form	The part of speech represented by a word meaning (i.e., verb, noun, pronoun, adjective, adverb, preposition, conjunction).
Frequency	How often a word occurs in a corpus. Although diverse statistical indexes are used to document word frequency, it is typically given as the number of appearances per a set number of words (most often, per million).
Headword	A derivative word that designates a word family. This definition, while specific to corpus linguistics, is similar to the more general use of headwords (or entry words) in dictionaries or encyclopedias.
Lexical	Relating to the vocabulary, words, or morphemes of written and spoken language.
Root	A word's primary lexical unit, which carries the most significant semantic content and cannot be reduced into smaller constituents.
Semantic	Relating to the meaning(s) of words or other symbols used in written and spoken language.
Token	Term used by linguists to reference a particular instance of a word.
Word family	A group of words that are closely enough related to one another to form a "family." Although words may be grouped into form-based (i.e., patterns of spellings) or meaning-based families, meaning-based families are used in the development of word lists and to guide vocabulary instruction. Typically, a meaning-based word family is made up of a base, or root, word and all its affixed forms (Graves, Ryder, Slater, & Calfee, 1987). However, it is important to note that linguists and other researchers use various (and sometimes divergent) procedures in identifying word families.

INTRODUCTION

One might assume that the designers of basal reading series (and, no doubt, other disciplinary texts) would wish to identify the most important words for teaching and learning vocabulary. Unfortunately, however, this does not appear to be the case. Hiebert (2005, p. 245) reported that of the 22 words targeted for vocabulary instruction in a fourth-grade basal reading series, students would rarely encounter a majority of the words (less than one occurrence per million words of text). This analysis highlights the challenge for vocabulary teaching and learning. Principled decisions about which words are worth teaching and learning are necessary if we are to devote precious instructional time to vocabulary instruction. Deciding which words to teach is the focus of this chapter.

In this chapter we first discuss the challenge of making principled decisions about teaching and learning vocabulary, especially for students who lag behind peers in vocabulary size and in their rate of independent vocabulary learning. We then describe the sequence in which word meanings are acquired and the general factors considered by linguists and others in developing word lists. We then turn our attention to the most widely used word lists and where these lists can be found. Finally, we outline the instructional implications of the information that we have gathered.

PRINCIPLED DECISIONS ABOUT TEACHING AND LEARNING VOCABULARY

One of the most challenging aspects of vocabulary teaching and learning in English (or any other language) is making principled decisions about which words are *most worth* teaching and learning. The vast number of words in the English language makes selecting the ones most worth teaching appear to be an overwhelming task. Goulden, Nation, and Read (1990) looked at the vocabulary represented in *Webster's Third New International Dictionary* (1963)—the largest English dictionary of its time—to identify the number of English word families. After excluding compound words, out-of-date words, abbreviations, proper names, alternative spellings, and dialect forms of words, they classified the remaining words into word families consisting of a root word, inflected forms, and transparent derivations (i.e., those with the same phonological characteristics of the root word, e.g., *acid–acidic, flame–flammable*). In all, *Webster's Third New International Dictionary* included approximately 54,000 word families. Of course, it not only would be virtually impossible to teach 54,000 word families to students but also would be far beyond the reach of students experiencing vocabulary difficulties—and even those who are not—to learn that number of word families. Of course, that continues to increase each year, since the English language, like most, is continually evolving over time.

Contemplating the vocabulary size of the typically well-educated individual is another way to think about how many words one might teach to students. Researchers and others have long sought to measure the vocabulary size of well-educated individuals (and other groups, such as English language learners). The methodological issues surrounding studies of vocabulary size have resulted in widely varying estimates, depending on how the researchers counted a word, how they sampled to select the words to assess, and how they assessed whether a person knows the word or not. In any case, an analysis conducted by Goulden and colleagues (1990) suggests that well-educated adult native speakers of English have a vocabulary of around 17,000 base or root words. While a much more manageable number than 54,000, 17,000 base or root words would still be too many to plausibly teach. Fortunately, research on vocabulary acquisition suggests that individuals learn the majority of word meanings through their natural reading habits (Nagy & Anderson, 1984; Nagy et al., 1985; Nagy & Herman, 1987).

Making Principled Decisions about Vocabulary Instruction

The results of studies of vocabulary reported by linguists and others (e.g., Biemiller, 2009; Nation, 1990) are useful in making principled decisions about which words are worth focusing on for teaching and learning vocabulary. The research reveals that 2,000 high-frequency root words make up approximately 87% of all words in texts, including academic

- 2,000 high-frequency words encompass approximately 87% of words in text.
- 500–800 academic words make up 10% of academic text.
- 1,000–2,000 discipline-specific words constitute most of the remainder.

ones (even university-level). An even smaller set of some 500–800 academic words (occurring widely across academic disciplines) has been identified as constituting an additional 10% of academic texts. Nearly 3% of text words are technical terms, which vary from one field to another, generally consisting of 1,000–2,000 discipline-specific words usually taught or acquired in the particular field of study. The remaining words in any text are considered to be low-frequency words that are generally mentioned only once or twice in a given text and, as such, do not usually merit specific teaching efforts.

Consider the text from a high school textbook presented in Figure 3.1. In this text, the high-frequency words are not marked. The academic words are marked with a single underline, while the technical words are indicated with a double underline. Approximately 87% of the words in the text are high-frequency words (unmarked). Another 10% of the remaining vocabulary consists of academic words (single underlined). Three percent of the words are discipline-specific (double underlined). Thus, students who know 2,000 high-frequency vocabulary words are equipped to master the vast majority of general words in academic texts, while knowing another 500–800 words provides the foundation for learning discipline-specific content.

Understanding the relative distribution of words in written text can be used to make principled decisions about which words to teach students. There are currently two major approaches that teachers can use to make principled decisions about which words to teach. One approach is to rely on available word lists that specify the relative *frequency and coverage* of words. Over the years, linguists have compiled word lists of the most frequently occurring words (e.g., Biemiller, 2009). Knowledge of an additional 500–800 academic words can significantly boost a student's comprehension of academic texts and activities, regardless of area (e.g., Coxhead, 2000). Educators (e.g., Marzano, 2004) have also compiled academic word lists. Teachers can use these various word lists to guide their vocabulary instruction.

A second approach to selecting words to teach has been outlined by Beck et al. (2002, 2008). This *"tier"* approach targets words for instruction that are frequently occurring and that are high-utility words for literate language users (Beck et al., 2008, p. 7). These authors distinguish among Tier One words like *happy* that children typically learn without instruction, Tier Two words that are central to their approach to vocabulary instruction, and Tier Three words that are low-frequency, specialized, and technical words. These Tier Three words have a narrower role in written language and can be taught when students encounter them, for example, in science or

MACHINES

Since earliest times Man has tried to conserve his energy whenever he has to do some work. By a variety of methods (many still in use today) men cut down on the size of the force, or forces, they had to apply to lift objects. Today Man has become more efficient in designing devices which enable him to transfer energy from one place to another extremely quickly, or to do useful jobs more easily. These devices are called machines. A machine is an energy transformer; it can change energy from one form to another (as an electric motor does), or it can hand energy on from one place to another (as a hydraulic press does).

You will have seen many machines around your home—a crowbar, hammers, a bicycle, wheelbarrow; even a sloping piece of board is a machine. Many other and more complicated machines can be seen in factories—pulley systems, presses, fork-lifts and the bewildering complex, automatic machines, sorting and assembling articles at high speed.

However, no matter how complicated the machine is, its parts, or components, are basically one or other of two simple machines—the lever and the inclined plane. The application of these simple devices has been used by Man for many thousands of years—you may have read how giant inclined planes were used during the construction of the Great Pyramid in Egypt.

1. A machine is an _____ (two words).
2. A complicated machine is just various combinations of two basic machines—the _____ and the _____ (two words).
3. Into what category of basic machine do each of the following fit: a spade; a car screw-jack; a hydraulic lift; a spanner; a winding road up a mountain; a human arm?

The lever

The lever (or, as you may have called it when you were younger, the see-saw) can be used to multiply forces or to produce turning effects (torques).

A screwdriver opening a paint-tin is a good example of a lever in action. The screwdriver is pivoted on a point (called the fulcrum), and you apply a force called the effort at the handle end, while the blade is pressing against the lid which is to be removed—the force caused by the lid being called the load.

The lever's input energy (E.S1) and its output energy (L.S2) are equal; as a machine it merely hands energy on; it neither creates nor destroys any. This does not prevent a lever from being very useful: it changes the force to a more convenient size (E is smaller than L, if S1 is bigger than S2); it alters the direction of the force; and it can transmit a force to any selected point.

FIGURE 3.1. High-frequency words, academic words, and low-frequency content-specific words. High-frequency words are unmarked; academic words are single underlined; discipline-specific words are double underlined. From Nation, *Teaching and Learning Vocabulary* (1990, pp. 14–15). Copyright 1990 by Heinle/ELT, a part of Cengage Learning, Inc. Reproduced by permission. *www.cengage.com/permissions.*

geography lessons or in other academic courses (Beck et al., 2002). A description of each tier and example words are presented in Table 3.1. Beck et al. (2002, 2008) define Tier Two words as those most important for vocabulary instruction. As the authors note, the three tiers do not directly correspond to levels of frequency. Teachers who select words for instruction based on the three-tier system need to use judgment in deciding which words fit within each category and their frequency and coverage (i.e., the degree to which the words are likely to occur across different areas or text types), because words at each of the tiers are not clearly identified.

It seems clear that there is value in knowing high-frequency and academic words. These words support comprehension of a wide range and large proportion of written language and school texts. Familiarity with high-frequency root words and academic words may be needed to bootstrap efficient access to and the learning of academic content as well as discipline-specific words encountered in various from reading contexts.

THE SEQUENCE IN WHICH WORDS ARE ACQUIRED

Another approach to vocabulary instruction considers the order in which words are typically acquired by children. Biemiller (2005) synthesized data from a number of studies to estimate the rate at which children acquire word meanings through the elementary school years (Anglin, 1993; Biemiler & Slonim, 2001; Dale & O'Rourke, 1981). Students acquire an average of 860 base or root word meanings per year from the first through third grades. The rate of acquisition increases somewhat, to 1,000

TABLE 3.1. Description of Beck, McKeown, and Kucan's (2002, 2008) Tier One, Two, and Three Words and Related Examples

Tier	Explanation	Examples
Tier One	• High-frequency basic words that are well known	*clock, baby, happy*
Tier Two	• High-frequency words used by mature language users across several content areas • Moderate- to high-frequency general words that occur across domains • Words with general high utility for literate language users • Words that play an important role in literacy • Words that characterize written text	*coincidence, absurd, hasty, perseverance*
Tier Three	• Low-frequency words, specialized vocabulary • Narrower role in literate language • Often conceptually challenging • Often limited to specific content areas	*nucleus, osmosis, archaeologist*

words annually, in the third through sixth grades. On average, children gain knowledge of some 10,000 words by the end of the sixth grade (Biemiller, 2005). As noted earlier, a well-educated individual typically is familiar with about 17,000 root words (Goulden et al., 1990).

Evidence from different study groups suggests that, regardless of their initial vocabulary, socioeconomic status, or language status, students acquire word meanings in roughly the same sequence (Biemiller, 2005). Biemiller (2005) reported that in adjacent grades certain words were understood, for example, by a majority of second-grade children while other words were understood by few or no children in the first grade. This pattern was evident across the elementary school grades and across the major risk groups. Additionally, the vocabulary size of English language learners in the fifth grade was similar to the overall average of third-grade students. Taken together, these findings suggest that students, regardless of initial vocabulary or language status, appear to acquire word meanings in roughly the same sequence. We believe that a similar process applies to students with learning disabilities, although their overall rate of vocabulary acquisition is probably slower than that of their grade-level peers.

The stable sequence of vocabulary acquisition most likely occurs because the word meanings learned early in a student's educational career are prerequisites to understanding word meanings absorbed later. In other words, as noted earlier, learning high-frequency root words may be necessary to boost efficient access to and the learning of less frequently occurring and more complex vocabulary. This observation suggests that teachers can predict reasonably well that children in need of vocabulary instruction should be initially learning word meanings from among those words that occur most frequently and have the widest coverage, followed by those that are less frequently occurring.

THE DEVELOPMENT OF WORD LISTS

Although the particular procedures used by developers of word lists to ensure the representativeness and adequate size of the corpus of interest and the criteria used for word selection differ, there are a number of general areas that are addressed in all cases (Biber, 1993). We highlight the four primary areas considered by linguists when developing word lists (see Figure 3.2).

1. Representativeness of the corpus
2. Organization of the corpus
3. Size of the corpus
4. Word selection criteria

FIGURE 3.2. Four areas considered by linguists when developing word lists.

Representativeness of Corpus

Research in corpus linguistics has shown that the linguistic features of texts differ across genres of text (e.g., newspapers, journals, textbooks), especially in vocabulary (Biber, 1990). To identify the vocabulary of a particular genre, the corpus must therefore contain texts that are representative of the varieties of genres they are intended to reflect.

Peculiarities in the vocabulary of an individual style or topic may be evident if long texts are used. Thus, the developers of word lists tend to use a variety of short texts (e.g., 200–500 words per sample) to enhance variation in and the representativeness of vocabulary to ensure that the text used in the corpus represents the vocabulary included in the full range of genres of interest. Additionally, developers include texts written by a variety of writers to help neutralize bias that may result from the idiosyncratic style of writers and to increase the number of words in the corpus. The goal is to ensure that the corpus contains a wide range of text types and authors so that the biases of a particular type or specific authors do not affect the resulting list of words.

Organization of the Corpus

All genres encompass a variety of subgenres. A particular word list should select words that appear across the various subgenres underlying the genre of interest targeted by the corpus. Organizing the corpus into coherent sections of proportional size (relative to the natural occurrence of text genres) allows the developer of the word list to identify the range of occurrence of the vocabulary words across the different genres and related subgenres of the corpus.

Size of the Corpus

The corpus of a word list should be large enough to ensure a reasonable number of occurrences of the words of interest. A corpus should include millions of running words (called tokens by linguists) to ensure that a very large sample of language is available (Sinclair, 1991). The exact amount of language required, of course, depends on the intended purpose and use of the word list; however, in general more language means that more information can be gathered about lexical items and more words in context can be examined in depth. In the past, linguists developed word lists by hand, which reduced the number of running words used in a particular corpus. The advent of electronic forms of print and statistical analysis programs has made possible the efficient analysis of large numbers of running words. For example, Coxhead's (2000) academic word list was based on some 4 million words.

Word Selection Criteria

An important issue in the development of word lists is the criteria for word selection, as different criteria can lead to different results. Defining what counts as a word is important in developing word lists. Word lists typically group words into word families (e.g., *analyst* would be counted as part of the same word family as *analysis*). Linguists tend to identify word families because comprehending regularly inflected or derived members of a family does not require much more effort by learners if they know the base or root word and are familiar with the basic word-building processes (Bauer & Nation, 1993). In general, when first establishing the criteria for including words, the developers of a corpus should carefully consider the purpose of the list and the specific learners for whom it is intended. Typical criteria include the regularity, productivity, and frequency of potential vocabulary candidates and the likelihood of students understanding the relationships of the words within a word family. For example, West (1953) considered frequency, coverage, ease or difficulty of learning, necessity (words that express ideas otherwise inexpressible through other words), and stylistic level (neutral unemotional words are easier to learn) when he developed the *General Service List (GSL) of English Words* (described in greater detail below).

WORD LISTS

The major theme of this chapter is that word lists are available that can be used by teachers and curriculum designers to make principled decisions about which words to teach students. This is especially true in the case of high-frequency root and academic words because the preferred selections are generally well defined and consistent across word lists. However, it is important to note that vocabulary curriculum designers and teachers do not necessarily need to teach all of the words in vocabulary lists. Rather, they can access these word lists when they design vocabulary instruction for students to judge whether the words they plan to teach are really important or not. Further, teachers should look closely at the word lists and word selection procedures used in commercially available vocabulary interventions.

In the compilation for this chapter, we have selected many of the lists most commonly cited and used by linguists, ones often *not* well known by practitioners. Anyone interested in teaching vocabulary should have an awareness of the featured lists and associated attributes. Historically, linguists have developed word lists for use in vocabulary instruction as well as for hypothesis testing and for validating linguistic rules. We acknowledge that teachers may not be able to easily access and use some of these lists for planning and augmenting their vocabulary instruction. Further, it is important to note that this list of lists is not exhaustive. We describe five major categories of word lists in the remainder of this section. We begin by describing word lists that are primarily based on frequency and, in most cases, coverage. We then describe a word list that details the familiarity of words across grade levels, independently of frequency. Next, we describe three word lists that focus on academic words. We do not include word lists that are discipline-specific, because these are not widely available and, besides, this specialized vocabulary may be best tailored to course content. Following the description of academic word lists, we provide an overview of two word lists that identify specific words for instruction. Finally, we provide an overview of the Corpus of Contemporary American English (*www.americancorpus.org*), the largest publicly available corpus of written text, which contains over 400 million running words. This corpus is continually updated and available online for analysis. This online corpus is relatively easy to search and could be used by those planning and augmenting their vocabulary instruction.

Word Lists Based Primarily on Frequency and Coverage

Title: *The Educator's Word Frequency Guide* (Zeno, Ivens, Millard, & Duvvuri, 1995).

Availability: Available in print and electronic (CD-ROM) forms.

Description: *The Educator's Word Frequency Guide*, which includes more than 154,000 words, represents the largest systematic word frequency count ever conducted. The words were drawn from text sampled across a wide range of content encountered by students in kindergarten through college. The overall goal was to develop a comprehensive word list from a corpus with wide coverage of actual text used in kindergarten through college.

Corpus: The word list is based on a count of a large and varied corpus of textbooks, works of literature, and popular works of fiction and nonfiction used in grades K–12 and colleges throughout the United States. The running words and associated text types included 4,853,287 words from language arts, 3,561,940 from social sciences, 1,940,249 from science and mathematics, 67,133 from fine arts, 628,667 from health and safety, 256,585 from home economics, 671,479 from trade and technical fields, and 4,870,122 from popular fiction and nonfiction literature. A word was generally defined as a string of graphic characters bounded on both sides by spaces. Graphic characters including letters, numerals, internal punctuation (e.g., hyphen, apostrophe), as well as mathematical symbols were included. Thus, a base or root word and its inflected variants all counted as separate entries. Upper- and lower-case letters were distinguished, resulting in separate entries for words that were capitalized and those that were not.

Word List Organization: Four statistics were calculated: *F, D, U,* and *SFI. F* is the frequency of a word's occurrence in the corpus. The *D* (dispersion) statistic provides an index of coverage (relative frequency) across content areas, based on the total corpus. Words that appear in only one content area have a *D* value of .0000. Words that appear across all content areas, regardless of frequency, have a *D* value of 1.0000. Values between .0000 and 1.000 indicate degrees of coverage between these extremes. *U* is the word's estimated frequency per million words in a theoretically infinite corpus rather than the corpus sample. The estimate of *U* is derived from *F* with an adjustment for *D*. It is believed that *U* better reflects the "true" frequency per million words and is useful for making direct comparisons to values given by other corpora. The *U* statistic is expressed as the frequency of the word per million words. The Standard Frequency Index (*SFI*) is derived from *U* to provide a more compressed and interpretable range of values than *U*. A word with *SFI* = 90 would be expected to occur once in every 10 words; one with *SFI* = 80 would be expected to occur once in every 100 words; and one with *SFI* = 70 would be expected to occur once in every 1,000 words, and so on. A convenient mental reference point is provided by *SFI* = 40, the value for a word that would occur once in a million words. Each positive unit of *SFI* represents an increase of about 25.9% in the probability of the word's appearance in the corpus.

The Educator's Word Frequency Guide presents four different lists of words and associated statistics. The first section, which is the most useful, is an alphabetical list of the 19,468 words with a *U* value greater than or equal to 1 in the total corpus. For each of the words, the *SFI*, *D*, *U*, and *F* statistics are detailed for the total corpus. In addition, the *F*, or frequency, at which the word occurred in grades 1 through 13 (college level) is detailed (i.e., the number of times it occurred in samples of text from books at each respective grade level). This information enables one to get a sense of when the words are most likely to be encountered by students across the grades. A sample listing for the word *affect* is presented in Table 3.2. The *SFI* of 58, *D* of .8517, *U* of 63, and *F* of 1254 indicate that "affect" occurred approximately once in every 10,000 words, occurred across a majority of the content areas in the corpus, would be expected to occur about 63 times per million words in a theoretically infinite corpus, and occurred 1,254 times in the corpus sample, respectively. Moreover, beginning in the second grade, students should increasingly encounter *affect* in written text as they progress through school.

The second section is an alphabetical list of the words with a *U* value *less than* 1 in the total corpus. This section provides the *SFI*, *D*, *U*, and *F* statistics for the total corpus, but the *F* values for the grade levels are not supplied.

The third section starts with an alphabetical list of words that begin with an apostrophe or are enclosed within single quotation marks. These are followed by words that begin with a dash. Words that start with a numeral (e.g., *10th*) and types that are composed solely of numerals (e.g., *1,000*) are listed next. Abbreviations are listed last. Only the *U* value for the total corpus is provided for each of these words.

TABLE 3.2. Sample Listing for the Word *Affect* from the First Section of *The Educator's Word Frequency Guide*

	Total corpus				Grade											
Word	SFI	D	U	F	1	2	3	4	5	6	7	8	9	10	11	12	13+
Affect	58.0	.8517	63	1254	0	2	12	18	39	46	50	53	59	67	78	87	129

Note. SFI, Standard Frequency Index (derived from *U*); D, index of coverage relative to frequency; U, estimated frequency of word in a theoretically infinite corpus; F, frequency of occurrence in the corpus. Numbers under each grade level indicate the actual frequency of occurrence of the word in the corpus of written text at each grade level.

The final section contains a rank-order listing of all of the words provided in the first two sections. This rank-order listing is based on unrounded U values for the words. The U value for the total corpus is provided for each word, and words with the same U value are listed alphabetically.

Title: *The American Heritage Word Frequency Book* (Carroll, Davies, & Richman, 1971).

Availability: Available in print form.

Description: *The American Heritage Word Frequency Book* listing includes approximately 87,000 words. The same definition for a word and statistics are used as those in the list in *The Educator's Word Frequency Guide* (Zeno et al., 1995). However, the words are drawn from text sampled across a wide range of content encountered by students in the third through ninth grades. The overall goal is to develop a comprehensive word list from a corpus with wide coverage of actual text used in the third through ninth grades.

Corpus: The corpus includes 5,088,721 total running words drawn from 500 word samples taken from a range of 1,045 texts (i.e., textbooks, workbooks, novels, poetry, general nonfiction, encyclopedias, magazines) encountered by students in the third through ninth grades. The running words and associated text types include approximately 1,870,500 words from reading, 606,500 from language arts, 389,500 from mathematics, 492,500 from social studies, 212,000 from spelling, 493,000 from science, 252,000 from music and art, 145,500 from home economics and industrial arts, 248,500 from library reference materials, 295,000 from popular magazines, and 6,000 from religious studies. Note that we have collapsed some of the content areas here. For example, we combined reading, reading supplementary, fiction, and nonfiction to form one "reading" category.

Word List Organization: *The American Heritage Word Frequency Book* uses the same four statistics that are used in *The Educator's Word Frequency Guide* (Zeno et al., 1995): F, D, U, and *SFI* (see the description above for each of the statistics). *The American Heritage Word Frequency Book* presents words alphabetically and by rank according to frequency. The *SFI*, D, U, and F statistics are detailed for the total corpus in the alphabetical list. The frequency of occurrence for the third through ninth grades is also presented. The words are listed in a column on the left side of the page. The F, D, U, and *SFI* statistics are provided for each word. The F statistic for each grade level (i.e., columns headed Gr 3, Gr 4, . . . , Gr 9) is also provided. With the exception of the order in which they are presented, the listing of the *SFI*, D, U, and F statistics for the total corpus and the F for each grade level parallel their presentation in *The Educator's Word Frequency Guide* (Zeno et al., 1995; see Table 3.2 in this volume). Unique to *The American Heritage Word Frequency Book*, the F for each of the content areas (e.g., reading, mathematics) is presented. Note that the authors caution against interpreting the grade level and content area breakdown because the total number of words sampled varied greatly by content area. For example, the number of words considered in the category of reading was over 1 million, whereas less than 5,000 words were considered in religion.

The rank-order list of words is straightforward. The list is not broken down by grade level or content area. The words are listed in order, based on their values of *U* and *SFI* (equivalent to one another in terms of ranking). Words with tied values are counted separately in the ranking.

Title: *The Teacher's Word Book of 30,000 Words* (Thorndike & Lorge, 1944)

Availability: Available in electronic form. Archived copy available at *www.archive. org/details/teacherswordbook00thoruoft*.

Description: The list in *The Teacher's Word Book of 30,000 Words* includes just 30,000 words. The overall goal of the authors was to identify the most frequently and widely occurring 10,000 words in the corpus, with a particular emphasis on the first 5,000 words. Although the word list is dated, the base word vocabulary of English changes slowly. Thus, the dated nature of the word list is not a significant problem for the most frequently occurring words. The value of this word list lies in its corpus base.

Corpus: The word list is based on a count of a large and varied corpus of 41 different text sources. The running words and associated text sources included some 625,000 words from literature for children; 3,000,000 words from the Bible and English classics; 300,000 words from elementary school textbooks; 50,000 words from books about cooking, sewing, farming, and the trades; 90,000 words from the daily newspapers; and 500,000 words from correspondence. A root word and its affixed forms were generally defined as a word family.

Word List Organization: A measure of the coverage and frequency of each word's occurrence was expressed in a "credit number." The credit number applies to approximately the first 10,000 important words (based on frequency and coverage) in the corpus (see Table 3.3 for an overview of the credit numbers associated with rank-order categories encompassing the most important 5,000 words). Additionally, in the case of the most important 5,000 words, the credit number in the detailed alphabetical listing is followed by a number and letter that indicate in which thousand and in which half of the thousand words the word belongs. For example, the word *approach* has a credit number of 43 and the letter 2a, indicating that it falls within the first half of the second 1,000 words, whereas the word *arrange* has a credit score of 35 and the letter 2b, signifying that it falls with the second half of the second 1,000 words. Finally, it is important to note that for convenience a list of the 2,500

TABLE 3.3. Credit Number and Associated Frequency Rank of Words for *The Teacher's Word Book of 30,000 Words*

Credit number	Approximate frequency rank of words
≥ 49	1–1,000
29 to 49	1,001–2,000
19 to 28	2,001–3,000
14 to 18	3,001–4,000
10 to 13	4,001–5,000

most widely and frequently occurring words, arranged in five sets of 500 each, are detailed separately at the end of the book (pp. 127–134).

Title: *A General Service List of English Words* (West, 1953)

Availability: Out of print. Electronic form available (*jbauman.com/gsl.html*).

Description: The *General Service List* included just 2,000 headwords. The overall goal of the author was to identify 2,000 headwords representing the word families thought to be of greatest "general service" to English learners. The GSL is unique in that each word item includes its affixed forms. For example, the headword *own* includes *own, owns, owned, owning, owner,* and *ownership*. Other word lists based on frequency would count each member of the word family as a separate entry. While not clearly defined, factors other than frequency and coverage were considered in selecting the headwords. Thus, the word list includes some low-frequency words that appeared to be the most efficient way to express an idea (e.g., *whistle, reproduce*). The GSL has had a wide influence for many years in the production of simplified text and vocabulary instruction for English learners.

Corpus: The corpus is a body of approximately 5 million words of English text. The text sources include a wide variety of types such as encyclopedias, magazines, textbooks, novels, essays, biographies, books about science, and poetry. The specific headwords associated with each source were not identified. The text sources were primarily drawn from those used for the word frequency lists of Lorge and Thorndike (*A Semantic Count of English Words*, 1938) and Lorge (*The Semantic Count of the 570 Commonest English Words*, 1949).

Word List Organization: The words in the *General Service List* are presented alphabetically along with derived forms of the word family. For each headword the parts of speech, or form for each word, are identified (e.g., *own* as an adjective, *own* as a verb). Frequency numbers are given for each word and the derived forms of the word family, along with their meanings. The frequencies were derived from *A*

Semantic Count of English Words (Lorge & Thorndike, 1938), which was later revised and published as *The Teacher's Word Book of 30,000 Words* (Thorndike & Lorge, 1944; described earlier).

Title: *The Brown Corpus of Standard American English* (Kucera & Francis, 1967).

Availability: Available in print and electronic forms (*www.usingenglish.com/resources/wordcheck/list-brown+corpus.html*).

Description: *The Brown Corpus of Standard American English* included over 50,000 words. The words were drawn from a varied proportional sample of English texts across 15 genres published in 1961. Later the authors reanalyzed the *Brown Corpus* to include parts of speech (Francis & Kucera, 1982). The overall goal, unlike the case with many of the lists reviewed, was not to identify the most frequently occurring set of words. Rather, the aim was to compile a corpus and basic analysis of words used in printed American English in the year 1961.

Corpus: The corpus is a body of over 1 million words of English text, divided into 500 samples of text of approximately 2,000 words each. The samples were drawn purposefully to ensure they were representative and proportional of the full range of genres published in America during 1961. The approximate running words and associated text types included 176,000 from the press (i.e., reportage, editorials, reviews), 34,000 from religion, 72,000 from skills and hobbies, 96,000 from popular lore, 150,000 from literary works, 160,000 from learned and scientific writings, 234,000 from fiction, 18,000 from humor, and 60,000 from miscellaneous text. This summary reflects some collapsing of genre categories. For example, the "fiction" category included general, mystery and detective, science, adventure and western, and romance and love story. There were a total of 15 genre categories. A word was defined as a continuous string of letters, numerals, punctuation marks, and other symbols (i.e., mathematical symbols) uninterrupted by a space.

Word List Organization: The *Brown Corpus* presents two primary frequency lists of words. The first word list presents all of the words found in the corpus in descending order of frequency. The second list also contains all of the words found in the corpus, but listed in alphabetical order. Words that begin with special symbols are presented at the end of the list. Each word entry in both lists is preceded by three numbers separated by dashes. The first number gives the actual frequency of the occurrence of the word in the corpus. The second number designates the number of genre categories in which the word appeared (i.e., 1 through 15). The final number gives the number of samples in which the word was found (i.e., 1 through 500). These latter two numbers are used to index the coverage of the word. For example, the most frequently occurring word, *the* is preceded by 69971–15–500; these notations indicate that it occurred 69,971 times in the corpus and appeared in all 15 genres and all 500 samples.

A Word List Based on Familiarity

Title: *The Living Word Vocabulary* (Dale & O'Rourke, 1981).

Availability: Out of print. A subset of 11,000 root word meanings from *The Living Word Vocabulary* are included in an Excel format word list on a CD that comes with the book *Words Worth Teaching* (Biemiller, 2009).

Description: *The Living Word Vocabulary* includes 44,000 words. A word was defined as a unit of meaning as presented primarily in *The World Book Encyclopedia Dictionary* (Barnhart, 1970), including its semantic variations (note that other dictionaries were also consulted). Thus, the number of meanings associated with a word varies widely depending upon the number of its semantic units identified in dictionaries. For example, *advert* has one meaning, whereas *affect* has three meanings. The overall goal was to develop a comprehensive analysis of the familiarity of the word meanings across grades 4, 6, 8, 10, 12, 13, and 16. The familiarity scores specify the percentage of students who know the word meanings.

Corpus: As noted above, the primary corpus for the word list was *The World Book Encyclopedia Dictionary* (Barnhart, 1970). However, the authors note that many dictionaries were consulted to find the different meanings of certain words and to derive simple and clear-cut definitions. These sources were not identified by the authors. The procedures for identifying which word meanings to test at each grade level were based on the use of several resources that provided graded vocabulary lists (e.g., *A Combined Word List*, Buckingham & Dolch, 1936).

Word List Organization: *The Living Word Vocabulary* presents the word meanings in an alphabetical list that includes two additional columns. The relevant grade and associated familiarity score (i.e., percentage of students that identified the correct meaning), given immediately to the left of the word, are presented for each word meaning. The overall goal was to list the earliest grade at which the familiarity score ranged between 67 and 84% for the various word meanings. For example, if a familiarity score for a given word meaning was 66% or lower in the fourth grade, it was assessed again in the sixth grade. If the familiarity score for a word meaning was 85% or above in the sixth grade, it was reassessed in the fourth grade. Thus, a majority of the words have familiarity scores of 67% or higher at the reported grade level. Additionally, the authors urge caution about assessing word meanings with familiarity scores below 50%. Chance alone would result in a familiarity score of 33% since a three-item multiple-choice format was used to assess familiarity). Thus, words with familiarity scores below 50% are considered to be difficult words.

Academic Word Lists

Title: *University Word List* (Xue & Nation, 1984).

Availability: Available in print and electronic forms (*jbauman.com/UWL.html*).

Description: The *University Word List* includes 836 word families. The word families were drawn from four available word lists. The overall goal was to identify words that occur frequently and widely in academic texts.

Corpus: The word list is based on an amalgam of four word lists. A list published by the New Zealand Council for Educational Research was used most extensively (Campion & Elley, 1971). This list was developed for a vocabulary subtest within a university entrance English test. The items were selected by analyzing 301,800 words from lectures published in journals and a cross-section of papers across the 19 disciplines with the largest enrollments in New Zealand. The second word list was the American University Word List, which was compiled for use for college-age English learners (Praninskas, 1972). This corpus included 272,466 running words drawn from 10 disciplines. The words from these lists were combined, and high-frequency base or root words were removed. This list was then checked against two lists developed by counting the words that foreign students annotated in their university textbooks (Ghadessy, 1979; Lynn, 1973). Approximately 70% of the words in each of these two lists overlapped with the combined word list. The high-frequency nonoverlapping academic words were then added to the combined word list. Only base words and not their derivations were included in the final list of academic words.

Word List Organization: The *University Word List* is ordered into 11 rank-ordered sublists (1 through 11) according to decreasing frequency. The number of words in each sublist varies from approximately 60 to 90 words. The occurrence of the words in Sublists 1 through 3 is approximately half of the total occurrence of all of the academic words identified in the corpus. Although Sublists 4 through 11 add relatively little to the overall coverage of the academic word families in the word list, they are nonetheless important, as these less frequent word families have wide coverage across the academic content areas and are unlikely to be acquired incidentally through reading. Examples from Sublists 1 and 11 are presented in Table 3.4.

TABLE 3.4. Examples of *University Word List* Words in Sublists 1 and 11

Sublist	Example words
1	*alternative, analyze, element, environment, tense, valid*
11	*accumulate, bulk, channel, fluid, luxury, ratio, switch, telescope*

Note. Sublist 1 words occur more frequently than those in sublist 11. Sublists 1 through 11 are in order of frequency of occurrence in the corpus.

Title: *Academic Word List* (Coxhead, 2000).

Availability: Available in print and electronic forms (*www.victoria.ac.nz/lals/resources/academicwordlist/default.aspx*).

Description: Coxhead's *Academic Word List* includes 570 word families. The words were drawn from a range of academic texts and content areas. The specific age range of the academic texts sampled was not specified. It appears that college-level texts were primarily used. The overall goal was to identify words that occur frequently and widely in academic texts. Additionally, two programs are available online (at *www.nottingham.ac.uk/~alzsh3/acvocab/index.htm*) that can be used to identify words from the *Academic Word List* that appear in any text (AWL Highlighter) and can provide practice in identifying academic words by replacing words from the list with a blank space to be filled out (AWL Gapmaker).

The *Academic Word List* is considered to be an update of the *University Word List* (Xue & Nation, 1984). There is an overlap of 435 word families (51%) between the *Academic Word List* and the *University Word List*. Some 401 word families occur only in the *University Word List* and 135 word families only in the *Academic Word List*. Coxhead (2000) reported that the explanation for the large number of word families occurring in the *University Word List* but not in the *Academic Word List* lies in the criteria for including word families in the latter list. Specifically, in the *Academic Word List*, members of a word family had to occur at least 100 times in the corpus. Approximately 150 of the word families found only in the *University Word List* occurred in the corpus less than 50 times. Further, the *University Word List* contains more than 133 word families that do not occur in all four sections of the corpus (i.e., these words have relatively limited coverage).

Corpus: The word list is based on a count of a large and varied corpus of academic textbooks, journal articles, psychology laboratory manuals, and other corpora (i.e., the *Brown Corpus*, Francis & Kucera, 1982; *MicroConcord*, Murison-Bowie, 1993). The running words from the sampled content areas included 883,214 words drawn from the arts, 879,547 from commerce, 874,723 from law, and 875,846 from science. A word family was defined as a word stem and all closely related affixed forms. Affixed forms included all inflections and the most frequent, productive, and regular prefixes and suffixes. Affixes included only those that could be added to stems that could stand as free forms (e.g., *specify* and *special* are not in the same word family because *spec-* is not a free form).

Word List Organization: Coxhead's *Academic Word List* is ordered into 10 rank-ordered sublists (1 through 10) according to decreasing word family frequency in the corpus. With the exception of sublist 10 (which includes 30 word families), each sublist consists of 60 word families. The words in the first three sublists occur with comparatively high frequency. The 60 words in Sublist 1 account for more than one-third of the total coverage of the entire word list. The next most frequently occurring

TABLE 3.5. Examples of Words from Coxhead's *Academic Word List*, Sublists 1 and 10

Sublist	Example words
1	*area, benefit, define, environment, factor, issue, research, vary*
10	*adjacent, forthcoming, integrity, levy, notwithstanding, panel, persistent*

Note. Sublist 1 words occur more frequently than those in sublist 10. Sublists 1 through 10 are in order of frequency of occurrence in the corpus.

120 words (Sublists 2 and 3) provide approximately 80% of the coverage that Sublist 1 does. Although Sublists 4 through 10 (as with the *University Word List*) add relatively little to the overall coverage of the academic word families in the word list, they are important as these less frequent word families have wide coverage across the academic content areas and are unlikely to be acquired incidentally through reading. Word examples from Sublists 1 and 10 are presented in Table 3.5.

Lists That Specify Words for Instruction

Title: *Words Worth Teaching* (Biemiller, 2009).

Availability: Available in print and electronic (CD-ROM) forms.

Description: The *Words Worth Teaching* word list includes 11,600 root words. The root words were drawn from the *Living Word Vocabulary* (Dale & O'Rourke, 1981; described earlier). The overall goal was to identify root words that should and should not be taught to students in the primary and upper elementary grades.

Corpus: The primary corpus for the word list was the *Living Word Vocabulary* (Dale & O'Rourke, 1981). To select the root words, 6,000 fourth- and sixth-grade root word meanings from the *Living Word Vocabulary* were used. Approximately 3,400 of these 6,000 word meanings were tested with samples of students in the third and fourth grades. Of these 3,400 word meanings tested, approximately 2,600 meanings were rated as either appropriate (i.e., 40% or more knew the meaning) or too advanced (i.e., < 40% of students knew the meaning) for instruction in the primary grades. Further, word meanings from the *Living Word Vocabulary* at the eighth- and tenth-grade levels that tested at over 80% familiarity with sixth-grade students were also included in the list of words that should be taught to students in the primary grades.

To identify words that should be taught to students in the upper elementary grades, word meanings that scored between 20 to 40% at the end of the second grade were assigned to the sixth-grade words. Furthermore, 3,000 eighth- and tenth-grade level root words in the *Living Word Vocabulary* were tested with samples of fifth- and sixth-grade students. Word meanings that 40–80% of students identified correctly were rated as appropriate to teach to upper elementary students, while those scoring at below 40% were deemed inappropriate to teach.

Word List Organization: The root word meanings are presented in two different forms (available on CD). The following six categories of words are identified in the first form:

1. Words known by most students at the end of the second grade.
2. High-priority words known by 40–80% of students by the end of the second grade.
3. Low-priority words known by 40–80% of students by the end of the second grade.
4. High-priority words known by 40–80% of students by the end of the sixth grade.
5. Low-priority words known by 40–80% of students by the end of the sixth grade.
6. Words known by fewer than 40% of children by the end of the sixth grade.

The second form includes the same word meanings organized alphabetically. Each word has a rating that indicates whether the word is appropriate for instruction or not. The same six categories represented in the first list of words are used.

Title: *Word Zones* (*www.textproject.org*).

Availability: Available in electronic form (*www.textproject.org/resources/word-zones-list*).

Description: The *Word Zones* word list includes 5,586 words drawn from released versions of fourth-grade standards-based tests. The overall goal was to identify 90% of the vocabulary included on tests, as this is a commonly used benchmark for instructional-level text difficulty. Additionally, a program is available online (*cehs07.unl.edu/reading/zone*) that can be used to analyze a text and identify the particular words that are included in each zone.

Corpus: The corpus for the word list was drawn from released versions of the fourth-grade standards-based tests from three states (Texas, New York, Florida) and the 2002 National Assessment of Educational Progress (NAEP). The identified words were then referenced with the *Educator's Word Frequency Guide* (Zeno et al., 1995; described earlier) to determine their frequency (U statistic). Words with frequencies of 10 or more occurrences per million words ($U \geq 10$) were considered for inclusion in the word list. On average, 92% of the unique words on the three states' and NAEP tests had frequencies of 10 or more occurrences per million words. The first 107 words with a frequency of 1,000 or more occurrences per million words were not considered because they tend to serve a grammatical function (identified as Zone 0—not recommended for instruction).

Word List Organization: The words are organized into four zones (1 through 4); corresponding to the respective grade level at which the words are first recommended for instruction (e.g., Zone 1 words are taught in the first grade). By Zone 4, approximately 80% of the entire word corpus of the *Educator's Word Frequency Guide* (Zeno et al., 1995), 90% of the corpus of *The American Heritage Word Frequency Book* (Carroll et al., 1971; described earlier), and 92% of the words on the standards-based tests from the three states and the 2002 NAEP are represented as suitable for prior instruction.

Two criteria were used to identify words for instruction within each zone. The first criterion centered on the semantic connections among words. An established semantic categorization scheme (composed of six categories, 0 through 5) was used (Nagy & Anderson, 1984). These categories were formed to answer the question "Assuming that a child knew the meaning of the immediate ancestor but not the target word, to what extent would the child be able to determine the meaning of the target word when encountering it in context while reading?" (Nagy & Anderson, 1984, p. 310). The first three categories (0 through 2) are described as semantically transparent. This means that the meaning of an unknown target word can be accurately ascertained based on knowing an ancestor word. The last three categories (3 through 5) are described as semantically opaque. This means that the meaning of an unknown target word cannot be ascertained based on knowing an ancestor word. The words included in the Word Zones fell within the first three categories (i.e., semantically transparent). The occurrences per million words in the word corpus for the *Educator's Word Frequency Guide* (Zeno et al., 1995) and the number of words per zone are identified in Table 3.6.

Title: *Building Background Knowledge for Academic Achievement* (Marzano, 2004).

Availability: Available in text form.

Description: The *Building Background Knowledge for Academic Achievement* word list includes 7,923 words drawn from various standards-based documents written by

TABLE 3.6. Occurrences per Million Words in *The Educator's Word Frequency Guide* and the Number of Words Per Zone

Zone	Occurrences per million words	Number of words
1	> 300	310
2	100–299	619
3	30–99	1,675
4	10–29	2,979

professional organizations and covering the full range of content areas (e.g., mathematics, science, history, social studies, language arts). The overall goal was to identify critically important background vocabulary words for academic achievement.

Corpus: The corpus for the word list was drawn from the national standards articulated by various professional organizations in documents on mathematics, science, history, social studies, English language arts, the arts, civics, economics, foreign language, geography, health, physical education, and technology. See Marzano (2004) for a complete listing of the documents used to identify the words.

Word List Organization: The words are organized into 11 subject areas: mathematics, science, English language arts, history (i.e., general, U.S., world), geography, civics, economics, health, physical education, the arts (i.e., general, dance, music, theater, visual), and technology. The words in each subject area are organized in four hierarchical levels linked to grade levels: Level 1 (K–2), Level 2 (3–5), Level 3 (6–8), and Level 4 (9–12). Table 3.7 presents the number of words recommended for inclusion per level in each of the subject areas. Marzano (2004) provides a complete list of the words for each subject area across the four levels.

TABLE 3.7. Number of Vocabulary Words across Content Areas and Levels

Subject area	Level 1 (K–2)	Level 2 (3–5)	Level 3 (6–8)	Level 4 (9–12)	Totals
Mathematics	80	190	201	214	685
Science	100	166	225	282	773
English Language Arts	83	245	247	223	798
History					
General History	162	560	319	270	1,311
U.S. History	0	154	123	148	425
World History	0	245	301	297	843
Geography	89	212	258	300	859
Civics	45	145	210	213	613
Economics	29	68	89	155	341
Health	60	68	75	77	280
Physical Education	57	100	50	34	241
The Arts					
Arts General	14	36	30	9	89
Dance	18	24	42	37	121
Music	14	83	67	32	196
Theater	5	14	35	13	67
Visual Arts	3	41	24	8	76
Technology	23	47	56	79	205
Totals	**782**	**2,398**	**2,352**	**2,391**	**7,923**

Note. From Marzano (2004). Copyright 2004 by ASCD. Reprinted by permission. *www.ascd.org*.

Corpus of Contemporary American English

The increasing availability of electronic text will no doubt continue to improve word list quality in the future. Along those lines, the Corpus of Contemporary American English (*www.americancorpus.org*) is a searchable corpus that currently includes over 400 million words drawn from more than 150,000 texts (1990 to the present), to which some 20 million new words are added each year. The corpus includes spoken sources (transcripts of unscripted conversations from TV and radio programs), fiction (short stories and plays from literary magazines, children's magazines, popular magazines, first chapters in edited books, movie scripts), nonfiction from popular magazines (news, health, home, gardening), and articles from newspapers (all sections from 10 newspapers from across the country) and academic journals (100 peer-reviewed journals). The development of the Corpus of Contemporary American English and its web interface parallels that of the British National Corpus (*www.natcorp.ox.ac.uk*). The web interface enables any user to easily search for exact words or phrases, parts of speech, or any combination of these. One can also search for collocates (surrounding words) within a 10-word range (e.g., all nouns near *faint*) and limit searches by frequency as well as compare the frequency of words and phrases by genre and time (i.e., different years). The web interface also allows the user to conduct semantically based queries of the corpus. There is a 5-minute guided tour available that demonstrates the major features and uses of the corpus.

INSTRUCTIONAL IMPLICATIONS

In order to allocate limited time in the school day to explicit instruction in word meanings, new vocabulary words must be chosen carefully. The instructional implications of this chapter center on this important choice. Let us consider the more prominent implications briefly:

1. Students acquire word meanings in a predictable sequence regardless of their initial vocabulary, any disabilities, or their original language status. This normal sequencing enables one to predict, at least in part, which words should potentially be taught, given students' current vocabulary levels. Knowing the familiarity of words at different grade levels helps teachers to select words that will be useful in the kinds of texts students are likely to encounter. Teaching words that students are likely to encounter increases the likelihood that they will both learn and retain these words as a result of multiple exposures not only during instruction but in subsequent written texts they encounter.

2. The majority of words in written text at all levels are made up of high-frequency base or root words. Knowing these words well helps to bootstrap students' efficient access to and learning of lower-frequency words. Although many children learn most root words without instruction, it may be necessary to teach

these words explicitly to English language learners and those with limited language exposure (e.g., children from disadvantaged socioeconomic environments).

3. A defined set of academic words (i.e., some 570–800) occur widely across all fields of study. High priority should be given to ensuring that students understand these academic words, given their importance to all disciplines or content areas. It may be important to teach these words to all students to boost their learning of academic content and discipline-specific words from more specialized reading contexts.

4. Becoming familiar with the high-frequency root and academic words should enable one to understand a majority of written text, regardless of level and area.

5. Two primary approaches are used to identify words for instruction. One approach (favored by Beck et al., 2002, 2008) suggests that instruction should target Tier Two words that are high-frequency words used by mature language users. An alternative approach is to focus on teaching root words typically known by a certain grade level (Biemiller, 2009) and certain academic words (Coxhead, 2000).

6. Finally, a number of word lists are available that often include web-based search capabilities for use in selecting high-frequency root and academic words important to teach and learn. The use of electronic search functions offers teachers and older students opportunities to take interesting side trips to investigate intriguing features and significant subsets of vocabulary. For example, teachers and students might explore the *Corpus of Contemporary American English* (*www.americancorpus.org*) to identify word pairings or groupings (collocates) that frequently occur in proximity to discipline-specific words they are learning. There is little doubt that word lists and other important tools for enhancing vocabulary instruction and learning will continue to benefit from technological advancements. The most useful and accessible word lists are identified in Figure 3.3.

---

1. *The Educator's Word Frequency Guide* (Zeno, Ivens, Millard, & Duvvuri, 1995). Identifies words based on frequency of occurrence in texts likely to be encountered in grades 1 through 13 (college level).
2. *Words Worth Teaching* (Biemiller, 2009). Identifies high-frequency words for instruction.
3. *Academic Word List* (Coxhead, 2000). Identifies academic learning words for instruction.
4. *Word Zones* (*www.textproject.org*). Identifies words for instruction based on fourth-grade standards-based tests.
5. *Building Background Knowledge for Academic Achievement* (Marzano, 2004). Identifies words across content areas for instruction.
6. *The Living Word Vocabulary* (Dale & O'Rourke, 1981). Indicates students' familiarity with different word meanings across the grades. Available in CD form with Biemiller's (2009) list of high-frequency words.

FIGURE 3.3. The most useful and accessible word lists.

CHAPTER 4

Early Approaches to Vocabulary Instruction

CHAPTER VOCABULARY

Response to intervention (RTI)   Integrates assessment and intervention within a multilevel prevention system designed to maximize student achievement. Within RTI, schools identify students at risk for poor learning outcomes, monitor student progress, provide evidence-based interventions, and adjust the intensity and nature of the interventions, depending on student outcomes. Most RTI utilizes a three-level approach: Tier 1, instruction for the general education classroom; Tier 2, more intensive, often small-group, instruction; and Tier 3, highly intensive and extended intervention for students who do not respond sufficiently well to Tier 1 or 2 efforts.

Standard protocol interventions   Interventions designed to address a common skill deficit for students who are struggling, including students with learning disabilities. These are often Tier 2 interventions designed to supplement the core Tier 1 instructional program. These interventions are typically provided in small groups by a teacher or tutor who has been thoroughly trained in the specific program or strategy.

INTRODUCTION

All of the early vocabulary and language development interventions described in this chapter rely on two interconnected instructional techniques to develop children's vocabulary. The first set of techniques is "evocative" in nature, encouraging children to play an active role during the instruction (Wells, 1985). For example, asking a child a "what" question is preferable to straight reading or to asking the child to point at some identified feature (e.g., a picture or word). The second set of techniques involves providing "feedback" to the child with information about vocabulary through such forms as expansion, modeling, correction, and praise to clarify meaning—for example, by asking a child "Can a ship sail over the sky?" in the story, followed by "Why wouldn't this make sense?," or by referring to his or her personal experiences ("Have you *packed* your own lunch before? What did you *pack*?"). These techniques provide children examples of slightly more advanced vocabulary than their own (Scherer & Olswang, 1984). These evocative and feedback instructional techniques along with "progressive changes" in vocabulary standards help to ensure improvement in the vocabulary and language skills of children (Wheeler, 1983).

The efficacy of the interventions described in this chapter has been established with relatively young children (i.e., preK–grade 3). Nevertheless, there is little doubt that the instructional elements included within the vocabulary and language development interventions described in this chapter can also be applied to older populations of students, including students at risk and those with language and learning difficulties. In the remainder of this chapter, we first describe picture and storybook interventions for vocabulary and language instruction, including suggestions for integrating such interventions and modifying them for diverse learners. Next, we describe a recently developed standard protocol approach to vocabulary instruction designed for response-to-intervention (RTI) and multitiered instruction delivery models. We also highlight general guidelines for enhancing instruction with the standard protocol approach. Finally, we outline the instructional implications for the information covered in this chapter.

PICTURE BOOK OR STORYBOOK READ-ALOUD INTERVENTIONS

Oral picture book and storybook reading (either with or without teacher explanation of word meanings) constitutes a significant source of vocabulary acquisition in the classroom (Elley, 1989). Thus, reading picture books or storybooks to children provides an excellent context for teaching vocabulary and language skills to children. (e.g., Crain-Thoreson & Dale, 1992; Wells, 1985; Whitehurst et al., 1988), and storybook reading may be implemented as a Tier 1 preventive vocabulary intervention. Teachers typically approach picture book or storybook reading with the intention of teaching vocabulary and language skills to children. Furthermore, research suggests that parents' (e.g., Cornell, Sénéchal, & Broda, 1988; Elley, 1989; Moerk, 1985) and teachers' (e.g., Coyne, McCoach, & Kapp, 2007; Leung & Pikulski, 1990) use of evocative and feedback instructional techniques have a positive impact on children's vocabulary and language skills.

Additionally, picture book or storybook interventions are pragmatic in that they are designed to fit naturally in the book reading opportunities provided daily to children by teachers. These interventions are typically used in conjunction with themes used by teachers to organize their picture book or storybook sessions with children. Thus, these interventions enable teachers to focus on theme-related vocabulary that they believe is important and use books available to them. The particular words and/or language skills are or are not identified a priori with the storybook or picture book interventions. Regardless, these interventions rely on the teacher to identify vocabulary and language skills for instruction.

We describe empirically validated interventions that rely on picture books or storybooks. Before proceeding, it is important to note that we focus on procedures that are used to improve the vocabulary and/or the language skills of students. These same procedures can be used to increase emergent readers' print knowledge through print referencing. Print referencing refers to techniques that can be used to increase emergent readers' knowledge about and interest in printed materials by highlighting the forms, functions, and features of print during storybook reading activities (see Justice & Ezell, 2002, 2004; Justice, Kaderavek, Fan, Sofka, & Hunt, 2009). Additionally, picture book and storybook interventions have been used to teach skills other than vocabulary, language, and literacy concepts. For example, Anderson, Anderson, and Shapiro (2004) used storybook reading to teach math concepts (e.g., size, counting) within the storybook. Most basically, picture book and storybook interventions are flexible in that teachers may use them to teach a wide range of concepts and skills. As such, these interventions can be used effectively to teach vocabulary and language skills to children.

Dialogic Reading

The essential elements of dialogic reading include the adult's:

- Providing language models.
- Asking questions to encourage the child to expand his or her language skills.
- Providing feedback to the child on his or her language or vocabulary choices.
- Eliciting increasingly sophisticated language from the child.
- Reflecting the interests of the child.

Dialogic reading is a Tier 1 preventive intervention designed to accelerate young children's language development that can be delivered by both teachers *and* parents (Whitehurst et al., 1988, 1994a, 1994b). Dialogic reading is based on the assumption that practice, feedback, and appropriately scaffolded adult–child interactions facilitate language development. Adults (parents or teachers) use specific techniques when reading picture books or storybooks with children. The adult provides models of language, asks the child questions, provides the child with feedback, and elicits increasingly sophisticated descriptions from the child, thus gradually enhancing children's vocabulary and language skills. The elements of this intervention program provide the foundation of many of the picture book- or storybook-based interventions described in this section.

The fundamental instructional techniques in dialogic reading are represented in the PEER sequence depicted below: Prompts, Evaluates, Expands, and Repeats. PEER adult–child interaction sequences should occur frequently throughout the reading of the picture book or storybook. Specifically, in PEER adult–child interactions, the adult:

1. *Prompts* the child to say something about the book. There are five types of prompts that are used in dialogic reading to begin PEER sequences. You can remember these question prompts by means of the acronym CROWD: completion; recall; open-ended; what, where, when, why, and how; and distancing question prompts (Whitehurst et al., 1994a, 1994b).

- *Completion question prompts.* Completion question prompts involve leaving a blank space at the end of or within a sentence and having students fill it in. These question prompts are used when rhymes or repetitive phrases are encountered. Example: "The loud noise made Jacob _____?"
- *Recall question prompts.* Recall question prompts involve asking about what happened in a book. These question prompts work for nearly everything except alphabet books. Recall question prompts can be used at the beginning, throughout, and the end of a storybook. Example: "Can you remember some things that happened to the dog Maddie?"
- *Open-ended question prompts.* Open-ended question prompts focus on the pictures or the major events in the books. These question prompts work best for books that have detailed illustrations. Open-ended question prompts are used most often when illustrations are encountered. Example: "What is happening in this picture?"
- What, where, when, why, *and* how *question prompts (referred to as* wh-*question prompts).* Wh-question prompts usually begin with *what, where, when, why,* and *how* questions about characters and events in the book. As with open-ended prompts, *wh*-question prompts focus most often on key aspects of the story. Again, *wh*-questions prompts work well for books that have detailed illustrations. Example: "What is this called?" or "Why is the boy running?"
- *Distancing question prompts.* Distancing question prompts ask students to relate the pictures or words in the book they are reading to experiences outside the book. These question prompts help students link what is being read with the real world. Example: "Did you ever play baseball like Jorge?" "What is it like to play baseball?"

2. *Evaluates* the child's response. When the response is correct, the adult should repeat the child's correct response and provide encouragement, indicating that the child is correct. When the response is incorrect, the adult should model a correct answer and have the child imitate that model. Additionally, the adult should provide feedback and praise (e.g., "good answer," "nice job") whenever the child responds substantively about the book.

3. *Expands* the child's response by rephrasing and adding information to it. The adult should model slightly more advanced language by repeating what the child says but with a bit more information or in a more advanced form. The best expansions add only a little more information so that the child is readily able to imitate the response. For example, if the child said "Boat float," the adult might say something like "Right, the boat is floating," or if the child said "Dog," the adult might say something like "Yes, a brown dog."

4. *Repeats* the prompt to make sure the child has learned from the expansion. The adult checks if the child has learned from the prompt, evaluation, and expansion sequence by repeating a prompt. The child's response should be accurate and more advanced than the initial response. For example, "Tell me again about what the boy is doing."

Overall, it is important for adults to reflect the interests of the children being taught by interacting with them about the things they find most interesting. Adults should engage children with the pictures they point at by talking about the story through the PEER sequence. It is also important to make reading fun by using a game-like turn-taking approach. Adults should balance the use of the PEER sequence with simply reading the story. Balancing the use of the PEER sequence with the reading of the story will help ensure that students stay fully engaged mentally throughout the picture book or storybook reading activities.

Interactive Book Reading

Interactive book reading (Wasik & Bond, 2001; Wasik, Bond, & Hindman, 2006) is a variation on the dialogic reading intervention described above. More specifically, interactive book reading embeds a specific focus on vocabulary instruction within the general language development process used in dialogic reading. Interactive book reading optimizes children's opportunities for learning vocabulary from book reading by ensuring that children encounter targeted vocabulary words (identified by the teacher) multiple times and in contexts beyond the pages of the book. Interactive book reading uses concrete representations of the vocabulary being taught to increase the salience of the word meanings being taught. As with dialogic reading, interactive book reading uses open-ended questions to encourage and engage children in a dialogue about the words being

> Interactive book reading is a variation on dialogic reading that targets vocabulary instruction.

taught as well as the book and other content. This approach to teach vocabulary to young children using explicit instruction of words together with meaningful practice is supported by a review of the effects of early vocabulary interventions (Marulis & Neuman, 2010).

Interactive book reading uses a three-step instructional sequence in conjunction with a prop box that contains two theme-related books and concrete representations of the target vocabulary being instructed. In brief, the sequence is to introduce the target vocabulary, read the storybook, and then ask reflection questions. The prop box is used over the course of several instructional sessions. The sequence is enacted during a picture book or storybook reading session that relies on dialogic interactions similar to those just described in the dialogic reading approach. The detailed sequence is:

1. *Introduce vocabulary*. The target vocabulary to be taught should be selected directly from the books used to explore a particular theme. The teacher identifies how each word is used in the book and develops a "student-friendly" definition by using everyday language understandable to students and examples of how the words might be used outside of the context of the storybook. If a word has other, less important, meanings, these are not mentioned during the instructional sequence.

During this first step, the target vocabulary is introduced prior to reading the book through use of the prop box. The prop box should contain books and objects organized around the specific theme or topic being discussed, such as "where we live," "feelings," or "the seasons." Specifically, each box typically contains two age-appropriate books carefully selected to ensure that they are related to the topic or theme and that share similar vocabulary to the picture book or storybook being read. Each box should also contain concrete objects that represent the target vocabulary in the books, which should be words thought to be unfamiliar to the children and yet necessary for the story's comprehension. For example, in a study reported by Wasik et al. (2006), the prop box for the "garden" theme contained two books, *The Carrot Seed* (Krauss, 1989) and *Jack's Garden* (Cole, 1995). The box also contained the following objects or replicas: seeds, a shovel, a rake, a small version of a garden hose, a watering can, insects, flowers, a stalk of corn, and a carrot. Pictures may be used as an alternative to the concrete object (Roberts, 2008). In this case, the target vocabulary was introduced by showing an 8" × 11" card with a picture from the storybook that illustrated the target vocabulary word. The target word was also written underneath the picture in large print.

The teacher uses the concrete objects that represent the target vocabulary and asks open-ended questions designed to actively engage the children and expand their understanding of the target vocabulary. The teacher begins by asking such questions as "What is this?" or "What do you call this?" The teacher then asks follow-up inferential questions like "What can I do with this?" or "Tell me what you know about this."

2. *Read the storybook.* Next, the storybook or picture book that includes the target vocabulary is then read, using the same instructional techniques as in the dialogic reading approach described earlier. Specifically, teachers use similar adult–child interactions as those described in the PEER interaction sequences discussed earlier. Although teachers highlight the targeted vocabulary prior to and call attention to it during the book's reading, the focus during the reading is not solely on the target vocabulary. Rather, the teacher uses the adult–child interaction sequences to help the children develop their language skills. The specific interactions described in the literature involve active listening, the modeling of rich language, and evaluative feedback.

3. *Ask reflection questions.* In the final step, after reading the story, the teacher asks a variety of reflection questions about the book and target vocabulary. These questions are also open-ended in nature, such as "What part of the book did you like the best," "Tell me why you think the boy did that," and "Have you ever done something like that?" The teacher might also generalize the learning by focusing on the targeted vocabulary during other parts of the school day (e.g., during art projects).

Ideally, the vocabulary that is targeted will be somewhat unfamiliar to students and yet important for comprehending the story. The related words and props (objects or pictures) should also be chosen carefully prior to undertaking the interactive book reading approach. This is in contrast to dialogic reading, in which the teacher tends to make decisions while reading the book based on the indicated interests of the children. As with dialogic reading, it is important to balance the time spent on teaching targeted vocabulary and related words with the actual reading of the story. Striking the right balance helps ensure that students stay engaged throughout picture book or storybook readings.

Repeated Interactive Read-Alouds

Repeated interactive read-alouds have been used to improve the vocabulary and language skills of children (Cornell et al., 1988; Hargrave & Sénéchal, 2000; McGee & Schickedanz, 2007; Pellegrini & Galda, 1982). Repeated interactive read-aloud interventions rely on open-ended adult–child interactions during book readings to develop the vocabulary and language skills of children. The primary difference between this approach and the dialogic reading or interactive book reading interventions described earlier is that the same book is read several times, thus providing opportunities for review and extension of the vocabulary and other literacy concepts taught during each read-aloud.

> Repeated interactive read-aloud approaches differ from dialogic reading and interactive book reading in that instruction is carried out through multiple readings of the same book.

The *first read-aloud* includes four components: book introduction, vocabulary support, analytical comments and questions, and postreading "why" questions. A description of each component follows.

1. *Book introduction.* The overall goal of the book introduction component is to make the main character(s) and the story problem or focus of the book explicit to children. This goal is based on research showing that effective readers begin to infer story problems from the start and use their tentative ideas about the problems to process story information (Van den Broek, 2001). The teacher initiates this component by showing children the book's front cover and, if possible, the back cover or end papers and title page. When the teacher shows these pages, he or she usually provides a general overview of the story problem or focus of the book. For example (cited in McGee & Schickedanz, 2007, p. 744), *Henny Penny* (Galdone, 1984) is about a hen who mistakenly believes that a piece of sky has fallen on her head. She is so upset by this event that she foolishly rushes with her friends to tell the king about this occurrence. Henny does not recognize the danger posed by the fox when he invites her and her friends to take a "short cut" through his cave (the story problem). The teacher explicitly states the story problem to the children when he or she shows them the front and back of the book (e.g., "This story is about a foolish hen who makes a big mistake. The hen thinks something bad is going to happen and runs with her friends to tell the king about it. The hen and her friends make a big mistake when they take a short cut through the fox's cave").

Teachers should not fixate on particular concepts of print (e.g., identification of the books' parts or the roles of the author and/or illustrator), as such emphases might divert the children's attention away from the key instructional goal of having them understand the story problems or focus of the book. This approach enhances the children's ability to attend closely to the meaning of the book as it is being read. Additionally, it is important that the teacher read with expressiveness, use gestures and dramatic pauses, vary the reading pace, and maintain eye contact with the students. These active read-aloud strategies effectively engage children during the book's reading.

2. *Vocabulary support.* The teacher selects 5–10 vocabulary words or phrases from the book that he or she wants to define or discuss during its reading. As is true with the interactive book reading approach, the words should be relatively unfamiliar to the students and yet critical to fully comprehending the story. The target vocabulary might include words that are not used in the storybook but that students need to enhance their comprehension of the story. For example, the words *mistake, catastrophe,* and *disaster* could be added to the discussion while reading *Henny Penny* (the story about the hen who thinks the sky is falling; Galdone, 1984). It is also important to select words that students are likely to encounter in other related books or that might be useful in similar contexts. The target vocabulary words or phrases are then highlighted in one or more of five ways:

- Insert a short phrase or sentence that defines or explains a word, such as "A *bank* is a place where people keep their money."
- Point out the salient parts of the story or the illustration that best clarifies the word or phrase meaning—such as point to any illustration of the bank as you read the word in the text.
- Use dramatic gestures, such as demonstrating the meaning of *flapping* by flapping your arms as you read.
- Use voice inflections, such as highlighting the humorous nature of a character by reading the text with a comical voice.
- Vary the pacing with which words or phrases are read, such as reading slowly to highlight the shuffling walking style of a character.

3. *Analytical comments and questions.* While reading, the teacher makes additional comments or poses questions that demonstrate his or her analytical thinking at three or four key junctures; ideally, these help the students to make useful inferences about the characters' thoughts, feelings, or motivations in the story. These analytical comments and questions may also be used to predict upcoming events in the storyline. Thus, the teacher uses this sequence of analytical comments and questions to enhance the children's comprehension of the story. The teacher initially uses language to signal the children's thinking by using such comments as "I'm thinking that Jorge is afraid because he doesn't like the dark." Then the teacher asks follow-up questions, such as "Why do you think Jorge will not like exploring the cave?" This deliberate teaching sequence of analytical comments and questions provides a natural context for the teacher to model analytical thinking and questioning that any ideal reader would do automatically while reading the story.

4. *Postreading "why" questions.* After reading the entire book, the teacher asks "why" questions that require the children to make inferences about and explain key story elements. The teacher then evaluates and expands on the children's responses. See the description of the evaluation and expansion questions and prompts described for dialogic reading.

The **second read-aloud** occurs a day or two after the first one. The goal of the second read-aloud is to further enhance the children's vocabulary, improve their comprehension of the story, and engage them in in additional analytical talk. The teacher begins the second read-aloud by reminding the students that they have read this book before and thus they will remember some things from the book. The teacher continues to highlight the same target vocabulary or phrases taught during the first read-aloud. However, the goal is to further develop children's understanding of the new vocabulary words or phrases. For example, in the first read-aloud we discussed with the children that "A *bank* is a place where people keep their money." During the second read-aloud the teacher might further elaborate that people use banks to save money for things they might want to buy in the future, like a car or a house.

Similarly, the analytical comments and questions are used to help the children make additional inferences about the story. During the first read-aloud, the comments and questions centered primarily on the main character(s) and points of the story. The analytical comments and questions during the second read-aloud might focus on the other characters or less prominent aspects of the story. The same sequence of analytical comments and questions used in the first read-aloud is used to further enhance the children's comprehension of the story. As with the first read-aloud, the teacher finishes the second one by asking "why" questions that require the children to make inferences about and to explain the story's elements. The teacher then evaluates and expands on the children's responses.

The **third read-aloud** occurs a day or two after the second read-aloud. The goal of the third reading is to provide the children opportunities to reconstruct their vocabulary knowledge and comprehension of the story. Once again, the teacher begins the reading by reminding the students that they have read this book before and that therefore they will remember certain things from the earlier readings. The teacher begins by asking the children questions about the title and/or the characters. The teacher then uses _wh_-question prompts—usually beginning with *what, where, when, why*, or *how*—about characters and events in the book. The teacher uses these _wh_-question prompts to help the children reconstruct key aspects of the story. During the third read-aloud the teacher continues to insert definitions and explanations of the target vocabulary and phrases. The teacher should extend some word meanings to a familiar context but not one included in the story.

Overall, each of the three read-aloud instructional sessions should build and extend the children's vocabulary, comprehension of the story, and the type of analytical thinking one employs when reading. The read-aloud instructional sessions are linked directly to one another, allowing for a progression in the vocabulary and language skills that are taught. Although perhaps most often used as a Tier 1 preventive intervention, the read-aloud interventions may also be used in Tier 2 applications for students who need more intensive or supplemental vocabulary instruction.

Extended Instruction

Extended instruction during storybook reading has been used to improve the vocabulary of children (Coyne et al., 2007). Extended instruction is designed to provide more intensive and expanded instruction in word meanings. Informed by research on effective vocabulary instruction (Bauman, Kame'enui, & Ash, 2003; Beck et al., 2002; National Reading Panel, 2000; Stahl & Fairbanks, 1986), extended

> Extended instruction provides explicit contextual and definitional vocabulary instruction designed to encourage in-depth processing of words. Extended instruction may especially help language-minority students and those with learning disabilities, who often need extended and supported opportunities to properly learn new words.

instruction is a robust approach designed to provide children rich information (i.e., beyond simple definitions) about words and their use and multiple opportunities for them to comprehend and employ the words through extensive practice with them. Extended vocabulary instruction is characterized by explicit instruction that includes using both contextual and definitional information, giving multiple exposures to target words in varied contexts, and encouraging in-depth processing of words rather than mere memorization of definitions. A critical feature of extended instruction is increasing the number of encounters with the target vocabulary by providing students maximum opportunities to interact with and discuss the target words in varied contexts beyond those introduced in the story.

Extended instruction consists of a three-step sequence: introduce and pronounce the target words, read the storybook, and engage in enhancement activities. The sequence relies on similar dialogic interactions as those described earlier for the dialogic reading approach. Furthermore, the same instructional sequence is replicated during three readings of the storybook. The detailed sequence follows:

1. *Introduce and pronounce the target words.* The target vocabulary to be taught should be selected directly from the books used during storybook reading. Ideally, the target words selected for instruction should be important for understanding the story, and yet unlikely to already be known by the students, and they should appear in contexts with sufficient information for students to infer their meanings. The teacher introduces each target word (referred to as a "magic word") encourages students to pronounce it prior to reading the storybook; typically, three words are introduced at a time.

2. *Read the storybook.* Students are encouraged to listen for each of the target words in the story. Students raise their hands when a target word is encountered in the story. The teacher then asks the student to identify the word and then rereads the sentence containing the word (e.g., "What word did you hear? Yes, *approaching*. 'And while busy gathering apples in the highest tree, he saw the wolf approaching.'"). The teacher then provides a child-friendly definition of the word (e.g., "*Approaching* means 'coming closer'."). The teacher then rereads the sentence and replaces the target word with its definition (e.g., "Now I'll say the sentence again with the words that mean *approaching*. 'And while busy gathering apples in the highest tree, he saw the wolf coming closer.'"). Finally, students are prompted to pronounce the target word (e.g., "Everyone say *approaching*.").

3. *Enhancement activities.* After the storybook reading, students engage in enhancement activities that provide them opportunities to interact with and discuss the words in rich and varied contexts beyond those offered in the story. Each activity begins with the teacher reintroducing the target words and reviewing how they were used in the story (e.g., "Remember, while the pig was busy gathering apples in the highest tree, he saw the wolf coming closer. What word means 'coming closer'? Yes! *Approaching* means 'coming closer.'"). Enhancement activities focus

on recognizing examples of target words (e.g., "I'll tell you about some things. If you think the following item is strong, say 'That's sturdy!' If you think it is not very strong, say 'Uh oh, that's not very sturdy!' A tall tower made of cards . . . this school . . . a big huge rock . . . a snowman on a hot sunny day"); answering questions about target words (e.g., "The girl looked across the yard and saw her friend running toward her. What word means 'coming closer'? Yes, *approaching*!"); formulating sentences with target words (e.g., "Everybody gets a turn making up a sentence with the word *approaching* in it. Start your sentence by saying, 'If I were approaching . . .'"); and responding to sentences containing more than one target word (e.g., "If a storm were approaching, would you go into a sturdy house?"). Teachers use dialogic interactions to encourage students to extend and elaborate on their initial responses. Finally, the teacher gives corrective feedback when necessary.

It is important to select the target vocabulary directly from the books used during the storybook reading. The words selected for instruction should be important for understanding the story and yet unlikely to be known by students, and they should appear in context with sufficient information for students to infer the meanings of the target words. The enhancement activities should be rich and varied, to ensure that the students understand how to use the word in everyday practice.

Suggestions for Integrating Picture Book and Storybook Interventions

Although there is little question that building children's vocabulary and language skills is important, it is just one of many learning goals that teachers must address during picture book or storybook reading (e.g., print referencing skills and comprehension skills are two others). Thus, educators may wonder how often they should focus on enhancing vocabulary and language skills. As a general guideline, our recommendation is that vocabulary and language development should occur whenever educators are reading picture books and storybooks with children. For example, many educators include a group read-aloud in the classroom curriculum for direct instructional purposes. Such inclusion provides an excellent opportunity to focus on vocabulary and language development instruction. Many of the research studies supporting the picture book and storybook interventions we have outlined here have involved children's participation in one instructional session per day for 3 or 4 days per week. This type of schedule suggests that picture book or storybook sessions focusing on vocabulary instruction should occur on a daily basis in small-group or large-group instructional sessions.

Within instructional sessions, the educator must be strategic in considering how many words to teach in each lesson while not detracting from the reading experience. As a general rule of thumb,

> Teach younger children one word and two to three related words per reading lesson.

targeting one word for instruction and two to three related words seems to be reasonable for younger students. The application of storybook interventions with older students might afford more opportunities to teach more words and associated related words in an effort to enhance children's vocabulary and content knowledge. The interactive book reading approach described above reduces the potential for detracting from the reading experience by teaching the words prior to and after the read-aloud. This approach reduces the amount of time devoted to teaching the target and related words during the actual read-aloud. Of course, detracting from the reading experience is less of concern when the intention is to enhance children's general language skills. In this case, the dialogic interactions play a large role in accomplishing this objective.

Modifying Picture Book and Storybook Vocabulary Interventions for Diverse Learners

Modifications for students with reading difficulties and for English language learners include:
- Slowing down the pace of instruction.
- Decreasing the verbatim reading and information statements.
- Repeating the definitions while also using child-friendly definitions.
- Increasing analytical questions and student opportunities for expansion.
- Pointing out the salient parts of the story or the illustrations that best highlight the new vocabulary being taught.

All of the picture book and storybook vocabulary interventions can be easily modified to accommodate diverse learners such as students at risk for reading problems and English language learners, and as noted may be used at the Tier 1 or 2 levels. These modifications involve the teacher's becoming more responsive to students by slowing down, decreasing his or her verbatim reading and information statements, simplifying and repeating definitions, and increasing his or her questions and expansions of children's responses (Crain-Thoreson & Dale, 1999). Additionally, it would be beneficial for the teacher to point out the salient parts of the story or the illustrations that help clarify a word or phrase meaning—such as pointing to an illustration of a bank as we read the word in the text, or using dramatic gestures to demonstrate the meaning of a word, or using physical props and pictures that represent the target vocabulary being taught.

Standard Protocol Early Vocabulary Instructional Program

Schools are increasingly using RTI intervention models to meet the needs of their students (see Fuchs, 2003, for a complete description of the characteristics of RTI models). The basic structure of RTI intervention models being used by schools include:

- Tier 1. Core instruction with opportunities for differentiated instruction, with classroom accommodations, if appropriate, provided in general education classrooms. Tier 1 programs are based on research principles and represent the primary prevention program.
- Tier 2. Supplemental empirically validated interventions for students at risk and students who are not responding to the primary prevention program. Tier 2 or secondary prevention is linked directly with the core instruction provided in general education classrooms. These approaches may include small-group tutoring.
- Tier 3. This tertiary prevention level is the most intensive level of intervention. Tier 3 instruction reflects focused individualized intervention often provided by a well-trained specialist. Tier 3 interventions may extend for longer periods of time and include lower teacher– or tutor–student ratios.

The use of small-group instruction delivered to students in need of supplemental instruction is central to RTI implementation (Vaughn, Linan-Thompson, & Hickman, 2003). Two types of interventions are used to deliver small-group instruction: individualized teacher-driven or standard protocol interventions. Although not originally conceptualized as such, the picture book and storybook interventions described earlier are examples of individualized teacher-driven intervention approaches that can be used at the Tier 1, 2, or even 3 level. Teachers guide all of the instructional decisions, based on an analysis of the critical instructional variables (e.g., target words and associated meanings). In contrast, standard protocol interventions involve the delivery of evidence-based programs that have been evaluated formally in efficacy or effectiveness trials. Standard protocol interventions are designed to be robust and flexible in terms of service delivery contexts and professionals. Although to date we know of only one early vocabulary intervention that has been conceptualized as a standard protocol Tier 2 intervention (described below), we believe that such interventions will become increasingly available, given schools' widespread use of RTI and multitiered service delivery models (Vaughn et al., 2003).

The primary advantage of standard protocol interventions is that they assure ample opportunities to impose quality control (Fuchs, Mock, Morgan, & Young, 2003). Another advantage is that schools can apply these interventions broadly across many student populations and settings. This approach therefore offers a highly efficient use of resource allocation, enabling large numbers of students to be accommodated into tiered interventions. A third and related advantage is that schools do not need to purchase any additional materials or conduct extensive staff development to assure high-quality implementation. Additionally, because many education professionals will have already had extensive training with the standard protocol intervention, they offer a built-in development resource for sustaining the intervention into the future as new professionals join the school's staff. Finally, standard protocol interventions can be implemented in a wide variety of instructional situations, including small groups within the general education classroom and special education as well as literacy support classrooms. In the remainder of this section we describe a standard protocol supplemental early vocabulary intervention that has been tested in an efficacy trial (detailed in *Early Vocabulary Connections: First Words to Know and Decode* (EVC; Nelson & Vadasy, 2007; see also Nelson, Vadasy, & Sanders, 2011; Vadasy, Nelson, & Sanders, 2011).

Although EVC (like the picture book and storybook interventions already described) relies on an interactive dialogic approach to teach word meanings, it has a number of unique instructional design features consistent with standard protocol interventions. First, 184 words that occur widely and frequently in K–1 grade-level texts were selected for instruction. Although familiar to most English-speaking students, certain high-frequency words may be less well known by English language learners (Beck, McKeown, & Omanson, 1987; Beck et al., 1982; McKeown et al., 1983, 1985; Nation & Waring, 1997). Because frequency is the characteristic most related to the likelihood a word will be decoded and understood (Adams & Huggins, 1985; Graves, Boettcher, Peacock, & Ryder, 1980; Graves et al., 1987; Solso & Juel, 1980), words selected for instruction were drawn from Biemiller's (1999) version of the Dale–Chall (Chall & Dale, 1995) list of 3,000 words commonly known by grade 4. Biemiller selected 2,300 root words from the list that are most useful in instruction. Biemiller and Slonim's (2001) sequence for acquisition of word knowledge supports the usefulness of the *Living Word Vocabulary* (Dale & O'Rourke, 1981) levels as a guide to selecting words for instruction. Words were selected from the developmentally sequenced Biemiller list. These words were then cross-checked with the K–1 Zeno lists (Zeno et al., 1995), which provide a measure (U) of word frequency per million words (weighted by an index of the dispersion, or distribution of the word across the various subject areas) sampled from texts students are likely to encounter at each grade level.

Second, because the intervention is conceptualized as a Tier 2 supplemental intervention for use in multitiered service delivery and RTI models, the high-frequency words selected for instruction were decodable based on typical K–1 alphabetic and phonics skills classroom instruction. The words selected for instruction were organized into a scope and sequence directly aligned with the typical introduction of consonants and vowels in core beginning reading curricula. This approach allowed the supplemental vocabulary intervention to be used in conjunction with existing stand-alone beginning reading curricula provided to all children in the classroom.

Third, instructional activities designed to teach word meanings are integrated with those used to reinforce the decoding skills being taught in the classroom. The integration of word meaning and decoding skill practice activities should enable students to link the supplemental vocabulary intervention with their core beginning reading instruction. This integration of instructional activities should also have a synergistic effect on children's acquisition of word meanings and decoding skills because of the key role of vocabulary knowledge in determining word reading efficiency (Lindsey, Manis, & Bailey, 2003; Nakamoto, Lindsey, & Manis, 2007; Verhoeven, 1990).

Finally, predictable instructional formats are used to ensure that both the teachers and the children become familiar with the routine and their respective roles in it (see the example lesson in Figure 4.1). The format not only guides the way and sequence in which teachers present the instructional activities but also provides the necessary instructional stimuli (e.g., child-friendly definitions for words, connected text highlighting the word meanings being taught, and decoding skills being reinforced) needed to teach each lesson. The use of predictable formats allows a wide range of educators to effectively use the supplemental vocabulary intervention program. Whitehurst (2002) concluded that high fidelity in implementing evidence-based curricula outweighs the effects of teacher background on student achievement.

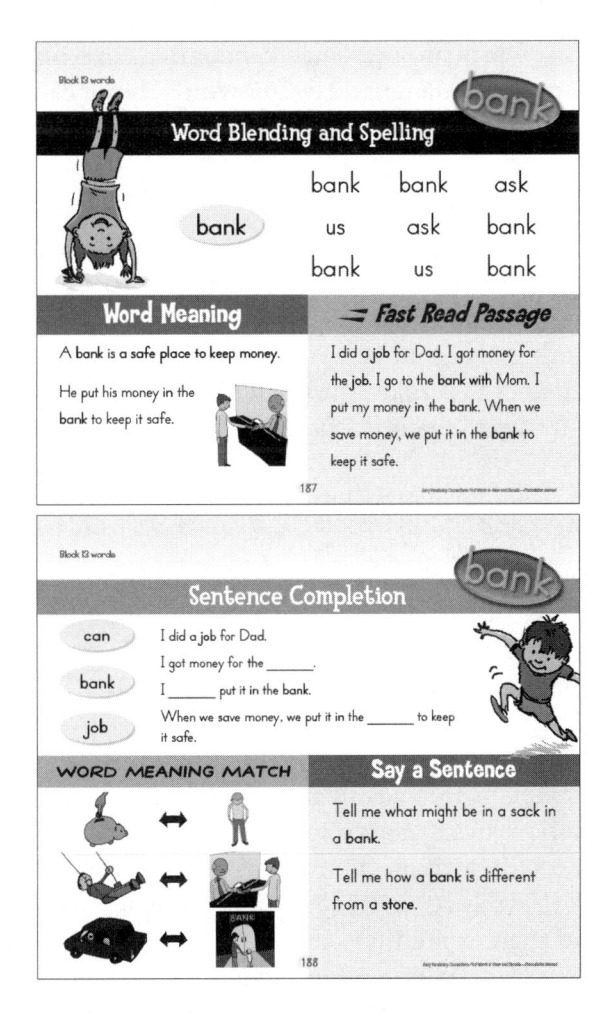

FIGURE 4.1. Example lesson from *Early Vocabulary Connections*. From Nelson and Vadasy (2007). Reprinted with permission from Sopris West.

The teacher uses a 12"×17" presentation manual to present the lesson to small groups of children. Each landscape-format page includes the activities for the lesson and is divided into two parts, with the instructional components presented on each side in large print. Because the program was designed for varied instructional situations and delivery by diverse educators (i.e., classroom teachers, resource teachers, paraeducators), the instructional activities have a predictable format. One target word is taught each day, which is a rate of vocabulary explicit instruction at which K–2 students can learn and retain word meanings well (Sénéchal, 1997). A brief description of each component is provided below. We encourage the reader to reference Figure 4.1 as he or she reads the description of each of the components.

1. *Word Blending and Spelling*. The primary instructional goals of the Word Blending and Spelling activity are to reinforce decoding skills by blending and spelling the target words. The Word Blending and Spelling activity requires students to blend target words, which are presented randomly (three times) within a serial list with two other previously taught distracter words (twice each). Multiple opportunities are designed to develop rapid unitized reading of words and phonetically accurate spelling.

2. *Word Meaning*. The primary instructional goals of the Word Meaning activity are to introduce the meaning of each target word and to have the student demonstrate understanding of the word in a scaffolded context with immediate teacher feedback. The Word Meaning activity presents child-friendly definitions of the target words. The meaning of each target word is depicted by an illustration and the word is used in a sentence to support the teacher's explanation of the definition. For example, the definition and sentence for the word *nap* is:

A *nap* is a short sleep during the day.
My baby sister takes a *nap* every afternoon.

Teachers help students understand the meaning of target words through active engagement. The teacher alternates between being the listener and the questioner for students' explanations of the meaning of target words. The directions for the Word Meaning activity follow.

- Read and explain the meaning of the target word to the students. Use the illustration and sentence to support your explanation. Follow your explanation with a recall prompt. Ask students, "Can you tell me what '_____' means or is?" Evaluate students' responses (e.g., "That's right") and then expand (or correct if necessary) students' responses by rephrasing and/or adding information.
- Repeat the recall prompt to give students another opportunity to talk about the meaning of the target word. Again, ask students, "Can you tell me what '_____' means or is?" Again, evaluate their responses (e.g.,

"That's right") and then expand (or correct if necessary) their responses by rephrasing and/or adding information.
- Ask students to think about other words that may have the *same* meaning as the target word: "Can you think of any other words that mean the *same* as '_____'?" Evaluate students' responses (e.g., "That's right") and then expand (or correct if necessary) students' responses by rephrasing and/or adding information.
- Ask students to think about words that have the *opposite* meaning of the target word. "Can you think of words that mean the *opposite* of '_____'?" Again, evaluate their responses (e.g., "That's right") and then expand (or correct if necessary) their responses by rephrasing and/or adding information.

3. *Fast Read Passage*. The primary instructional goals of the Fast Read Passage activity are to reinforce students' understanding of the meaning of target words and provide an opportunity to reinforce decoding skills through successful and independent oral reading of decodable text. The Fast Read activity requires the students themselves to read a short passage that uses the target word in a context that is decodable and meaningful to young children. While most of the passage is written to be decodable based on the letter sound sequence used in the program, the last sentence in each passage is a less decodable sentence meant for the teacher to read. This last sentence confirms the meaning of the target word by using the context of the passage. For example, the passage for the word *nap* consists of three decodable sentences and one less decodable sentence:

The cat had a nap.
The cat had a nap on Nan's cap.
The cat had a nap on a cap!
The cat did not sleep long—he just had a nap.

The teacher and student first read aloud each passage together. The teacher–student read aloud is then followed by a student read-aloud. Each read-aloud is repeated until students can read the passage fluently and show comprehension of the text containing the target words. Students are asked to think about the meaning for the target words prior to each read-aloud. The teacher checks for understanding at the end of each read-aloud.

4. *Sentence Completion*. The primary instructional goals of the Sentence Completion activity are to reinforce students' understanding of the meaning of target words and to develop comprehension sequencing skills (i.e., arranging items or events in correct order). The Sentence Completion activity requires students to "fill in the blanks" in a cloze procedure task. The cloze procedure requires the student to use the sentence context to choose the appropriate word that goes in the blank. Students use clues from the context to supply the correct one of three words that

have been deliberately removed from the text. This cloze task also provides scaffolded syntactic awareness practice, requiring the students to use the words in the correct position in a sentence. The task is scaffolded by having students choose the correct word from a small restricted set of three words. Students are instructed to say the appropriate word that goes in the blank. For example, the Sentence Completion activity for the word *nap* is as follows.

Sentence	**Word Choices**
The cat had a nap.	
The cat had a _____ on Nan's cap.	cap
The cat had a nap on a _____!	nap
The _____ didn't sleep long—he just had a nap.	cat

5. *Word Meaning Match.* The primary instructional goal of the Word Meaning Match activity is to check students' understanding of the meaning of target words. The activity requires that students correctly identify the illustration depicting the target word from a pair of possible alternatives. The teacher helps the child describe and extend his or her understanding of the attributes of the illustration that best communicates the meaning of the target word. Three pairs of alternatives are presented in each lesson.

6. *Say a Sentence.* The primary instructional goals of this activity are to reinforce students' understanding of the meaning of the target words. Activities 1–5 (described above) are primarily recognition tasks, whereas the Say a Sentence activity requires the student to use the word orally. Unique prompts are provided for each word so that teachers do not need to extemporaneously create an appropriate and engaging prompt. When possible, the prompt requires the student to discriminate between two taught words (e.g., for the words *hot* and *damp*, the prompt is "Tell me how *hot* is different from *damp*"). Prompts vary in the degree to which they challenge students, and they enable the teacher to individualize instruction for students within a group. Some prompts are easier and require students to discriminate between two choices (e.g., "Tell me if *ham* is a meat or a vegetable"), while other prompts challenge students to use the correct word in context (e.g., "Tell me what it is like if the light is *dim*"). Teachers use the unique prompt provided for each word to promote conversation about the word, including encouraging child talk, promoting active listening, and providing feedback. The prompts are constructed to help students use the target words in a correct and meaningful context. The teacher alternates between being the questioner and the listener for responses that require the student to use each target word in a sentence.

Overall, *Early Vocabulary Connections* is a standard protocol supplemental early vocabulary intervention designed to simultaneously promote both the vocabulary and decoding skills of children. There are two levels of the program: Level 1, First Words to Know and Decode (Nelson & Vadasy, 2007); and Level 2, Important

Words to Know and Spell (Vadasy & Nelson, 2008). Level 2 builds directly on the vocabulary knowledge taught in Level 1. *First Words to Know and Decode* is designed for children who are just learning to read, while *Important Words to Know and Spell* is intended for children who are consolidating their decoding skills. Like Level 1, Level 2 is a complete scope-and-sequence process with all instructional stimuli. The 380 words in Level 2 are introduced in pairs to facilitate teaching and learning. The word pairs are based on semantic (e.g., *office–desk, bridge–river*), opposite (e.g., *peace–war, question–answer*), or other word relationships (e.g., *much–cost, how–way, very–often*). Teaching the words in pairs enables teachers to build semantic relationships within the word categories and to increase the instructional efficiency of each lesson. Pairing words also helps children establish an initial conceptual network for each word.

Suggestions for Enhancing Student Success

EVC is designed to be used with small groups of children. Some tips for organizing small groups of children for EVC instruction include:

1. Sit the children on chairs in a curved row in front of the teacher. It is important that the children be able to see the teacher presentation manual without much effort. This arrangement also ensures that the teacher is able to observe the children closely.
2. Children who need the highest degree of instructional scaffolding should be placed directly in front of the teacher. This approach will better enable the children to pay close attention, thus providing them additional instructional support.
3. The teacher should assign seats individually, helping to ensure that the children sit where they will benefit most from the instruction. Assigning seats also minimizes the amount of time needed to transition from the preceding instructional activity.
4. Get into the lesson quickly. Present each instructional activity as it appears in the presentation book, and keep up a brisk pace within and across the lessons.

This small-group instructional format requires that teachers employ a combination of group and individual student responses. Teachers should use a group signal to cue students when to respond in unison (i.e., a choral response) and should then call on individual students (in individual turns) to respond throughout the lesson. Although the teacher should engage all students individually throughout the lesson, he or she should focus primarily on those students who struggle the most in acquiring word meanings and decoding skills. Teachers should monitor these most instructionally needy students to assess the groups' acquisition and consolidation of word meanings and decoding skills. Teachers should not move to individual turns until the group as a whole sounds confident in their responses. This approach increases the success rate of the instructionally needy students. We recommend the following signal procedures for each of the instructional activities to engage and cue students to respond in unison. Of course, the purpose of using these cues is to maintain a pace that enables the teacher to introduce one new word each day during limited instructional time. Suggested signal cues for each EVC instructional activity are detailed in Table 4.1.

SUMMARY

Research indicates that language and vocabulary development plays a significant role in classroom learning experiences (Holbrook, 1983; National Reading Panel, 2000). The language and vocabulary interventions described in this chapter provide teachers a number of ways to enhance language and vocabulary development in the classroom. With the exception of *Early Vocabulary Connections* (Nelson & Vadasy, 2007), all of these interventions require the teacher to identify the vocabulary for instruction, develop the new words' meanings, and identify any props or scaffolds required for instruction. In contrast, EVC is a Tier 2 standard protocol approach to vocabulary instruction that is linked directly to the core beginning reading program. This standard protocol includes all of the program materials needed for instruction and provides simultaneous instruction in vocabulary and practice in decoding skills. This linkage between the two is important because vocabulary knowledge plays a key role in word reading efficiency (Lindsey et al., 2003; Nakamoto et al., 2007). All of the interventions rely on interactive dialogic approaches and feedback instructional techniques to build and expand children's understanding of the vocabulary being taught. A brief summary of the procedures used to identify vocabulary, the primary instructional procedures, and the number and types of exposure to vocabulary for each of the vocabulary instruction interventions described in this chapter are presented in Table 4.2. General instructional implications that can be drawn from the early vocabulary interventions described include:

1. The teacher provides a student-friendly description, explanation, and example of the target word meaning. Definitions in themselves are not sufficient for students to learn the meaning of words. However, conversation-based descriptions, explanations, and examples are useful for students' initial learning of word meanings and how they are used. This process can be supported with physical gestures (when applicable), props, and illustrations.
2. Evocative and feedback instructional techniques play a central role in all of the early vocabulary intervention approaches. Evocative techniques encourage children to take an active role during instruction, whereas feedback practices such as expansion, modeling, correction, and praise are used to clarify and further elaborate the word meanings.
3. Students should have opportunities to use the vocabulary independently.

TABLE 4.1. Signal Cues for EVC Instructional Activities

Instructional activity	Signal cue
Word blending and spelling	Use a verbal prompt (e.g., "Ready") and physical prompt (i.e., finger pointing at the first letter of the initial word) to engage students. Then say "Begin" and slowly slide your finger under the letters within the word to prompt children to blend the letter sounds, and then say the word fast in unison. Move to the next word after a short pause, and slide your finger under the letters within the word, and so on. There is no need to say "begin" at the start of each word if your pacing is consistent and smooth within and across the words.
Word meaning	Use a verbal prompt (e.g., "Ready") and physical prompt (i.e., raised palm) to engage students. Then drop your hand to prompt students to respond in unison. Identify responses provided by students (they will differ somewhat in this activity) to use in your evaluation and discussion of their responses.
Fast read passage	Use a verbal prompt (e.g., "Ready") and physical prompt (i.e., finger pointing at the first letter of the initial word) to engage students. Then say "Begin" and slide your finger under the word in the passage to prompt children to read the passage in unison. Use the word meaning signals to prompt students to respond to questions that stimulate student use of the target words.
Sentence completion	Use a verbal prompt (e.g., "Ready") and physical prompt (i.e., finger pointing at the first letter of the initial word) to engage students. Then say "Begin" and slide your finger under the word in the passage to prompt children to read the sentences in unison. Use the word meaning signals to prompt students to respond with the appropriate word that completes the sentence.
Word meaning match	Use a verbal prompt (e.g., "Ready") and physical prompt (i.e., finger pointing at an illustration) to engage students. Then say "Does this picture show the meaning of . . . ?" Move to the next picture after a short pause, and repeat the prompt, and so on. Actively engage students throughout this activity. There is no need to say "Begin" at the start of each word if your pacing is consistent and smooth across the illustrations.
Tell or write a word meaning message	Use a verbal prompt (e.g., "Ready") and physical prompt (i.e., raised palm) to engage students. Then drop your hand to prompt each student to respond individually. Discuss the responses provided by the students (each student's response will differ in this activity) and provide feedback that evaluates each response.

TABLE 4.2. Summary of Instructional Attributes

Intervention	Identification of vocabulary	Primary instructional procedures	Number and types of exposure to vocabulary
Dialogic reading	Selected from the book, based on the natural interest of the children during the book reading	Interactive dialogic approach during the book reading	Exposure during the book reading
Interactive book reading	Selected (unfamiliar words important for comprehension of the story) from the book by the teacher prior to the book reading	Vocabulary introduced prior to the book reading with the use of props, interactive dialogic approach during the book reading, and use of reflection questions after the book reading	Minimum of three exposures (before, during, and after the book reading)
Repeated interactive read-alouds	Selected (unfamiliar words important for comprehension of the story) from the book by the teacher prior to the book reading	Vocabulary introduced and expanded upon by using the interactive dialogic approach during three book reading sessions across several days and through enhancement activities after the final book reading	Multiple exposures across three read-aloud sessions
Early Vocabulary Connections	184 decodable root words that frequently occur in K–1 texts (organized by the typical introduction of consonants and vowels in core reading programs)	Vocabulary introduced and expanded upon by using an explicit and interactive dialogic approach during instructional activities and through independent student use of the words	Minimum of six exposures across the instructional activities

Students' acquisition of word meanings are enhanced when they construct their own explanations and use of the words. It may be important for this self-assertiveness to occur not only in the context of the instruction (e.g., the story reading) but also in other contexts in which new words are used.
4. Students' acquisition of vocabulary is enhanced through multiple exposures. In other words, students should encounter vocabulary several times during and outside of the lesson.

CHAPTER 5

Evidence-Based Instructional Approaches for School-Age Children

Specific Important Word Meanings

CHAPTER VOCABULARY

Academic words Words that occur regularly in academic texts in a wide variety of subject areas. These are words that do not often occur in everyday and informal conversation. They are often abstract, frequently used to talk or write about ideas or research (e.g., *element, contribute, concept, assume*). Academic language generally relates to schooling and education.

Tier Two words "Words that are of high frequency for mature language learners and are found across a variety of domains" (Beck et al., 2002, p. 8) (e.g., *expedition, prosperous, savored, menace, lavish, cunning*).

INTRODUCTION

Vocabulary knowledge becomes increasingly important once students master early word reading skills and begin to "read to learn." When students are learning to decode words, they need to *know*—in the sense of recognizing spoken words, the words that are used in everyday spoken language. Early readers rely on their oral vocabulary skills to understand the words that they decode. In the texts they read, beginning readers encounter primarily words that are familiar and decodable, generally high-frequency words already in their oral vocabulary—words like *dog, cat, play, red,* and *house*. However, as students begin to read longer and increasingly more difficult texts in grades 3 and 4, they soon encounter words that do not necessarily occur in conversation and that they have not encountered before in speaking and listening. These include longer and more interesting words that occur in children's literature, like *crumpled, relished*, and *tampering*. These also include words that occur in school texts across the content areas, like *rotate, major, dimension*, and *generate*. Because students must be able to understand at least 95% of the words in a text to comprehend it, gaps in their vocabulary knowledge of these word types begin to limit their comprehension. Students at risk for reading problems, with learning difficulties, and from diverse language backgrounds are most likely to experience these gaps in word knowledge that create obstacles to comprehension.

Researchers recommend that teachers prepare students for the more challenging texts that await them by introducing primary grade children to words that constructively build their vocabulary and that they are about to encounter in print (Biemiller & Boote, 2006; Biemiller & Slonim, 2001; Robbins & Ehri, 1994). Chapter 4 described approaches to teaching vocabulary to young children, generally RTI Tier 2 approaches for students at risk for limited vocabulary knowledge. This early vocabulary instruction prepares children for increased reading and writing demands. School-age students need to understand certain words that are often used across school texts, including the finer distinctions in the meanings of related words (for example, understanding the difference between a *bad* person and an *unprincipled* person, or the difference between *typical, mediocre*, and *average*). By grades 3–4, students begin to need knowledge of specialized vocabulary (words like *stem, root, petal*, or *planet, rotate, system*) that appears in their content area reading. Finding opportunities to gradually introduce these words to young children makes sense. Good readers have very large vocabularies. Further, it often takes up to 12 separate encounters with a word (speaking, reading, writing, or hearing it) to learn it well and be able to use it. A broad and deep vocabulary base supports reading and also enables students to express themselves clearly in writing. These are reasons for early elementary school instruction to build vocabulary. For students who begin to fall behind their peers early on in vocabulary learning, especially students at risk or with learning disabilities, prompt efforts to promote vocabulary knowledge are particularly important. Without such direct instruction, these students are less likely to acquire new vocabulary, have greater difficulty remembering new word meanings, and may ultimately need remedial instruction to make new vocabulary a part of their personal lexicon.

In this chapter we describe two research-based approaches to direct vocabulary instruction of school-age children. Both approaches build on early findings that effective vocabulary instruction must include sufficient firsthand practice with the words and their meanings (Kame'enui, Carnine, & Freschi, 1982; Jenkins, Matlock, & Slocum, 1989; Pany, Jenkins, & Schreck, 1982). However, as noted in Chapter 2, instruction in meanings alone does not provide students with the desired depth of word knowledge. The two approaches described in this chapter go well beyond brief exposures to definitions, providing contextual information as well about words, with multiple exposures and activities that engage students in deep and extended processing in both speech and writing (see Stahl, 2005). The first approach, developed by the researchers Beck, McKeown, and Kucan (2002, 2008), is often known as "rich" or "robust" vocabulary instruction. This approach is characterized by intensive instruction to develop in-depth word knowledge. It targets instruction in particular types of words that are regarded as important and useful and that therefore warrant extra instructional time. The rich and robust vocabulary approach was developed and is most often used as a key Tier 1 vocabulary intervention. The second approach, a schoolwide vocabulary intervention for middle school students, is in the process of being developed and studied by Catherine Snow and her colleagues (Snow, Lawrence, & White, 2009) at the time of this writing. It is also a primary Tier 1 intervention, targeting instruction in *academic* words. Both of these approaches to vocabulary development are intensive, involving extended and active interactions with the target vocabulary. Each approach identifies a specific category of words for instruction. The approaches differ, however, in certain important ways, such as their starting point for choosing words and their involvement of either classroom or schoolwide staff. Both approaches describe activities that engage students in active and deep processing. These activities require students to make connections between words, to employ them in diverse contexts, and to use them to express themselves and their thinking about important issues. These are the routes students must travel to fully understand a new vocabulary word and be able to use it correctly.

RICH AND ROBUST VOCABULARY INSTRUCTION

There is broad consensus on the strong link between vocabulary knowledge and reading comprehension. Given the large number of students (especially ones from ethnic and language-minority groups and those with learning disabilities and low levels of language skills) who chronically lag behind their peers in vocabulary knowledge, and with gaps in word knowledge that only increase over time (Biemiller & Slonim, 2001), researchers have long sought to identify superior approaches to teaching vocabulary. Researchers Isabel Beck, Margaret McKeown, and Linda Kucan developed the "rich vocabulary instruction approach" to offer teachers a method of improving children's vocabulary knowledge of useful and mature words as well as developing their skills in learning related words in context. A defining feature of this approach is actively engaging students in processing new words in their natural context. Word definitions are only the starting point in learning words, merely preparing students for repeated encounters with the words and ever deeper levels of processing. The underlying assumption is that this type of engagement develops semantic network connections and also facilitates learning related words from context (McKeown, Beck, Omanson, & Pople, 1985). Imbedded in these activities is implicit instruction directed toward reasoning with words and text (e.g., "Could a *philanthropist* be a dictator?") that likely strengthens children's comprehension.

The rich vocabulary approach is based on a presumed causal link between the knowledge of word meanings and reading comprehension that rests on two hypotheses. First, the *instrumentalist hypothesis* holds that ready access to word meanings has a direct impact on reading comprehension (Anderson & Freebody, 1981). Second, the *access hypothesis* holds that the accuracy and speed of retrieving knowledge of words is also important for comprehension (Mezynski, 1983). This access hypothesis is implicitly linked to Perfetti's (1985) *verbal efficiency theory*: reading comprehension is compromised when lexical processes, such as accessing the meanings of words, are not automatic. The procedures for this rich vocabulary

> **Tier Two Words**
>
> - Words that characterize written text.
> - Words that are not common in everyday conversation.
> - More sophisticated than everyday words.
> - Very useful words for learning from texts.
> - Words that students with lower language and literacy skills are less likely to know.

approach were initially tested in two core studies (Beck et al., 1982; McKeown et al., 1983), and these studies are widely cited in the research literature. The studied instruction targeted words that were "judged likely to be unknown, yet useful and interesting" (McKeown et al., 1983, p. 6). These words were later identified as "Tier Two" words, "words that are of high frequency for mature language learners and are found across a variety of domains" (Beck et al., 2002, p. 8; Beck & McKeown, 1985). The target word corpus for this approach has definitionally become these Tier Two words. The "rich" vocabulary instruction approach has been used in other storybook reading interventions for primary grade children, including repeated read-alouds with first graders at risk for reading difficulties (Maynard, Pullen, & Coyne, 2010), and read-alouds that include direct instruction of advanced vocabulary (Beck & McKeown, 2007).

The Target "Rich" Words

Beck et al. (2002, 2008) created a now widely used three-tier framework to select words for this explicit instruction. In this framework, Tier One words are the high-frequency words that most students know, learn on their own, and usually do not need to be taught explicitly. Tier Three words are low-frequency words used in specialized contexts and best taught when students encounter them in learning about a topic. Tier Two words are of moderate to low frequency, characterize sophisticated language use, and are useful in literate discourse. Tier Two words also represent concepts that are familiar to students and that can be clearly explained in simple language. As noted in Chapter 3, there is no formal list of Tier Two words, and teachers must identify and select these words from the texts being used in the classroom.

Perhaps the most noteworthy finding of Beck et al.'s (1982) initial study was the significant effects of rich vocabulary instruction on both proximal (words actually taught in the program) *and* distal (words not taught in the program) vocabulary knowledge *and* reading comprehension. The study showed that the approach had significant positive effects on students' reading comprehension and vocabulary knowledge, as measured by norm-referenced tests as well as experimenter-developed tests of vocabulary knowledge. One important and sobering finding from this study is that at least 12 encounters with target words were needed to produce significant comprehension gains. In this study, instruction included 14 weeks of 5-day cycles (at 30 minutes per day) in which 8–10 words each week were introduced, practiced, and tested for mastery. Each cycle featured a variety of instructional activities, including defining, sentence generating, classifying, producing oral and written responses, timed games, and forming semantic and affective word relationships. The routine below outlines typical activities in a 5-day cycle for four specific words taught in the 1982 study (*accomplice, novice, philanthropist,* and *virtuoso*).

- *Day 1 (Monday): Defining words, forming word associations.* The entire set of 8–10 words is defined. The teacher reads the words and describes the contexts in which the words appear. The teacher then reads student-friendly definitions of the words, and students write the words in their vocabulary log. Then the teacher provides opportunities for the students to interact with the words and meanings. The teacher may show word cards and have students pronounce the words. The class may play a word association game to explore word relationships (e.g., the teacher takes the four target words, presents a clue word related to one of the target words—say, *crook* for *accomplice, teacher* for *novice, charity* for *philanthropist,* and *violin* for *virtuoso*—and then asks the students how the two words are related; students then justify their responses). The teacher may lead a game that taps students' affective associations with the target words (e.g., the teacher says the target word and asks students to say "yay" or "boo" to show how they feel about the word, with students defending their responses). These activities are repeated for each of the words in the 5-day cycle.

- *Day 2 (Tuesday): Sentence completion activity.* Students complete sentence stems for the target words that require students to reason and evaluate the use of the words in different contexts (e.g., "The *accomplice* swore he would never break the law again because . . ." "If I were a *philanthropist* I would . . ." "When the *virtuoso* violinist was a *novice*, she . . ."). One sentence stem is presented and discussed for each word in the cycle. The teacher divides the class into teams for a game to match each new word with its definition. Teams aim for both accuracy and speed.

- *Day 3 (Wednesday): Generate contexts and situations.* Students engage in activities to generate contexts and situations for the target words. For example, for the following words the students choose the appropriate response for each question:

"Would an *accomplice* be more likely to rob a bank or enjoy babysitting?"
"Would a *novice* writer be teaching or taking a writing class?"
"How would someone walk *cautiously* on an icy sidewalk?"
"Where would you be likely to find a *virtuoso* tuba player?"

Students justify their responses and then think of one added behavior for a word like *accomplice* ("An *accomplice* to a bank robber sometimes drives the getaway car"; or "An *accomplice* might get caught, and the judge might send him to jail").

- *Day 4 (Thursday): Game to develop speed of word and meaning retrieval.* Students play "Ready, Set, Go," a game intended to develop speed in matching the new vocabulary words with their definitions. Students draw lines connecting the words to the definitions, with a partner recording the time. Each student completes four laps, trying to beat his or her previous time. Alternatively, students engage in an activity intended to help them think about the words in new ways: "Could an *accomplice* be a *hero*?" "Would a *hermit* likely be an *accomplice*?" "Would a *miser* give away his money to charity?" "Would you pay $50 to go see a *virtuoso* or a *novice* pianist?"

- *Day 5 (Friday): Word test.* Students are assessed on the words taught within the cycle by having them complete a multiple-choice word knowledge task, and then the teacher reviews the words with the students as needed.

In a subsequent 2008 book, Beck, McKeown, and Kucan expanded on the questions and examples about their vocabulary approach. For example, in this volume they discuss the when and how of teaching these words. They advise preteaching only those words that are essential for understanding the text, and they recommend teaching Tier Two words after the first reading of the text. For example, after reading a passage on drought and the environment, vocabulary instruction might elaborate on the meanings and usage of Tier Two words from the text, like *barren, precarious,* and *parched*. The teacher provides user-friendly definitions based on the COBUILD dictionary definitions that are more accessible to students who are totally unfamiliar with a word.

After the words and meanings are introduced before or after the reading of the text in which they occur, the teacher provides additional examples of the words in new contexts. As noted earlier, students must typically encounter a new word multiple times and in different contexts in order to truly know and "own" the word. The opportunities to actively process the words build upon cognitive theory and also help to heighten motivation and engagement in vocabulary learning. Although the activities in this approach are varied, they typically occur in a pattern that is predictable for both teachers and students. Instruction begins with introducing the words' meanings, and after the student interacts with the words in diverse ways, subsequent tasks require more active processing of the words, increased use and evaluation of the words in varied contexts, and accessing the words and meanings in real-time interactions.

This whole approach is fully described for teachers in the initial book, *Bringing Words to Life* (Beck et al., 2002), and the later one, *Creating Robust Vocabulary* (Beck et al., 2008). In their 2008 volume, the authors provide extended examples and teaching scripts, and recommend specific grade-level novels and corresponding lists of target Tier Two vocabulary words. For example, the authors outline a week of instruction for teaching the following set of eight words that appear in the assigned reading for the class novel: *benevolently, ironic, subtle, preoccupied, sarcastic, philosophical, nonchalantly,* and *inevitable*. Examples of activities for each day include:

- *Day 1.* The Teacher refers to the part of the text in which the target word *benevolently* was used:

"In Chapter 1, we read that 'The judge smiled *benevolently*.'"

Next the teacher defines the word:

"A *benevolent* principal would be very understanding and willing to help students."

Then the teacher asks the class to interact with the word and to evaluate sentences in which the word is used. The teacher requires students to explain their responses, and an important aspect of this exercise is to help them make their thinking steps more explicit, that is, to help students learn how to make connections and integrate new word meanings.

"If I say something that might be *benevolent*, say 'That's *benevolent*!' If not, don't say anything:
 "Offering to help someone move into their new home.
 "Ignoring a person who is having trouble with a suitcase.
 "Interrupting someone who is trying to explain her problem.
 "Asking someone if he has a ride home from the game."

- *Day 2.* The teacher prompts the students to think about features of each of the eight target word meanings with the following question about the word *benevolent*:

"Would a *benevolent* person be likely to ignore a cry for help? Why or why not?"

The students work in groups with a teacher prompt to develop contexts or examples about each word:

"Tell about someone whom you think of as *benevolent*."

- *Day 3.* The teacher asks students to complete analogies for each of the focus words, including *benevolent* and *preoccupied*:

"Someone who is *benevolent* is not mean or selfish; someone who is *preoccupied* is not. . . ."

Students work with a partner to create other analogies with pairs of vocabulary words, like *benevolent* and *sarcastic*. One set of partners creates an incomplete analogy, and another pair completes the analogy. The teacher reviews the word meanings, and students create explanations for each word. The class discusses the students' explanations and decides which explanations make the most sense. Students write the explanations in their vocabulary logs.

- *Day 4.* Students work in pairs to complete sentence stems (see below). Students share their work with the class and discuss which sentences provide strong contexts for the focus words:

> "Our gym teacher can be described as *benevolent* because . . ."
> "The *sarcastic* comment made the girl feel . . ."
> "Because I did not study for the test, it was *inevitable* that . . ."
> "It was *ironic* that she ordered the pork chop on the menu because . . ."

Students work in small groups to reread assigned sections of the class novel and respond to comprehension questions that include the focus words. Finally, the teacher may ask the students to find examples in songs or outside readings that feature the focus vocabulary words.

- *Day 5.* The teacher and students review the eight vocabulary words, and students are tested on the words' meaning on either a true-or-false test or a test of sentence stems that students must complete.

Unique Features of Professional Development

In Beck et al. (2008) the authors outline professional development for robust instruction for four grade-level categories: K–3, 4–5, 6–8, and 9–12. For each grade span, the book provides a specific grade-level text and a typical sequence of activities. For example, for grades 4–5, the authors outline the sequence of activities for:

- Selecting Tier Two words.
- Contextualizing the words, based on their use in the story.
- Crafting student-friendly definitions.
- Creating contexts for using the words that go beyond the text.
- Developing follow-up activities (with a menu provided).
- Constructing an assessment.

Key Features of the Rich and Robust Vocabulary Approach

- Teach important and interesting words that can be learned in the context of studying a specific novel.
- Teach words intensively, providing multiple exposures to the word in varied classroom activities.
- Create opportunities for students to use the new words in speech and writing, to interact with the words, and to consider the new words' relationships to other words.

For each activity above, the authors create an exercise for the teacher or reader to practice the steps in planning this type of instruction, one based on the study of a preselected class novel:

- *Engage.* Complete each activity. For example, the teacher or reader may select the Tier Two words *gregarious* and *garnished* from the sample reading passage.
- *Compare.* Compare the reader's choice to the author's choice. For example, the authors explain why they chose the word *gregarious* for instruction (because it reflects middle school students' experiences in talking about friendly and outgoing people) and why they did not choose the word *garnished* (because it is most typically used in association with food and might not have broader applications for middle school students).
- *Consider and reflect.* The authors add a rationale for each activity and word choices and provide questions to guide the teacher's choice of activities for instruction. For example, the authors compare various types of definitions for Tier Two words (e.g., from traditional dictionaries vs. a COBUILD dictionary) and point out features to help teachers craft student-friendly definitions. The authors also provide examples of how to make COBUILD definitions even more "student-friendly."

THE WORD GENERATION PROGRAM

> **Academic Language Features**
>
> Academic vocabulary includes discipline-specific words (e.g., *fulcrum, hypotenuse*) as well as general academic words (e.g., *analysis*, conclusion). The latter general academic words are high-leverage words to teach because they occur frequently across content areas. Academic language is characterized by:
> - Conciseness.
> - A high density of information-bearing words.
> - Dense grammatical structures.
> - Reduced use of personal pronouns.
> - The use of an impersonal authoritative voice.
> - General rather than specific claims (Snow, 2010).

In 2002, Harvard education professor Catherine Snow and a team of colleagues, including collaborators from the Boston public schools, set out to improve middle school literacy. Many of the middle school students in Boston, as in many urban districts serving large numbers of at-risk students, were reading below grade level. The research team developed the Word Generation program in response to the widening gap in Boston students' vocabulary and background knowledge. Many students' limited word and concept knowledge had prevented them from understanding what they read and from learning new words in their school texts. The Word Generation program is unusual in its schoolwide approach to vocabulary development. Implementation involves the collaboration of school teams, including literacy coaches, English as a second language teachers, and classroom teachers. The schoolwide organization of the program is particularly appropriate for the types of words that are taught in the program. Word Generation has a focus on academic vocabulary, words that occur across diverse content areas. The researchers chose these words because they are often neglected. Unlike such specialized words as *photosynthesis* or *mitochondria*, academic words don't "belong" to a specific discipline or content area. Often highly abstract, academic words are used to express relationships, describe communication processes (e.g., *respond, implicate, debate, publish, convince*), or talk about research and knowledge (e.g., *theory, derive, interpret, conduct, justify, element*). The words used in the Word Generation program are derived from Coxhead's (2006) *Academic Word List* (see Chapter 3 for a detailed description of this list). These all-purpose academic words are extremely useful for effective discussion and debate. They support student thinking about school content and are necessary for more advanced cognitive processes (e.g., classifying information, expressing relationships, communicating with an academic or scientific audience).

In using the *Word Generation* program, teachers should seek to:

- *Select a corpus of generative words.* The researchers chose academic words from a well-established list of 570 academic word families (Coxhead, 2006). The words are useful to teach explicitly and intensively because they occur across subject areas. These often abstract words are difficult to learn from context or from dictionary definitions (e.g., *amnesty, eligible, alter, equity, perspective, constrain, proceed*). A powerful and motivation building feature of the program is that the starting point for instruction was the topics around which instruction was designed. The specific words included in the program were those that could be productively used and taught to discuss high-interest and often controversial topics that included:

> Should the government fund stem cell research?
> Should the school day be extended?
> Should shopping malls be allowed to institute teen curfews?
> Should stores use paper or plastic bags?
> Should English be the official language of the United States?
> Should there be censorship of libraries and popular music?

Although the topics may not directly reflect those included in the regular curriculum, they offer teachers an opportunity to help students examine important, timely, and often controversial topics connected with subject areas.

- *Ensure repeated exposures.* The program is structured to provide 15 minutes per day on the weekly topic and words. Each Monday, the teacher introduces a topic paragraph and five focus words for the week. Activities are outlined for students to interact with the words each day of the week (see sample weekly schedule below). The weekly paragraphs are selected for their relevance to middle school students and generally relate to humanities, science, and math topics. Written at the sixth-grade reading level, they deal with real-world issues, encouraging students to engage in stimulating discussion and writing.

- *Provide opportunities for students to use the words.* The program includes 24 week-long units. Each unit outlines in-depth instruction for five academic words. Activities for each day of the week include:

> The teacher introduces the topic, reads the topic paragraph, introduces the words and meanings, and leads a class discussion based on guiding comprehension questions.
> The teacher introduces multiple meanings of the words and leads a discussion on similarities and differences in the meanings.
> The teacher posts four position statements on the week's topic, and the students choose a statement to discuss with peers. The groups take turns defending their positions and engage in practicing the focus words.
> The teacher conducts a math or science activity to discuss the general versus content-specific meanings of the target words.
> The week typically ends with a writing activity in response to a writing prompt on the week's topic. Again, students are encouraged to use the focus words in their writing.

- *Present the words in semantically rich contexts.* The meanings of abstract academic words like *theory* and *constrain* are difficult to teach with dictionary definitions. As we noted in Chapter 2, dictionary definitions are themselves often abstract and difficult to explain to students unfamiliar with the words. These words are most effectively understood by seeing them used in many different illustrative contexts.

Word Generation builds upon the way students learn much of their vocabulary—from context. Instruction offers students practice and feedback in using context effectively to understand unfamiliar words.

- *Teach word learning strategies.* Strategy instruction is incorporated into the Word Generation activities. For example, students learn about multiple meanings and to be aware of how a word is used in different contexts. The program also teaches students about morphological relationships, roots, cognates, and how to evaluate the usefulness of context to derive word meanings.

Word Generation provides instruction in strategies students can take away to continue building their academic vocabularies. This strategy instruction is provided in contexts that afford opportunities for both teacher modeling and learning from the ways that other students use context successfully.

- *Provide learner-friendly definitions.* Dictionary definitions are particularly inadequate in helping students understand the meaning of these often abstract academic words. *Word Generation* provides explanations of the words and examples of the words in clear contexts—more effective methods of helping students understand their meanings.

- *Expand each word's semantic mapping.* Teachers are encouraged to begin instruction with the core meaning of the word. However, because many of these academic words have shades of meaning and may be used in different academic contexts, it is important to help students notice these meaning variations. For example, the word *constant* may be used to mean "steadfast and loyal" but it is also used in mathematics to mean "a quantity with a fixed value."

When students engage in deeper levels of semantic processing, word meaning is encoded in their memory with more supporting information than a simple definition (Craik & Lockhart, 1972b). This feature builds on research on how a learner integrates knowledge of new word meanings with his or her own existing and developing semantic frameworks (Beck et al., 1987).

- *Encourage word awareness.* As the developers point out, the goal of Word Generation is not limited to teaching only the words included in the curriculum. There are far more words that students must learn than can be taught directly, and word awareness and word learning strategies are also instructional objectives of the program. Activities are designed to heighten students' word awareness and to help them be successful in learning more words through incidental exposure. Students keep a vocabulary log of the focus words they are learning.

Classroom vocabulary instruction is acknowledged as the first level of a "cognitive apprenticeship" involving word learning (Resnick, 1989). Encouraging students' independent discovery of new words is a feature of many vocabulary approaches, and these approaches typically include students' use of vocabulary notebooks.

- *Encourage experimentation and expect mistakes.* Word Generation developers emphasize that students must be encouraged to *use* the words in order to get feedback on their use. Students must feel safe to make mistakes when they first begin to use new words. Professional development clearly outlines specific teacher "moves" that support these student trials in word learning. For example, one effective teacher "move" is revoicing. Teachers found that when they were first teaching a word to their middle school students, the students often provided responses that were unclear or confused. For one thing, these students are often inexperienced in discussing substantive topics. When student responses are not clear, the teacher repeats part or all of the student response and asks the student to verify whether the teacher's interpretation is correct or not.

Word Generation Teaching Strategies

- Academic words are difficult to learn incidentally.
- Many academic words can only be well understood in context (e.g., *justify, inherent, crucial, infer*).
- Learning requires many examples as well as practice in using the words in context.
- *Word Generation* creates opportunities for students to use these words to discuss timely topics.
- Teacher strategies ("moves") help teachers identify what students already know about the word or concept and what they still need to learn.
- Teachers help students use words in discussions that readily engage them and sharpen their reasoning skills.

This "move" helps teachers keep students engaged, pushes students to use their reasoning skills, and gives students credit for how they used the word. Other "moves" that are introduced in the program are described below. The teacher goal is to create interactions in which students feel safe in attempting to discuss a controversial topic that requires using new vocabulary. The program design takes into account that many middle school students have not thought about or discussed the often controversial topics. The authentic debates create opportunities for students to learn and practice both vocabulary and reasoning skills—something that students must increasingly do to make sense of more difficult reading texts.

This practice in experimenting with new words is a particularly important feature because of the unreliability of context in revealing word meanings. The odds that a student can learn a word from a single encounter in context are between 1 in 20 and 1 in 7 (Herman, Anderson, Pearson, & Nagy, 1987; Nagy et al., 1987; Shu, Anderson, & Zhang, 1995).

Unique Features of Professional Development

Training for teachers in Word Generation procedures includes one special feature to support specific and varied student scaffolding strategies. This feature is the use of teacher strategies to elicit student responses, help students make obvious their reasoning for their statements, and require students to go deeper in their thinking about topics. These specific strategies are called "moves," and the teacher "moves" used in the program include:

- *Revoice.* The teacher repeats a student's response in order to have him or her verify whether the teacher interpreted the response correctly.
- *Say more.* This request allows a student to add more to a peer's earlier response, often providing an opportunity for quiet or less confident students to contribute.
- *Repeat.* This is an often challenging instruction that requires a student to reformulate a peer's earlier statement. Because students must anticipate being called upon, they must pay close attention in order to be prepared to "repeat." This simple move heightens students' level of listening.
- *Agree/Disagree.* This instruction requests that students explain why they agree or disagree, thus requiring them to hear and weigh one another's statements carefully.
- *Why do you think?* This move requires students to explain how they arrived at their position—whether through evidence, by citing the text, or by using text features. This explanation enables students to lay bare their thinking and helps all students better understand how people develop their positions on important issues.
- *Wait time.* This move affords opportunities for the quiet, reticent, and less

confident students to formulate their statements and then contribute to the discussion.

Professional development also prepares teachers to elicit students' "accountable talk" about the topics. This process involves deriving relevant information from the text, using the context to make informed guesses at word meaning, connecting the new vocabulary words to prior knowledge, listening carefully to peers, and showing students how to rationalize and defend their responses.

Sample Weekly Schedule

The schoolwide collaborative aspect of Word Generation is illustrated in a sample weekly schedule of the program. Generally, the focus words are introduced in a paragraph passage on Monday. On Tuesday through Thursday, students engage in content-area activities involving the focus words. On Friday, the students complete a writing activity with the focus words. In the following example, teachers spent 15 minutes each day on a Word Generation activity. The daily 15-minute activities in this week's unit were designed to be conducted by the student's English, social studies, science, and math teachers.

- *Day 1.* The English teacher introduces the topic passage and describes the five target words by using student-friendly definitions. The teacher employs a set of comprehension questions to guide class members in both understanding the passage and discussing their views on the topic.
- *Day 2.* The social studies teacher posts four position statements on the topic. The students choose a position and then group themselves to discuss their positions. The students practice identifying the reasons and evidence underlying their positions.
- *Day 3.* The science teacher provides a science-related passage to give students added practice in using the words in different contexts and in different forms. The teacher may involve students in interpreting data and drawing conclusions.
- *Day 4.* The math teacher presents mathematics problems that are related to the weekly topic and that feature the target words in a math context.
- *Day 5.* The English teacher gives students a writing prompt for a persuasive essay on the week's topic. Students are encouraged to include the focus words in their essay.

Connecting Vocabulary Learning across Subjects and across the School Day

- Explicitly plan and support student discourse on important topics that are meaningful, and actively engage the students in debate and critical thinking.
- Create opportunities to teach and guide students in using new vocabulary and concepts to discuss important topics.

Word Generation materials are available for field testing, and teachers can register to use them through the program's website. The program includes a teacher guide and related professional development material, including extensive website resources (see *wordgeneration.org*).

Research on Word Generation

Preliminary evidence suggests that the Word Generation program is effective in building academic vocabulary knowledge in middle school students. In a quasi-experimental study, Snow et al. (2009) tested Word Generation in five schools, with three schools in the same district that did not use the program serving as controls. Schools undertook to use the program voluntarily, with the Word Generation schools serving a large proportion of students from low-income and language-minority backgrounds. The study involved students in grades 6–8. The researchers found that students who received Word Generation instruction learned more of the taught words than students in the comparison schools. Data from one school serving a large number of language-minority students supported the benefits of the program for language-minority students. Researchers suggested that the complex skills taught in Word Generation (i.e., deep reading, thoughtful discussion, debate, and writing about engaging topics) were related to performance on the state achievement test. As noted, the study design had a number of limitations, and the researchers are currently conducting an experimental study of the curriculum in a larger implementation.

SUMMARY

In this chapter we described two vocabulary programs for school-age students. The instructional conditions of the "rich and robust" vocabulary approach are widely recommended and have been drawn upon in many vocabulary programs. The features provide a framework for teaching a set of Tier Two words that are familiar to mature language users.

The Word Generation program takes a schoolwide approach to vocabulary and literacy development for middle school students. The starting point for the program is a set of current issues that spark civic engagement and debate and topics that interest adolescent students. These issues enable students to use the focus words in the types of contexts in which the words are typically used—to discuss and analyze ideas and to communicate about knowledge. The program is structured so that repeated exposures to the words are provided, in part through schoolwide involvement in vocabulary learning.

These two evidence-based vocabulary programs, one classroom- and one school-based, reflect research-based principles for vocabulary learning that have important implications for classroom vocabulary instruction.

INSTRUCTIONAL IMPLICATIONS

1. Two categories of words are regarded as especially worthy of explicit vocabulary instruction for school-age students: *Tier Two words* that characterize literate discourse and mature language use and *academic words* that occur widely in school texts across the various disciplines. Both of these types of words occur more frequently in written text than in conversations and are less likely to be learned from exposure to the media or through conversations.

2. The instructional design and preliminary research findings on both programs support the benefits of teaching vocabulary intensively through the respective program activities. Both programs include activities that provide multiple exposures to the target words. Both programs require intensive student engagement and interaction with the words and related concepts.

3. Vocabulary knowledge, in particular for low-frequency and academic words, is intricately related to comprehension. Science texts, for example, often define concepts using general academic words that students may not know. Further, many of these words are *polysemous*, that is, have shades of meaning that depend on the context. Students need practice in matching the correct meanings to different contexts in school texts.

4. Particularly for language-minority students and students with more limited vocabulary skills, vocabulary development can best be fostered through firsthand interactions with the new words in discussions and through practice in reasoning and writing about related topics. These activities provide the repeated word encounters often required to learn challenging vocabulary. Research on vocabulary learning for second-language learners also specifically concludes that depth of vocabulary knowledge is best acquired through repeated exposures and a long-term approach to instruction. Second-language learners generally require 5–20 repeated exposures to a new word, and the periodic review of previously taught words is especially crucial to their long-term retention of new vocabulary (Nation, 1990). Effective learning is most closely associated with instruction that maximizes students' firsthand engagement with the words.

CHAPTER 6

Independent Vocabulary Learning Approaches

CHAPTER VOCABULARY

Context	The text surrounding an unfamiliar word.
Keyword method	A method used to remember word meanings by associating the unfamiliar word with a word already known and connecting the meaning of the new word with an image associated with the known word.
Mnemonic	Memory-enhancing. Mnemonic devices are used often in foreign language learning.
Morpheme	The smallest meaningful part of a word (e.g., in the word *childish*, there are two morphemes: *child* and *-ish*).
Morphemic	Having to do with the small individual parts of a word.
Semantic	Having to do with the meaning of a word, phrase, or sentence.
Semantic features analysis	A method used to teach vocabulary and comprehension by analyzing the features of a set of related words.
Semantic mapping	A method used to teach vocabulary and comprehension by laying out the relationships among a group of related words.

INTRODUCTION

One approach to building vocabulary is to directly teach individual word meanings. In Chapter 5 we described two RTI Tier 1 preventive primary intervention approaches for teaching the meanings of two specific groups of words, Tier Two and academic words. The *rich vocabulary* approach is widely utilized by *classroom* teachers to provide instruction in Tier Two vocabulary—words that are used by mature language users—while *Word Generation* is a unique *whole-school* approach to teaching academic vocabulary that students encounter across their various subject areas. These two approaches both offer useful principles for organizing vocabulary instruction at the classroom and school levels.

There are other widely used and perhaps more discrete classroom techniques for teaching individual words. Much of the research on these techniques has been conducted with special populations of students, including students with learning disabilities and those learning English as a second language. The evidence for the efficacy of these techniques varies greatly, but most incorporate aspects of these agreed-upon principles of effective vocabulary instruction:

- Provide the definition of the word.
- Provide examples of the word used in different sentence contexts.
- Engage students in active processing and analysis of the word.
- Provide multiple exposures of the word in varied contexts.
- Engage students in discussions about the word's meaning (see Graves, 2009; Stahl & Fairbanks, 1986; Stahl & Nagy, 2006).

In the first part of this chapter, we describe several cognitive strategies that help students understand groups of related words. We outline the basic components of these semantic strategies and the research on their effectiveness.

The research we earlier reviewed on vocabulary size makes clear the limits of trying to directly teach all of the individual word meanings a student must learn. The time required to teach an individual word is estimated at between 5 and 26 minutes, far more time than is available to teach the 3,000–4,000 word families that students need to learn annually in grades 3–12 (Jenkins et al., 1989; Nagy & Herman, 1987). To be effective lifelong vocabulary learners, all students need successful independent strategies for learning vocabulary from context.

Therefore, in the second part of this chapter, we review the research on teaching students strategies to use context in learning word meanings. The average-skilled student who reads at least 15–30 minutes a day encounters many unfamiliar words that can be learned through context to build a strong reading vocabulary. Some students develop strategies for learning vocabulary through context with minimal explicit instruction in these learning strategies. However, students who read less and who struggle with reading problems are less likely to acquire new vocabulary words in this way. They are also less likely to develop effective independent strategies for word learning. Researchers have considered approaches to help these students improve their vocabulary. The goal of the context use approaches is to teach students a set of skills they can apply when they are reading independently. As students become independent skilled readers, these contextual analysis strategies are often used in tandem with looking up words in the dictionary. Instruction in dictionary use helps students locate the right words to find a meaning and to take advantage of information in dictionary entries that builds word knowledge and supports the productive use of new vocabulary.

Finally, we also review research on *mnemonic* techniques for remembering taught vocabulary, in particular research on the *keyword method*. These mnemonic strategies are also used to help students remember important concepts in the content areas (e.g., systems of scientific classification, the periodic table of the elements, the chronological order of the U.S. presidents).

SEMANTIC APPROACHES TO VOCABULARY INSTRUCTION

Semantic techniques are used to activate student background knowledge and to develop better understanding of the underlying concepts represented by vocabulary words. These approaches are based on a hypothesis that seeks to explain the relationship between vocabulary and reading comprehension. This *knowledge hypothesis* holds that vocabulary knowledge reflects an underlying appreciation of the concepts that account for the strong connection between vocabulary and comprehension (Anderson & Freebody, 1981). Semantic approaches are used to develop depth of knowledge of both words and concepts. These approaches are especially helpful in teaching words and concepts that encompass abstract and complex ideas—such as *democracy, conservation*, and *evolution*. Teaching the definitions of these words is only the first step in helping students understand their meaning and proper usage in diverse contexts.

Semantic approaches are used most effectively to teach groups of vocabulary words related to a specific topic (e.g., new vocabulary words that appear in a text on plate tectonics might be *core, magma, molten, mantle, crust, plate, tectonics, subduction, earthquake, volcano,* and *continent*). Instruction sometimes begins with a brainstorming session to generate words related to the target word or concept.

Two of the most widely used semantic approaches are *semantic mapping* and *semantic features analysis*. We briefly consider how each of these approaches is used and taught.

Semantic Mapping

Semantic mapping is a useful activity that can help students learn words and understand how groups of words are related. It is most often used with Tier 1 content-area instruction and can readily be incorporated into a lesson on a new content area topic—such as, say, forms of government or types of fish or dinosaurs. New words are categorized into topics with other words the students know. These groups of words are then analyzed in terms of how they are similar and different. One approach to semantic mapping has four steps:

1. *Brainstorming.* The teacher and class members generate terms related to the main topic or target word.
2. *Mapping.* Terms are then organized into a map by using categories that the teacher and students specify.
3. *Reading.* When the map is complete, the class reads the text on the topic.
4. *Reviewing the map.* After reading the text or studying the topic, class members revisit the map and add terms or categories, referencing the map while discussing the text (see Stahl & Nagy, 2006, pp. 84–85).

Semantic maps create word networks that reflect how our brain organizes and stores words and information. For example, the group of words about the topic of plate tectonics might be organized in a semantic map that relates the words to features of the earth's surface.

Semantic Map on Plate Tectonics

Earth layers or location	Earth movement or eruption
magma	tectonics
core	subduction
crust	earthquake
plate	volcano

The following example of a semantic map features a group of words from the *Academic Word List* (Coxhead, 2006). These words are related to the concepts of "texts" and "publications" and can be grouped for instruction into the following categories:

Semantic Map of Academic Words

Types of publications or texts	Parts of a text	Features of texts
manual	chapter	author
issue (of journal)	text	theme
thesis	draft	format
document	margin	bias
book	appendix	topic
journal	chart	paragraph

Discussion of these words can then focus on understanding the differences among the words and how they relate to one another. Students might discuss, for example, who might be the author of a *thesis* or a *journal* or a *manual*. Who are the audiences for a *manual*, a *thesis*, a *book*? What information might you find in an *appendix* or a *chart*? What kinds of *texts* would a student use? A lawyer? What kind of information would you find in a *manual*?

Semantic Features Analysis

Semantic features analysis, another vocabulary technique easily integrated into Tier 1 classroom instruction, is used to compare the characteristics of a related group of words. The teacher outlines a grid that lists the words on the left side, and the characteristics or features that differentiate the words across the top of the grid. The students then review the grid, discussing whether other features should be added. Then the teacher completes the grid with the class, taking each word and deciding whether to place a plus or a minus sign in the column beneath each feature, depending upon its applicability. This type of analysis requires students to consider and discuss the qualities of each member of the category. In what ways are the members similar and how are they different. At the end of the discussion, the students try to summarize the information in the grid. With continued instruction in the topic, the students add categories to the grid. A basic semantic map can be used as the first step in a semantic features analysis. This example shows a partially completed grid.

Semantic Features Analysis Chart for the Study of Fossils

	Bone	Footprint	Burrow	Leaf	Shell	Pollen
Mold				+	+	−
Cast	+			+	+	−
Imprint		+	−	+		
Petrification						
Whole animal or plant	+			+	+	

In this example, the types of materials that can be preserved in a type of fossil formation are listed across the top of the grid. The types of fossil formations are listed in the left-hand column of the grid. Class members would discuss these features and fill in the grid by determining which materials could be preserved in the fossil formation types listed. Many templates for semantic maps and semantic features analysis charts are available online. Both semantic mapping and semantic features analysis require time to set up. These approaches are most appropriate for teaching groups of words that support reading and understanding important concepts in science or social science.

Research on Semantic Approaches

In a review of vocabulary instruction for students with learning disabilities (Jitendra et al., 2004) based on 10 group design studies, these semantic approaches were found to be very effective (mean effect size = 1.10), superior to traditional vocabulary instructional methods (e.g., dictionary lookup, direct instruction), and also had large follow-up effects (mean effect size = 0.94), although transfer effects (to untaught words) were moderate. A series of studies on teaching these semantic strategies to students with learning disabilities was conducted by Candace Bos and her colleagues (e.g., Bos, Allen, & Scanlon, 1989; Bos & Anders, 1990, 1992; Bos, Anders, Filip, & Jaffe, 1989). In one of these studies, Bos and Anders (1990) studied the use of semantic maps and semantic features analysis with junior high students with learning disabilities. In the semantic mapping condition, the teacher and students constructed a hierarchical map to represent a list of concept-related vocabulary words from a passage on fossils. For example, a semantic map on fossils (including the words *remains, sedimentary, preserve, minerals, fossil, uplifting*, and *erosion*) was organized, based on how fossils are formed. In the semantic feature analysis condition, the teacher and students constructed a relationship matrix that described superordinate and subordinate concepts represented by the vocabulary words. For example, a matrix on fossils may include the superordinate category of "rocks," under which the word *sedimentary* would be discussed. Teachers and students in the study interacted and discussed the maps and matrices. Compared to students in a definition-only condition, the students who received the interactive semantic strategies instruction scored higher at posttest on vocabulary and comprehension multiple-choice items. The two types of semantic instruction shared several features of many effective vocabulary approaches, specifically:

- The activities required the students to activate their background knowledge and to interact with their peers in sharing the information.
- Students had to make predictions about the relationships between the concepts and then to confirm their predictions.
- In-depth instruction occurred through students' discussions about the words in the various textbook contexts for their study of fossils.

In a recent review of vocabulary interventions for students in grades pre-K–12 and their impact on reading comprehension (Elleman et al., 2009), the studies that featured higher levels of discussion were associated with larger effects on vocabulary outcomes. This review also found that students with reading problems made more than three times the gains in comprehension as compared to students without reading problems. Semantic approaches offer an effective Tier 1 vocabulary intervention for at-risk students, including English language learners, and for students with learning disabilities.

USING CONTEXT TO LEARN WORD MEANINGS

Students derive and learn many new word meanings incidentally under normal reading conditions (Nagy et al., 1985). It is estimated that students learn about 15% of the unfamiliar words they encounter (Swanborn & de Glopper, 1999). Students can learn to become more successful in deriving words from context (Fukkink & de Glopper, 1998; Kuhn & Stahl, 1998). They may use *word-level* context clues found in the small parts of words (morphological analysis), and they may use cues from the *textual context* surrounding the unfamiliar words (contextual analysis).

Morphological Analysis

Teachers often incorporate instruction in morphological analysis into their classroom Tier 1 instruction, either as part of literacy or content area reading. Skilled readers figure out word meanings by using context clues. One approach is to analyze the immediate word context and study the parts of the word. This morphological approach is also known as structural analysis. Morphemes are the smallest meaningful parts of a word, including the root, prefix, suffix, or inflected ending. Each of these small word parts may provide clues to the word meaning. When White, Power, and White (1989) set out to find out how many affixed words students actually encounter and what proportion of them could be figured out (in terms of their meaning) solely through morphological analysis, they found that students encounter a dramatic increase in the number of words with common prefixes between grades 3 and 7. They found that the meaning of many words *cannot* be determined based solely on knowledge of the most familiar root meaning. But they also concluded that about 80% of affixed words can be successfully analyzed by taking them apart and that instruction related to prefixes is the most useful.

Students with a proper understanding of morphology are able to derive the meanings of most complex words and also tend to be good readers (Carlisle, 2000; Nagy & Anderson, 1984). In a recent study (Carlisle & Fleming, 2003), students' skills in analyzing morphologically complex words measured in the first and third grades significantly contributed to their skill in understanding complex words and reading comprehension 2 years later. Related research suggests that morphological analysis also contributes importantly to the growth in students' vocabulary throughout the elementary school grades (Nunes & Bryant, 2011; White et al., 1989; Wysocki & Jenkins, 1987).

Students can be taught to break an unfamiliar word into parts, to identify the meaning of each part, and then to put the parts back together to arrive at a word's meaning. However, morphological analysis alone does not always lead students to a word's complete and full-bodied meaning, and young and less skilled students may often overlook important semantic and syntactic clues. True morphological awareness may also reflect students' relative skills in reading derived words, and morphology's relation to word reading and decoding skills increases during the elementary grades.

Analyzing word parts appears to be most usefully undertaken beginning in middle school (Anglin, 1993). Students are better able to read derived words that are high frequency and *phonologically transparent* (in which the pronunciation of the base word does not change in its derived form) than less frequent words in which the base word is more difficult to recognize. Examples of phonologically transparent and opaque derived words are:

Phonologically Transparent
grow–growth
art–artist
active–activity
interpret–interpretation

Phonologically Opaque
heal–health
nature–naturalist
major–majority
reserve–reservation

Words may also be either orthographically transparent (i.e., retaining the spelling of the base word in their derived form) or orthographically opaque. Examples of these types of derivations are:

Orthographically Transparent
heal–health
converge–convergence
herb–herbal
liberal–liberalize

Orthographically Opaque
strong–strength
abstain–abstinence
crime–criminal
retain–retention

When the spelling or pronunciation of the base word changes in its derived form, it is more difficult for students to find or recognize the root word and sort out the word's meaning.

The most valuable morphemic units for instruction are roots and affixes. As noted in Chapter 2, high-frequency prefixes are extremely worthwhile to teach, as their spelling and meaning are relatively consistent (White et al., 1989), there are comparatively few of them, and yet they are used in many words. The majority of prefixed words feature some 20 prefixes. The recommended guidelines for morphological analysis include explicitly teaching the meanings of high-frequency prefixes and providing guided practice in using the prefixes to figure out word meanings. For example, one should teach the prefix *dis-* in the following way:

1. Read and discuss a group of root words to be practiced: *regard, obedient, own, satisfy.*
2. Explain the meaning of the prefix (*dis* = not, reverse), and discuss how the prefix changes the meaning of the root words.
3. Attach the prefix (*dis-*) to each root word, discuss, and have students try to derive word meanings (i.e., for *disregard, disobedient, disown, dissatisfy*).
4. Use the prefixed words in sentences.
5. Have students practice deriving the meanings of additional words with the target prefix (e.g., *dishonest, dislocate, disbelief, disassemble*) (see Edwards, Font, Baumann, & Boland, 2004; Graves & Hammond, 1980).

Most Useful Prefixes to Teach

un-
re-
in-
dis-

There are several provisions one should note in teaching morphological analysis. Students may be confused or misled by prefixes that have multiple meanings.

For example, the prefix *un-* may mean "not" or it may mean "back." If the student assumes that *un-* always means "not," it will lead to misunderstanding the words *unclasp* and *unload* for example. There are other hazards, and not all words can be literally taken apart and analyzed to produce an accurate meaning, for example: *undulate, under, rebus, region, distaff, district.*

Because morphological analysis is one part of a broader context-use strategy, its use has been studied both as a separate strategy and in combination with context analysis. Baumann and his colleagues (Baumann, Edwards, et al., 2002; Baumann, Edwards, Boland, Olejnik, & Kame'enui, 2003) studied the benefits of teaching either morphological analysis or contextual analysis, or both, to middle school students. They found that the former helped students figure our individual word meanings while the latter helped students infer the meanings of unfamiliar words in contexts used in the study. They found that middle school students were able to apply the combined morphological and contextual analysis strategies to identify the meanings of unfamiliar words in the textbooks used in the study. Training to recognize morphemic units may also have spelling benefits. Students with learning disabilities often experience difficulty in spelling derived words, recognizing root words, and learning the spelling patterns of affixes. With instruction and practice in word structures and their spellings, students with learning disabilities improve in their spelling of complex words (Arnbak & Elbro, 2000; Nunes, Bryant, & Olsson, 2003; Tsesmeli & Seymour, 2008). In these studies students ranged in age from 7 to 15 years.

Morphology and Language-Minority Students and Students with Learning Disabilities

More recent research suggests that morphological awareness is also important for English language learners and makes a significant contribution to their reading comprehension. It may be that students with higher levels of morphological awareness are better able to process complex words in texts that support comprehension. Students with morphological awareness may have more complete word knowledge at the phonological, orthographic, and semantic levels. In their study of language-minority students through grades 4–5, Kieffer and Lesaux (2008) found that the relative knowledge of derivational morphology predicted reading comprehension for language-minority students in grade 5, indicating that morphological training may help language-minority students improve in English reading comprehension through its strong relationship with vocabulary knowledge. They recommend explicit instruction in morphological analysis in the context of vocabulary instruction, including high-frequency affixes, roots, and attention to how the pronunciation and spelling of words may be transformed in derived word forms (Kieffer & Lesaux, 2007). A review of research on morphology-related interventions supports its benefits for vocabulary and comprehension, indicating that students with learning difficulties benefit from direct instruction in morphological analysis (Arnbak & Elbro, 2000; Reed, 2008).

Contextual Analysis

Skilled readers also figure out the meanings of individual words by analyzing the surrounding context. As we noted in Chapter 1, experts agree that most of students' word learning occurs during independent reading (Nagy et al., 1987). As they read, good readers use clues in the text to figure out the meanings of new words they encounter. One way to help less skilled readers take advantage of context is to teach students how to use context cues successfully. These approaches provide students with explicit instruction in how to look for clues around the unfamiliar target word that may help one figure out its meaning. Contextual analysis is a strategy that is difficult to master, thus requiring explicit instruction and intensive practice across subject areas and grade levels.

Many contextual analysis approaches teach students to recognize two types of clues: syntactic and semantic. Syntactic clues refer to the word order in the sentence and the syntax of the word (i.e., whether it is a noun, verb, or adjective). For example, in the following sentence:

The boy who won the contest took on a *supercilious* attitude.

the word *supercilious* may be unfamiliar to the reader. Yet, using syntactic clues, the reader can at least determine that it is an adjective that describes the boy's attitude. By reading on to the next sentence in the text, the student may obtain more context clues that help him or her to derive the meaning:

After the contest the boy would not even talk to his friends, and acted like he was too good to spend time with them.

Combining the syntactic cue that the word describes the boy with this added context information, the student may be able to figure out that *supercilious* means "scornful."

The textual context provides varying levels of support for learning a new word meaning. Some contexts are helpful and provide multiple clues to word meaning—for example, a context that provides a direct synonym (e.g., "The rat poison was *efficacious*, or very effective in ridding the house of the pests"). Another type of helpful context provides a contrast that helps the student to derive the meaning of an unfamiliar word (e.g., "The new housekeeper was *assiduous* in cleaning the house, unlike the previous housekeeper, who was careless and undependable"). Other context cues may aid one in other ways in deducing word meanings—for example, if an unknown word appears a number of times in the text or if the unknown word occurs near the cue in the text. Other contexts are less helpful or even misleading and make it difficult for a student to infer the meaning of an unfamiliar word (e.g., "The sound was *plangent*" or "The reporter was *obsequious*"). Obviously, context cues vary in their usefulness, and many contexts are insufficiently rich in their details to be of much help in deriving meanings. Moreover, students vary greatly in their skills in using context to decipher the meaning of unknown words.

Several strategies suggesting how best to use context cues to unlock word meanings have been studied. These strategies include teaching students context cue types. For example, context clue types taught in one study (Baumann, Edwards, et al., 2003, p. 464) were:

1. Definition clues (e.g.," When the sun hit its *zenith*, which means *right overhead* . . .").
2. Synonym (e.g., "Captain Jackson's uniform was *impeccable*. In fact, it was so *perfect* . . .").
3. Antonym (e.g., "The soldier was very *intrepid* in battle, in contrast to the person next to him, who was quite *cowardly*").
4. Example (e.g., "*Tigers, lions, panthers, and leopards* are some of the most beautiful members of the *feline* family").
5. General (e.g., "*Patriotism* was a *very strong force* in the South. People *loved their part of the country* and were *very proud to be a Southerner.*").

Context use instruction is typically provided to middle school and older students. In many studies the students are taught to use a basic strategy. For example, in one study, (Carnine, Kame'enui, & Coyle, 1984, p. 197) students were taught a rule: "When there's a hard word in a sentence, look for other words in the story that tell you more about the word." In another study (Jenkins et al., 1989, p. 221), students were taught to use a helpful five-letter mnemonic, SCANR:

1. **S**ubstitute a word or expression for the unknown word.
2. **C**heck the context for the clues that support your idea.
3. **A**sk if substitution fits all context clues.
4. **N**eed a new idea?
5. **R**evise your idea to fit the context.

Contextual Analysis Steps

- Find the unknown word.
- Is it defined in the context?
- Look for clues within the same sentence.
- Look for clues in nearby sentences.
- Guess the word's meaning.
- Check to see if it makes sense in the sentence.
- If there are no clues, or if your guess does not fit, check the dictionary.

Because contexts vary in the quality and quantity of clues they provide to a word's meaning, students should learn to check their guess to be sure it makes sense in the context of the sentence and the overall text.

Research on Context Use Instruction

Reviews of research on teaching students to infer meanings from the surrounding context support the conclusion that explicit instruction in context use *does* help students learn to infer word meanings (Fukkink & de Glopper, 1998; Kuhn & Stahl,

1998). The average effect of this instruction appears to be moderate ($d = 0.43$; Fukkink & de Glopper, 1998). As we noted, contexts that are not revealing do not lend themselves to using context clues, and some readers lack skills in using the clues. Two important influences on students' productive use of context to learn vocabulary are their previous knowledge of vocabulary related to the subject and their background knowledge about the subject itself (Carlisle, Fleming, & Gudbrandsen, 2000).

Fukkink and de Glopper (1998) found that context clue instruction was effective, although the studies did not clearly show that this instruction generalized beyond the clue types taught and the contexts used. Teaching strategies to derive meanings from context may be effective, in particular when students are given adequate practice in applying the strategies. For example, in one study, moderate (practicing 15 words a day for 11 sessions) or high (practicing 15 words a day for 20 sessions) levels of practice were needed to be effective in deriving meanings of words from context (Jenkins et al., 1989).

Many of these approaches entail rather extensive procedures. Students must practice finding clues to meaning in the passage, then using the clues to guess the word's meaning, and then evaluating whether their guess makes sense in the immediate context. Pressley, Disney, and Anderson (2007) pointed out one overlooked finding from the context use studies reviewed by Kuhn and Stahl (1998), namely, that control students in four of the studies who were instructed to simply try to figure out the meanings of the words in the texts (they were not instructed in the use of context clues) did as well as the respondents who were given instruction. The amount of time needed to teach students to use different types of context clues has led other vocabulary experts to question its costs and benefits, and Stahl and Nagy (2006) recommend teaching students comprehension monitoring techniques instead. Although most of the research on context clues has been conducted for its use as a Tier 1 classroom intervention, it may be used as a Tier 2 or 3 intervention when students have persistent difficulties in using context effectively, and when more intensive or individualized intervention is warranted.

USING THE DICTIONARY AND OTHER REFERENCES

Students who read as widely and actively as they should inevitably encounter many words with which they are not familiar. They must be able to use a dictionary effectively. Some readers keep a dictionary handy as they read, while others list words to look up later. Sometimes dictionary definitions end up confirming a reader's initial hunches about meaning—but, again, other times they introduce the reader to new and unexpected ideas. Although dictionaries are valuable tools, they are complex resources that students need to learn to use correctly and effectively.

Dictionaries are designed to include a lot of information about a lot of words in as little space as possible. A single word entry may include multiple meanings, the parts of speech, synonyms, word origins, and examples of the word used in various sentences. The conventions that have developed to compress this information into a brief dictionary entry make it wise for students to seek out training in its proper understanding. Students (as well as many adults) are often unaware of how dictionaries are organized and what kinds of information about words they contain. Students with limited language or reading skills may find dictionary definitions especially bewildering and unhelpful.

Of greatest interest to students when they consult a dictionary is the definition. As we noted earlier, dictionary definitions are often disappointingly unhelpful, in particular for students who have not been introduced to how dictionary definitions are structured. Definitions must be written to be very concise to save space and to include many entries. Further, definitions may contain words that are also unfamiliar to the student (e.g., *haj*—A **pilgrimage** to Mecca). Words are often defined in terms of superordinate and subordinate relationships (e.g., *habeas corpus*—one of a variety of **writs** . . .), making them unhelpful to understand if the student is not familiar with the larger family of things (i.e., *writs*).

In spite of their limitations, dictionaries are important resources, and vocabulary experts offer recommendations for teaching students to use these references. First, choose the best dictionary to match the student's age(s) and skills (see Table 6.1). Students will progress through a variety of dictionaries during their school years. The grand *Oxford English Dictionary* (OED) may be an excellent and beloved match for the university English major. Younger and less skilled students are better matched to a dictionary with these two important features:

- *User-friendly definitions*—written in complete sentences with common words.
- *Examples*—well-selected examples to show how the word is used in typical contexts and grammatical patterns.

As others also recommend, the *Collins COBUILD dictionaries* (there are many versions—*Student's Dictionary, Learner's Dictionary*), first designed for English language learners in the United Kingdom, are written to reflect contemporary patterns

TABLE 6.1. Comparison of Learner Dictionaries and Traditional Dictionaries

Learner dictionaries	Traditional dictionaries
More complete information on pronunciation.	Very concise definition.
Words are defined in complete sentences, using simple words.	Often describes the word in relation to larger categories, requiring an understanding of terms used in the definition.
More examples of the word used in sentences that illustrate common usage.	Includes etymology of the word.

Note. Based on Scholfield (2006).

of speech and writing. Definitions are complete sentences that sound like natural speech (e.g., "A *hedonist* is someone who believes that having pleasure is the most important thing in life"). The *Longman Dictionary of Contemporary English* (1995) is another recommended learner dictionary.

Dictionary Entries

The dictionary *entry* is the explanation of the word meaning. The style and content of dictionary entries vary widely, and it is useful to make students aware of these differences. Many words have more than one *meaning* or *sense*, and dictionaries handle this problem in different ways. Some dictionaries include all senses in one entry, while other dictionaries have a separate entry for each part of speech. Most dictionaries organize the meanings in order of frequency. The length of dictionary entries for words with multiple meanings makes it challenging for English language learners or lower-skilled students to locate the correct meaning. For example, a student may encounter the word *master* in the following sentence:

The *master* led the students in their daily lessons.

Confronted with as many as 15 noun meanings for the word *master*, the student may easily choose a meaning (e.g., "one who defeats another") that does not match the word's use in this sentence (i.e., "a male schoolteacher"). Students are more successful in looking up words in the dictionary when they know to use the context of the word to guide their inferences about its meaning.

The example above illustrates one problem with having students learn a list of new vocabulary words by looking up their meanings in the dictionary. As Stahl and Nagy (2006) recommend, dictionaries are most useful when students learn to use them as most adults use them—as a resource to consult when they need to look up or confirm the meaning of a word they encounter in reading. Students can then first use the textual context to "guess" the part of speech and meaning, use the dictionary to scan the senses (or various meanings) and then choose the sense that best matches the textual context. Nagy (2006) has also emphasized this role of context in second-language learning. With limited research on the benefits of teaching students how to use context effectively, Nagy recommends a focus on overall text comprehension rather than word learning: using the context to figure out the meaning of unfamiliar words when possible, and using a dictionary as a resource when context fails and a word is important for understanding or is used frequently and is central to understanding the text. This habit or practice of making inferences to figure out a word meaning actively involves the student in thinking about the word and may help deepen his or her word knowledge.

Strategies in effective dictionary use are a feature of English as a second language instruction, and the second-language research offers several guidelines that have general value for Tier 1 classroom instruction:

1. Introduce students to how dictionaries are organized.
2. Teach students when it is most useful to use a dictionary (e.g., to confirm the student's guess based on context; to understand a word that is key to the passage).
3. Review the key or style manual for the dictionary with the students so that they can use it more effectively.
4. Encourage students to use the dictionary to look up a word after (1) analyzing the use of the word in context to identify the part of speech and (2) making an initial "guess" of word meaning based on the context (Scholfield, 2006).

What the Research Says about Learning Vocabulary through Dictionary Definitions

A consensus has evolved, based on research and reviews of vocabulary instruction, that learning definitions in isolation is not an effective way to teach vocabulary (see Fischer, 1994; Stahl & Fairbanks, 1986). For example, research by Miller and Gildea (1987) illustrates the limits of having students look up word meanings in the dictionary. Students were trained to look up dictionary definitions for unfamiliar words and to compose a sentence using each word. About half of the sentences the students wrote were "odd" and idiomatically unacceptable (e.g., "I was *meticulous* about falling off the cliff"). Students often substituted one part or aspect of the definition for the full word meaning. Miller and Gildea's research suggests that teachers should specifically *prepare* students to use dictionaries effectively as independent learning tools. Because vocabulary learning from dictionaries has its limitations (i.e., depth of word knowledge is not acquired through reading the dictionary), the challenge is to teach students how to integrate dictionary and contextual information to assign each usage a correct meaning based on context clues and constraints. Many students need teacher modeling and practice in varied contexts to successfully develop this strategy.

REMEMBERING THE MEANINGS OF WORDS: MNEMONIC TECHNIQUES

Vocabulary growth depends upon learning words—either through direct instruction in the meanings or from context—and then *remembering* the meanings of the words. Students (and many adults) have difficulty remembering words and concepts they have learned. *Mnemonic* (memory-enhancing) techniques are strategies that students can use to remember new words they have learned. Mnemonic strategies work by creating a mental link or association between the word and its meaning.

Keyword Method

One widely studied mnemonic strategy is the *keyword strategy* (Pressley, Levin, & McDaniel, 1987). Students use this strategy to pair a new word with its meaning, often using an image that helps the student remember the meaning of the word. Or, the student may think of a word that sounds like the new word to help cue the meaning. The keyword method requires the learner to process more than one feature of a word—often both meaning and sound—and to form useful word and picture associations that cue word meaning. Three basic steps of the keyword method are *recoding* the new word into familiar keywords that sound similar, *relating* the new word to pictures or images, and using these images and the keyword to *retrieve* the new word meaning (Scruggs, Mastropieri, Levin, & Gaffney, 1985). In their review of research on vocabulary instruction for students with learning disabilities, Jitendra et al. (2004) found keyword approaches to be very effective for students at risk for reading problems and students with disabilities, with large effect sizes for both maintenance tasks (recall at follow-up) and transfer tasks (e.g., a measure of comprehension or independent use of strategy).

To see how the keyword technique is used (taking an example from Mastropieri, Scruggs & Fulk, 1990), suppose that a student has just learned the word *oxalis*, a clover-like plant. The student might choose a keyword that sounds similar to *oxalis* and that can be easily pictured, like the word *ox*. Then the student might form a picture of an *ox* eating a clover-like plant. The student learns to think of the keyword (*ox*), recall the mental picture of the ox, and use this information to recall the meaning of *oxalis*, a clover-like plant. The keyword method is also used in teaching both older students and students who are English language learners (Mastropieri, 1988; McCarville, 1993). Keywords can be used to remember second-language (L2) words that are difficult to learn. In this case, the student thinks of a keyword in his or her first language that sounds like the new L2 word and then creates an image that links the new L2 word with the keyword. Taking an example from Nation (2008), a Thai student learning the English word for *council* (a group of people elected to govern) might use a Thai phrase that sounds like the word *council* and means

---

The Keyword Method: Using Imagery to Connect Words and Definitions

- *Example*: Using the keyword method to teach terms related to a topic on glaciers.
- *Target word*: *eskers*—long, winding ridges of sediment from streams under or within a glacier.
- *Recode*: Find part of the word or another word that is familiar to the student (e.g., *whisker*), that sounds or looks like the target word (*esker*), and that the student can picture.
- *Relate*: Form an image of the recoded word (*whisker*) and relate it to the definition of *esker*, imagining a long, thin cat whisker.
- *Retrieve*: When the student sees the glacial term *esker*, he or she thinks of the keyword (*whisker*); pictures a long, thin cat whisker; and links to the definition (Mastropieri, 1988).

"uncooked rice." Then the student pictures the meaning of *council* as a group of people meeting around a table of uncooked rice. Keyword methods, which have been studied primarily for teaching word meanings, also promote definition recall and word comprehension. The strategy has not been used to develop depth of word knowledge or to promote transfer (i.e., learning of untaught words). Keyword and other mnemonic strategies are useful in both Tier 1 classroom instruction and more intensive Tier 2 or 3 instruction for students with learning disabilities (see below).

As Nation (2008) notes, the keyword technique is limited only by the student's imagination. However, others have noted that it is difficult to find pictures and acoustic mnemonics already known by the student for many words (Kamil & Hiebert, 2005). It can be time-consuming to develop materials for keyword instruction. We find that the research on the keyword method for remembering new vocabulary is substantive. For example, in a study by Mastropieri et al. (1990), adolescent students with learning disabilities who were taught keywords for both concrete and abstract words were able to remember the meanings and provide the correct word in a sentence context significantly better than students in a direct explanation condition. The researchers underscore the success of the keyword method for students with learning disabilities and other students demonstrating limited semantic knowledge and difficulty in acquiring abstract vocabulary. The method is associated with better recall of word meanings and better comprehension of concepts being learned through the method.

Yet, as Kamil and Hiebert (2005) note, although research supports the keyword method, it has its limitations. For example, Pressley and his colleagues conducted a number of studies of the keyword approach and found that, while it had immediate strong effects on word learning (e.g., Pressley, Levin, Kuiper, Bryant, & Michener, 1982), the method had little impact on teaching practice (Pressley et al., 2007). The inordinate teacher or student preparation required for keyword learning and the fact that many words do not readily lend themselves to learning via this method likely account for its not being used more widely.

Research on Mnemonic Strategies

The keyword method, which is used across content areas to help students recall word meanings and concepts, has been widely studied. One team of researchers that conducted many studies of teaching mnemonic strategies to students with learning disabilities also reviewed research on these approaches (Scruggs & Mastropieri, 2000). The research they reviewed showed that these memory-enhancing strategies have large effect sizes across grade levels, disability conditions, and content areas. These effects were large for studies conducted in lab settings as well as in classrooms. The keyword strategy has been found to help students with learning disabilities remember new content terms and their attributes (e.g., dinosaur names, social studies events, science terminology; e.g., Mastropieri, Scruggs, Bakken, & Brigham, 1992; Veit, Scruggs, & Mastropieri, 1986).

Several general reviews synthesized findings across vocabulary interventions for students with reading difficulties and students with learning disabilities. In a review of studies of mnemonic strategy instruction for students with special needs, the overall effect size was large ($d = 1.62$; Forness, Kavale, Blum, & Lloyd, 1997), and these approaches have also been found to be effective when implemented with students with learning disabilities. In a review entirely focused on studies of vocabulary instruction for students in grades 4–12 with learning disabilities (Jitendra et al., 2004), six group design studies included in this review showed that keyword or mnemonic approaches were superior to more traditional vocabulary instruction methods when testing for both maintenance effects and transfer effects. The effect sizes for these keyword or mnemonic interventions were large (mean ES = 1.93). The National Reading Panel (2000) reviewed studies of the keyword method and found that it has benefits for word recall. In their meta-analysis of vocabulary instruction studies, Stahl and Fairbanks (1986) found that keyword methods had positive effects for both definition recall and contextual vocabulary knowledge (which measures word use in various contexts).

CHAPTER 7

Vocabulary Assessment

CHAPTER VOCABULARY

Assessment	The process of collecting data for the purpose of making decisions about individuals and groups.
Benchmark	Student performance standards.
Construct	The specific knowledge and/or skills measured by a test.
Criterion-referenced test	An assessment in which student performance is compared to an expected level of mastery in a content area.
Diagnostic	An assessment used to determine an individual student's unique strengths and weaknesses.
Item	The type of task or query on an assessment that is used to test a specific area of knowledge or skill.
Outcome	A postintervention assessment used to document and/or evaluate the efficacy of an instructional program.
Progress monitoring	Repeated measurement of academic performance to inform instruction of individual students in both general and special education classes in grades K–8. It is conducted at least monthly to (1) estimate rates of improvement, (2) identify students who are not demonstrating adequate progress, and/or (3) compare the efficacy of various types of instructional techniques in order to design more effective individualized instruction.

Reliability	The consistency of test scores over time, across raters, or across items that measure the same construct.
Screening	An assessment used to identify students who are not acquiring skills or knowledge at an appropriate rate.
Standardized measure	An objective measure that is given and scored in a uniform manner.
Validity	The extent to which a test measures what it is purported to measure.
Vocabulary breadth	The quantity of words about which students may have some level of knowledge.
Vocabulary depth	How much students know about a word (e.g., meaning, usage).

INTRODUCTION

The focus of this chapter is on vocabulary assessment. *Assessment* is defined as "the process of collecting data for the purpose of making decisions about individuals and groups" (Salvia, Ysseldyke, & Bolt, 2007). Most fundamentally, the goal of assessment is to support student learning. There are four major types of assessment that provide different kinds of information that are inextricably tied to instruction: screening, progress monitoring, diagnostic tests, and outcome assessments. These assessment types also relate to implementing RTI models and identifying and intervening on behalf of students at risk for reading problems and with learning disabilities. First, the purpose of universal screening is to identify students who are not successfully acquiring vocabulary knowledge at an appropriate rate and therefore are in need of supplemental and/or specialized instruction. Screening measures are designed to be used ideally with all students to efficiently determine which children are acquiring vocabulary knowledge at the expected rate and, importantly, those who are not. Universal screening—in which student performance and progress are reviewed on a regular basis and in a systematic manner to identify students who are either progressing as expected, at some risk for school failure, or at high risk of or experiencing school failure—plays a critical role in current multitiered RTI models. In such models, educators typically administer the universal screening assessments to all students three times a year in order to identify those at risk for reading problems and also demonstrating low academic performance. The data from the screening measures are used for two purposes, the first of which is to assess the effectiveness of the core curriculum and instruction being provided to all students. According to RTI intervention models, some 80% or more of all students in a school should show adequate progress in the core curriculum and instruction program. The second purpose is to identify students who are not making such adequate as these students need supplemental instruction in the form of Tier 2 interventions.

Second, the purpose of progress monitoring, which also plays a key role in multi-tiered and RTI models, is the ongoing use of assessment procedures to determine the extent to which students are benefitting from classroom instruction and for monitoring the effectiveness of the core curriculum as well as secondary and tertiary interventions. A fundamental assumption of RTI is that students benefit from high-quality instruction—that is, a majority of students learn and achieve the vocabulary skills and understand the content taught in the core curriculum and instructional program. For students who are not sufficiently responsive to these, secondary and tertiary vocabulary interventions can be provided, and, again, students' responses to these interventions are regularly monitored. Thus, progress monitoring is a valid and efficient tool for gauging the effectiveness of instruction, determining whether instruction modifications are necessary, and providing important information for eventual classification and placement decisions. Information about progress monitoring is rapidly expanding.

Third, the purpose of diagnostic assessment procedures is to determine individual students' unique strengths and weaknesses. Diagnostic measures are used to identify the specific strengths and weaknesses of students who display significant delays in attaining grade-level vocabulary knowledge. This information can then be used to more directly target vocabulary instruction. Diagnostic assessments also are used to classify or specify a particular area of disability. Diagnostic assessments are most often conducted by team members as part of a referral for special education.

Finally, the purpose of outcome assessment procedures is to document and evaluate how effective intervention programs are in teaching students. Outcome measures are designed to document and evaluate the effectiveness of vocabulary instructional programs, individually or overall. Of course, vocabulary outcome measures play a large role because schools are under increasing pressure to improve the outcomes of students in all areas. Recent updates to the Individuals with Disabilities Education Improvement Act of 2004 (IDEA; Public Law 108-446) and the No Child Left Behind Act of 2001 (NCLB, 2001) require schools to assess student outcomes on a regular basis. There is little doubt that the accountability focus will not change in future reauthorizations of these federal education laws.

In the remainder of this chapter, we first discuss differences in conceptions of vocabulary knowledge. We then provide an overview of the dimensions of vocabulary assessment that teachers can use to design and evaluate vocabulary assessments. Next, we describe vocabulary screening and progress monitoring measures and procedures. This description is followed by a discussion of vocabulary diagnostic and outcome measures, including a discussion of how to get the most out of them and where to locate them. We follow this description with basic information on some of the more commonly used vocabulary and language measures. Finally, we describe some emerging technology-based vocabulary screening and progress monitoring measures that will be available to educators in the near future.

DIFFERENCES IN CONCEPTIONS OF VOCABULARY KNOWLEDGE

At the outset it is important to note that there is disagreement about what it means to fully know a word and what kind of knowledge this is. Differences in the types of test items and aspects of vocabulary knowledge are reflected in the constructs measured through vocabulary assessment tools (see descriptions of the specific tests later in this chapter). Richards (1976) defined vocabulary knowledge as including both the morphological and syntactic properties of a word and word frequency and breadth., Nation (1990) argued that a person's knowledge of a word should entail both receptive and productive (expressive) knowledge—in sum, all aspects of what is involved in knowing a word's form, position, function, and meaning. Nation's definition is further elaborated in Table 7.1.

TABLE 7.1. Aspects of Knowing a Word Associated with the Receptive and Productive Domains

Aspect	Domain	Attribute
Form		
Spoken	Receptive	What does the word sound like?
	Productive	How is the word pronounced?
Written	Receptive	What does the word look like?
	Productive	How is the word written and spelled?
Position		
Grammatical patterns	Receptive	In what patterns does the word occur?
	Productive	In what patterns must we use the word?
Collocations	Receptive	What words or types of words occur with the word?
	Productive	What words or types of words are used with this word?
Function		
Frequency	Receptive	How common is the word?
	Productive	How often should the word be used?
Appropriateness	Receptive	Where would one expect to encounter the word?
	Productive	Where can one use the word?
Meaning		
Concept	Receptive	What does the word mean?
	Productive	What word should be used to express a particular meaning?
Associations	Receptive	What other words does this word make one think of?
	Productive	What other words could be used to express the meaning?

Note. Based on Nation (1990).

Most vocabulary measures present individual words and elicit students' responses that are scored as either correct or incorrect (Beck et al., 2002). For example, a student is asked to identify the correct response to the question "What does the word *suggestion* mean in the paragraph?" Others argue that vocabulary knowledge, however, is not typically all-or-nothing (Nation, 1990; Phythian-Sence & Wagner, 2007). Several gradient models have been proposed to account for multiple levels of vocabulary knowledge (e.g., Dale & O'Rourke, 1981; Stahl, 1986). For example, Dale and O'Rourke (1981) described the four possible levels of knowledge of a word's meaning, ranging from no familiarity to knowing how to use the word in multiple contexts (see Chapter 1).

A number of scales of vocabulary knowledge use similar gradient models of word knowledge (e.g., Joe, 1995; McNeill, 1996; Scarcella & Zimmerman, 1998). A typical scale of vocabulary knowledge often takes the form of "Yes/No" self-assessment items or multiple-choice numbers corresponding to specified levels of knowledge. These scales are often used by learners to self-assess their knowledge of a list of words. For example, the student would circle the response related to his or her self-assessment of knowledge of a particular word.

0 = I do not know this word.
1 = I have seen this word before but do not know its meaning.
2 = I have seen this word before, and I think I know its meaning.
3 = I know this word and can use it when I speak or write.

Self-assessment scales of vocabulary measures can be used easily by teachers to assess their students' vocabulary knowledge. Nelson and Marchand-Martella (2005) developed a self-assessment scale that teachers can use to assess students' acquisition of vocabulary knowledge taught in the Multiple Meaning Vocabulary program. The self-assessment asks the students to address the question "How much do I know about this word?" prior to and after instruction (see Figure 7.1). The students indicate which level of the Dale and O'Rourke (1981) scale of word knowledge applies to each word:

> Vocabulary assessments tend to emphasize the measurement of vocabulary breadth or depth.

1. "I never saw the word before."
2. "I've heard of the word, but I don't know what it means."
3. "I think I know it—it has something to do with . . . "
4. "I know the word—it means _____ in this context."

In summary, vocabulary assessments tend to emphasize the measurement of vocabulary breadth or depth. Vocabulary breadth refers to the quantity of words about which students may have some level of knowledge. The number of item queries employed in such measures enable teachers and others to sample a relatively large number of words. Multiple-choice assessments or standardized tests

Target Word: _____

How much do I know about this word? (Student makes one check mark in each column)

Before the Lesson		After the Lesson	
1. I never saw it before.	___	1. I never saw it before.	___
2. I've heard of it, but I don't know what it means.	___	2. I've heard of it, but I don't know what it means.	___
3. I think I know what it means. It has something to do with _____.	___	3. I think I know what it means. It has something to do with _____.	___
4. I know what the word means. It means _____.	___	4. I know what the word means. It means _____.	___

FIGURE 7.1. Example of self-assessment scale used in Multiple Meaning Vocabulary program. Adapted from Nelson and Marchand-Martella (2005). Adapted with permission from Sopris West.

at the end of instructional blocks are used to measure vocabulary breadth (see the example of the multiple-choice query, or item, in Figure 7.2). Tests used to measure breadth can target words from a particular story or content unit or can cover words learned over the course of the academic year in a given content area or even words found in state-mandated outcome measures or diagnostic measures that sample words from a wide corpus. Vocabulary depth, on the other hand, refers to how much students know about a *particular* word. Tests used to measure it are designed to assess students' gradient knowledge of words, as described above and depicted in the example in Figure 7.1.

Dimensions of Vocabulary Assessment

Three assessment dimensions are relevant in designing and evaluating vocabulary assessments (Read, 2000). Used by teachers in determining the nature of commercial assessments or in designing classroom measures, these three dimensions may

> *Chronic* means
>   A. lasting for a long time [correct answer]
>   B. dissatisfied
>   C. decreasing
>   D. effective

FIGURE 7.2. Example of a multiple-choice vocabulary item.

be described as (1) discrete–embedded, (2) selective–comprehensive, or (3) context independent–context dependent.

Discrete–Embedded

Discrete vocabulary measures treat students' knowledge of a word as an independent construct. In other words, the measure focuses exclusively on word knowledge (see Figure 7.2 for an example of a discrete vocabulary item). Such measures, as noted above, can be targeted in assessing either vocabulary breadth or depth. In contrast, embedded vocabulary assessments treat students' knowledge of a word as embedded within the word's application in larger constructs of composition, conceptual schema, or comprehension of the word's meaning. In other words, an embedded measure of vocabulary assesses vocabulary within some larger construct (see Figure 7.3 for an example of an embedded vocabulary item). It is important to note that a variety of different item formats are used with both discrete and embedded vocabulary measures. For example, anecdotal record keeping is another type of embedded measure. In this case, a teacher keeps notes on vocabulary use by students, recording their vocabulary preferences in discussions, writing assignments, and other types of assessments.

Selective–Comprehensive

Selective measures test small samples of words. An assessment that measures students' vocabulary knowledge for a story or content unit would be on the selective end of the continuum. On the other hand, mandated state tests and diagnostic tests are comprehensive in that they draw vocabulary items from a large general corpus of words. Such tests would be on the comprehensive end of the continuum.

Context Independence–Context Dependence

Context-independent vocabulary assessments present the word as an isolated element (see Figure 7.2 for an example), while context-dependent vocabulary measures

---

What does the word *suggestions* mean in the following paragraph?

"Your uncle is very funny." Jorge said. This did not help Linda, who was having difficulty identifying a humorous person she could write about for her English composition class. Jorge tried to give her some other *suggestions*. "What about a famous comedian or something funny that happened to someone that was reported in the press?" Jorge asked.

    A. questions
    B. difficulties
    C. reasons
    D. options [correct answer]

FIGURE 7.3. Example of an embedded vocabulary item.

present the word in its surrounding context. This dimension has to do with the need of students to engage with context in order to derive a meaning partially based on how the word is presented. For example, among context-dependent multiple-choice items, all potential choices should represent a plausible definition of the word. Students must be able to identify the correct definition based on how the word is used in the particular passage (see Figure 7.4 for an example).

> Vocabulary assessments designed to measure students' ability to use words in context must move toward the embedded, comprehensive, and context-dependent ends of the continua of these three dimensions.

Screening and Progress Monitoring Measures

As noted above, multi-tiered and RTI service delivery models are increasingly being used by schools to prevent and ameliorate learning and behavior difficulties (American Association of School Administrators, 2009). Such models integrate assessment and intervention within a multi-level prevention system to maximize student achievement and reduce behavior problems. With RTI, schools identify students at risk for poor learning or social outcomes, provide evidence-based interventions, monitor students' subsequent progress, adjust the intensity and nature of those interventions based on the students' responsiveness, and identify those with unremediated learning problems or other disabilities (for a complete description of the elements of RTI service delivery models, see National Center on Response to Intervention, 2010).

Universal screening and progress monitoring play a central role in such service delivery models. Screening and monitoring of learner performance is reviewed on a regular basis and in a systematic manner to identify students who are progressing as expected, at some risk for learning difficulties, and at high risk of or experiencing learning difficulties. Universal screening relies on assessment procedures that are characterized by the administration of quick, low-cost, repeatable evaluations of critical academic skills.

Given the importance of vocabulary to reading comprehension and communication in general, it is important for schools to identify students with, or at risk for, vocabulary difficulties. As with diagnostic and outcome measures, it is critical to choose screening and progress monitoring vocabulary measures that are psychometrically sound and feasible. Although there are a number of psychometrically

What does the word *air* mean in this sentence?
John set his shoes on the porch to *air* them out.
   A. a person's appearance
   B. a light breeze
   C. ventilate [correct answer]
   D. invisible gas that surrounds the earth

FIGURE 7.4. Example of a context-dependent vocabulary item.

sound norm-referenced vocabulary measures that can be used for screening (specific examples are discussed later in this chapter) we would argue that only a few of them are feasible for universal screening. More generally, these norm-referenced measures are unlikely to be used as a part of regular school practices because they are resource-intensive, utilizing additional personnel, time, materials, and money. However, such measures could be used as a potential screen for individual students. It appears none of the norm-referenced vocabulary measures is available for progress monitoring. Before going on, we note that doubtless there will be advances in the development of vocabulary and screening measures in the future.

The National Center on Response to Intervention (*www.rti4sucess.org*) identifies and reviews the technical adequacy of curriculum-based measurement (CBM) screening and progress monitoring measures for use by schools. Currently, in contrast to a number of well-developed CBM screening and progress monitoring probes in reading, mathematics, and written language for elementary school students, there appears to be only one technically adequate CBM screening and progress monitoring measure available to "directly assess" students' vocabulary growth, namely, Dynamic Indicators of Basic Early Literacy Skills, Word Use Fluency (DIBELS WUF: Good & Kaminski, 2003). The DIBELS WUF measure is an individually administered test of vocabulary and oral language that can be used in grades K–3. The student is presented a word and asked to use the word in an appropriate sentence. The score is the number of correct words used in correct utterances (i.e., sentences that accurately convey the meaning of the word) in 1 minute. Benchmark standards are currently not available for the WUF. Tentatively, students in the lowest 20% of a school district using local norms should be considered at risk for poor language and reading outcomes, and those between the 20th and 40th percentile mark should be considered to be at some risk.

The WUF can be used for progress monitoring to determine the extent to which students are benefiting from classroom instruction and for monitoring effectiveness of the core curriculum as well as supplemental interventions. The primary purpose of progress monitoring with the WUF is to determine whether the vocabulary instruction is effective in improving the students' learning rate to an appropriate level. Decision rules are used to determine when students might no longer require supplemental vocabulary instruction and when the instruction needs to be modified or changed. The progress monitoring process includes the following four steps (see *dibels.uoregon.edu* for a complete description of the WUF progress monitoring procedures):

1. Establish an expected growth rate in a specified period of time. This goal can be accomplished by creating intraclass/-school/-district comparisons (i.e., comparing an individual student's score to the class, school, or district mean or median) and by creating expectancy tables that incorporate scores on end-of-year examinations or high-stakes assessments.
2. Assess all students' progress on a frequent basis (one to two times per week).

3. Chart the results and analyze students' progress on a regular basis.
4. Use preset rules to determine when a student is not adequately responding to an intervention (a common rule is that four consecutive data points below a goal line warrant a change in intervention, while four above the goal line warrant raising the goal or decreasing the amount of time to achieve the goal). Today, teachers have available to them a number of free or commercially available graphing programs. In these programs, an educator, can for example, enter a student's name and grade, the type of CBM measure administered, goal lines, the dates of periodic progress monitoring, and the progress monitoring data. Additionally, educators can track when instructional or goal line changes are made. The program can be printed easily and serve as a communication tool for educators, students, and parents.

Vocabulary matching is another CBM measure that may be used to screen and assess students' acquisition of vocabulary (Espin, Busch, Shin, & Kruschwitz, 2001). Vocabulary matching involves creating vocabulary matching probes made up of 22 vocabulary terms and 20 definitions. The two additional terms serve as distractors (see Figure 7.5 for an example of vocabulary matching items). Terms and definitions can be drawn at random from terms being taught over a specified period of time. Vocabulary terms appear on the left side of the page and are arranged alphabetically to allow students to easily locate the terms. Short definitions (15 or fewer words) appear on the right side of the page. Students are given 5 minutes to read the terms and definitions and to match each term with its definition. The vocabulary matching probe can also be read to students. In this case, only the terms are provided on the probe. The teacher then reads the definitions, and students identify which term matches the definition being read.

Additionally, given the very strong relationship between vocabulary and reading comprehension (Nation, 2009), schools may use available CBM Maze reading

	Term		Definition
1. _F_	Classical conditioning	A.	A resource that is important for a country's industries or national security.
2. _B_	Empathy	B.	Feeling as another person does.
3. _D_	First world	C.	A part of the personality concerned with right and wrong.
4. _E_	Socialization	D.	Wealthy industrialized nations.
5. _A_	Strategic resource	E.	Process through which an individual learns the rules of society
6. _C_	Superego	F.	Pairing of neutral stimulus with an unconditioned stimulus so they produce the same response.

FIGURE 7.5. Vocabulary matching example. Based on Espin, Busch, Shin, and Kruschwitz (2001).

comprehension measures as a proxy for vocabulary. CBM Maze is a multiple-choice cloze task that students complete while reading silently. Typically, the first sentence of a 150–400 word passage is left intact. Thereafter, every seventh word is replaced with three alternative words inside a parenthesis. One of the words is exactly the same one from the original passage. The student attempts to identify the correct word for each item. The very nature of CBM Maze measures requires vocabulary knowledge to successfully complete it. CBM Maze measures are available at the following websites:

dibels.uoregon.edu
easycbm.com
www.aimsweb.com
www.interventioncentral.org

Diagnostic and Outcome Measures

Diagnostic and outcome measures typically provide an array of useful scores for evaluating students' vocabulary knowledge and language skills (e.g., age-equivalent, percentile, and standard scores). There are two things you can do to get the most out of diagnostic measures. It is important to study the nature of the query items in the measurement. Diagnostic and outcome measures can vary widely. For example, one measure of vocabulary might ask students to identify the meaning of a word in context, while another might require them to identify the meaning of a word in a multiple-choice query. In this case, the scores derived from the measures would reflect two very different types of vocabulary knowledge.

Additionally, as noted earlier, there is widespread disagreement about what it means to fully know a word and what kind of knowledge that constitutes. These different aspects of vocabulary knowledge are reflected in the constructs measured through vocabulary assessments (see the descriptions of the specific tests later in this chapter). Because of these differences, it is important to study the assessment items carefully to get a sense of their nature and what the score tells us about a child's performance. It is also important to study the pattern of correct and incorrect items. For example, examining the protocol can determine whether, for example, student performance might differ among the various word forms (e.g., verbs, nouns, adjectives). Such a conclusion requires analysis of the actual protocol to identify the specific items a child got wrong versus right.

LOCATING DIAGNOSTIC AND OUTCOME MEASURES

Three widely available sources may be used to locate assessment measures one might employ. These resources can be accessed either online or in university and public libraries. They are:

1. *Tests in Print* (*www.unl.edu/buros*) provides a comprehensive bibliography of all known commercially available assessment measures that are in print (approximately 3,000). A useful feature of *Tests in Print* is that it serves as an index for the *Mental Measurement Yearbook* test review series (also at *www.unl.edu/buros*).
2. *Test Link*, which is the Educational Testing Collection Database, is a valuable resource for identifying commercial as well as noncommercial assessment measures (over 20,000; *www.ets.org*). Noncommercial measures are those that appear in books and professional journals.
3. The *Mental Measurement Yearbook* series is the premier source for independent reviews of all available assessment measures, commercial as well as noncommercial (*www.unl.edu/buros*). The *Mental Measurement Yearbook* series is published by the Buros Institute for Mental Measurements. Each review is consumer-oriented, to encourage appropriate use of the measures. The *Mental Measurement Yearbook* series can also be used to locate measures.

EXAMPLES OF VOCABULARY AND LANGUAGE SKILLS MEASURES

In this section we provide basic information (i.e., author, publisher, year of publication, administration time, availability of computerized scoring, descriptions, primary use, standardization, scores, reliability, validity) on available vocabulary and language skills tests. No systematic process was used to identify the tests. Rather, we selected tests that appear to be frequently used by researchers. We generally selected tests that targeted (1) receptive vocabulary, (2) expressive vocabulary, (3) both receptive *and* expressive vocabulary, (4) comprehensive language skills, (5) psycholinguistic skills, and (6) comprehensive achievement measures that include vocabulary subtest(s).

List of Tests Described

Receptive Vocabulary
- Peabody Picture Vocabulary Test—Fourth Edition (PPVT-4; Dunn & Dunn, 2007)
- Receptive One-Word Picture Vocabulary Test—2000 Edition (ROWPVT; Brownell, 2000b)

Expressive Vocabulary
- Expressive Vocabulary Test—Second Edition (EVT-2; Williams, 2007)
- Expressive One-Word Picture Vocabulary Test—Revised (EOWPVT-R; Brownell, 2000a)

Receptive and Expressive Vocabulary
- Comprehensive Receptive and Expressive Vocabulary Test—Second Edition (CREVT-2; Wallace & Hammill, 2002)
- Oral and Written Language Scales (OWLS; Carrow-Woolfolk, 1995)

Comprehensive Language Skills
- Comprehensive Assessment of Spoken Language (CASL; Carrow-Woolfolk, 1999)
- Test of Language Development—Primary, Fourth Edition (TOLD-P:4; Newcomer & Hammill, 2008b)
- Test of Language Development—Intermediate, Fourth Edition (TOLD-I:4; Newcomer & Hamill, 2008a)
- Clinical Evaluation of Language Fundamentals—Screening Test, Fourth Edition (CELF-4; Semel, Wiig, & Secord, 2003)
- Clinical Evaluation of Language Fundamentals—Preschool, Second Edition (CELF-P2; Semel, Wiig, & Secord, 2004)
- Test of Narrative Language (TNL; Gillam & Pearson, 2004)

Psycholinguistic Skills
- Bankson Language Test—Second Edition (BLT-2; Bankson, 1990)

Comprehensive Achievement Measures That Include Vocabulary Subtest(s)
- Woodcock Reading Mastery Tests—Revised—Normative Update (WRMT-R/NU; Woodcock, 1998)

Test Descriptions

Receptive Vocabulary

Peabody Picture Vocabulary Test—Fourth Edition (PPVT-4)

Authors: Lloyd M. Dunn and Douglas M. Dunn.

Publisher: Pearson.

Year: 2007.

Age range: 2.6 through 90+ years.

Administration time: 10–15 minutes.

Computerized scoring: Yes (optional).

Description: The PPVT-4 is an individually administered, norm-referenced assessment of an individual's receptive single-word vocabulary. The query items sample words that represent 20 content areas (e.g., actions, tools) and parts of speech (i.e., nouns, verbs, or attributes) across all levels of difficulty. The measure is available in two parallel forms (A and B), each containing training items and 228 test items. The forms consist of four full-color pictures as options on a page. For each item, the examiner says a word and the examinee responds by selecting the picture that best illustrates that word's meaning.

Primary use: Screening, diagnostic, outcome asssessments.

Standardization: Approximately 5,500 individuals were included in the validation studies. The norm sample closely matches 2004 census data for demographic variables and clinical diagnosis or special education placement. Standardization was conducted in fall 2005 and spring 2006 to obtain fall and spring grade-based norms. The PPVT-4 was conormed with the Expressive Vocabulary Test, Second Edition (EVT-2; Williams, 2007).

Scores: (1) Age- and grade-based standard scores; (2) Growth Scale Values (GSVs); (3) Percentiles; (4) Stanines; (5) Normal Curve Equivalents (NCEs); and (6) Age and grade equivalents.

Link: *psychcorp.pearsonassessments.com.*

Receptive One-Word Picture Vocabulary Test (ROWPVT)

Author: Rick Brownell.

Publisher: Academic Therapy Publications.

Year: 2000.

Age range: 2.0 through 18.11 years.

Administration time: 20 minutes.

Computerized scoring: No.

Description: ROWPVT is a norm-referenced, individually administered assessment used to assess English hearing vocabulary. ROWPVT assesses receptive vocabulary by showing the subject four color pictures and presenting a stimulus word. The subject is asked to identify the picture that depicts the word's meaning. The items and stimuli become progressively more difficult. Examinees are permitted to respond in English or Spanish. Results can be compared to those obtained from the Expressive One-Word Picture Vocabulary Test—Revised, to explore developmental differences in receptive versus expressive language. A Spanish bilingual edition is also available.

Scales: Receptive Vocabulary.

Primary use: Screening, diagnostic assessments.

Standardization: The ROWPVT was originally standardized on a sample of 1,128 children in the San Francisco Bay area, California. The sampling, based on 1970 U.S. Census data, reflected representation in regard to range and level of ability. The 2000 edition norms were based on a nationally representative sample of 2,327 children from 220 sites across 32 states. The demographic characteristics of the standardization sample are representative of the school-age population of the United States. The test was conormed with the Expressive One-Word Picture Vocabulary Test—Revised (EOWPVT-R).

Scores: (1) Standard scores; (2) Percentile ranks; (3) Confidence intervals; and (4) Age equivalents.

Link: portal.wpspublish.com/portal/page?_pageid=53,69179&_dad=portal&_schema= PORTAL.

Expressive Vocabulary

Expressive Vocabulary Test—Second Edition (EVT-2)

Author: Kathleen T. Williams.

Publisher: AGS Publishing/Pearson Assessments.

Year: 2007.

Age range: 2.6 through 90+ years.

Administration time: 10–20 minutes.

Computerized scoring: Yes (optional).

Description: The EVT-2 is an individually administered, norm-referenced test of expressive single-word vocabulary and word retrieval. The test items sample words that represent 20 content areas (e.g., actions, tools) and parts of speech (i.e., nouns, verbs, or attributes) across all levels of difficulty. The measure is available in two parallel forms (A and B) that are administered individually, each with 190 items of increasing difficulty. Each form contains training items consisting of four full-color pictures as options on a page. For each item, the examiner presents a picture and reads a stimulus question. The examinee responds with a one-word label, answers a specific question, or provides a word that fits the picture.

Primary use: Screening, growth monitoring, diagnostic, outcome assessments.

Scales: Expressive vocabulary and word retrieval.

Standardization: Normative data were compiled for a sample of almost 4,000 individuals. The norm sample closely matched 2004 census data for demographic variables and clinical diagnosis or special education placement. Standardization was conducted in fall 2005 and spring 2006 to obtain fall and spring grade-based norms. The EVT-2 was 100% conormed with the Peabody Picture Vocabulary Test—Fourth Edition (PPVT-4; Dunn & Dunn, 2007).

Scores: (1) Age- and grade-based standard scores; (2) Growth Scale Values (GSVs); (3) Percentiles; (4) Stanines; (5) Normal Curve Equivalents (NCEs); and (6) Age and grade equivalents.

Link: www.pearsonassessments.com/HAIWEB/Cultures/en-us/Productdetail.htm?Pid= PaEVT.

Expressive One-Word Picture Vocabulary Test—Revised (EOWPVT-R)

Author: Rick Brownell.

Publisher: Academic Therapy Publications.

Year: 2000.

Age range: 2.0 through 18.11 years.

Administration time: 20–30 minutes.

Computerized scoring: No.

Description: The EOWPVT-R is an individually administered, norm-referenced test used to assess verbal expression of the English language. To administer the EOWPVT-R, the examiner presents a series of pictures that the examinee is asked to name, usually with one word. The items become progressively more difficult and are discontinued when the examinee can no longer name the pictures correctly. Materials are available in both English and Spanish editions.

Scales: Expressive Vocabulary.

Primary use: Screening, diagnostic assessments.

Standardization: Norms are based on a nationally representative sample of 2,327 children from 220 sites across 32 states. The demographic characteristics of the standardization sample are representative of the school-age population of the United States. The test was conormed with the Receptive One-Word Picture Vocabulary Test (ROWPVT).

Scores: (1) Standard scores; (2) Percentile ranks; (3) Scaled scores; (4) Stanines; and (5) Age equivalents.

Link: portal.wpspublish.com/portal/page?_pageid=53,69175&_dad=portal&_schema= PORTAL.

Receptive and Expressive Vocabulary

Comprehensive Receptive and Expressive Vocabulary Test—Second Edition (CREVT-2)

Authors: Gerald Wallace and Donald D. Hammill.

Publisher: Pro-Ed.

Year: 2002.

Age range: 4 through 89.11 years.

Administration time: 20–30 minutes.

Computerized scoring: No.

Description: The CREVT-2 is designed to measure receptive and expressive oral vocabulary and identify deficiencies in oral vocabulary, discrepancies between receptive and expressive vocabulary, and progress in instructional programs. The CREVT-2 is available in two equivalent forms (A and B). For the Receptive Vocabulary Subtest, the examiner requests that the subject choose the photo related to the stimulus words presented. The subject chooses from photographs of common, everyday objects (animals, methods of transport, occupations, clothing, food, personal grooming items, tools, household appliances, recreation items, and clerical materials). In the Expressive Vocabulary Subtest the subject is encouraged to provide details about particular stimulus words that pertain to the same themes used in the Receptive Vocabulary Subtest.

Scales: Receptive Oral Vocabulary, Expressive Oral Vocabulary.

Primary use: Screening, progress monitoring assessments.

Standardization: The CREVT-2 was standardized on 2,545 individuals, including the normative samples for the CREVT and CREVT—Adult version. The normative sample closely represented the U.S. Census data in regard to gender, geographic region, ethnicity, race, urban/rural residence, and special population. Norms were stratified by age.

Scores: (1) Standard scores; (2) Percentiles; and (3) Age equivalents.

Link: www.proedinc.com/customer/productView.aspx?ID=2172 (portal.wpspublish.com/portal/page?_pageid= 3,69923&_dad=portal&_schema=PORTAL).

Oral and Written Language Scales (OWLS)

Author: Elizabeth Carrow-Woolfolk.

Publisher: AGS Publishing/Pearson Assessments.

Year: 1995, 1996.

Age range: Listening Comprehension (LC) and Oral Expression (OE) subtests: 3 to 21.11 years; Written Expression (WE) subtest: 5 to 21.11 years.

Administration time: 30–65 minutes; LC: 5–15 minutes; OE: 10–25 minutes; WE: 15–25 minutes.

Computerized scoring: Yes.

Description: The OWLS is a norm-referenced assessment designed to measure listening comprehension (LC), oral expression (OE), and written expression (WE). The WE scale can be administered individually or with groups. The WE measures the use of handwriting, spelling, punctuation, modifiers, phrases, and sentence structures as well as the ability to communicate meaningfully in writing. The examiner presents oral, written, and pictorial prompts, and subjects respond in writing. The LC is an individually administered subtest designed to assess receptive language by having subjects identify a picture that corresponds to the stimuli presented. The OE assesses expressive language by having subjects generate language in response to verbal stimuli. The OWLS offers an Oral Language Composite score and a Language Composite score.

Scales: Written Expression, Listening Comprehension, Oral Expression.

Primary use: Diagnostic assessments.

Standardization: A total of 1,985 subjects aged 3 through 21 years were assessed at 74 sites across the nation. Of that total, standardization was based on the 1,795 subjects most representative of 1991 U.S. Census data. The sample was controlled for age, gender, race, geographic region, socioeconomic status, and special populations.

Scores: (1) Age- and grade-based standard scores; (2) Percentile ranks; (3) Stanines; (4) Normal Curve Equivalents (NCEs); and (5) Grade and age equivalents.

Link: *www.pearsonassessments.com/pai/ca/RelatedInfo/OWLSTechnicalInformation.htm*.

Comprehensive Language Skills

Comprehensive Assessment of Spoken Language (CASL)

Author: Elizabeth Carrow-Woolfolk.

Publisher: AGS Publishing/Pearson Assessments.

Year: 1999.

Age range: 3 through 21.11 years.

Administration time: 30–45 minutes.

Computerized scoring: Yes (optional).

Description: The CASL is an individually administered, norm-based assessment designed to measure the language processing skills of comprehension, expression, and retrieval in oral language. The CASL battery is composed of 15 tests designed to assess four areas of language: Lexical/Semantic, Syntactic, Supralinguistic, and Pragmatic. The number of tests taken depends on the age of the examinee. Supplementary tests provide additional diagnostic information.

Primary use: Screening, diagnostic, identification assessments.

Standardization: A total of 2,750 children and young adults aged 3 through 21 were tested at166 sites nationwide. Based on the U.S. census data from 1994, the sample was controlled for gender, race, geographic region, and socioeconomic status. After item analysis, a representative sample of 1,700 subjects was used for the normative scores.

Scores: (1) Age-based standard scores; (2) Percentiles; (3) Normal Curve Equivalents (NCEs); (4) Stanines; and (5) Test-age equivalents.

Link: psychcorp.pearsonassessments.com/HAIWEB/Cultures/en-us/Productdetail.htm?Pid=PAa3580; www.pearsonassessments.com/NR/rdonlyres/E56A4DA9-DF5C-4760-8FA2-220065C369AE/4310/caslinternet1.pdf.

Test of Language Development—Primary, Fourth Edition (TOLD-P:4)

Authors: Phyllis L. Newcomer and Donald D. Hammill.

Publisher: Pro-Ed.

Year: 2008.

Age range: 4.0 to 8.11 years.

Administration time: 1 hour.

Computerized scoring: Yes.

Description: The TOLD-P:4 is an individually administered assessment designed to identify children with language disorders and isolate areas of deficit in language development. The TOLD-P:4 has nine subtests that measure various aspects of oral language: picture vocabulary; relational vocabulary; oral vocabulary; syntactic understanding; sentence imitation; morphological completion; word discrimination; word analysis; and word articulation. The results of these subtests can be combined to form composite scores for the major dimensions of language: semantics and grammar; listening, organizing, and speaking; and overall language ability.

Primary use: Screening, diagnostic assessment.

Standardization: In 2006-2007, the TOLD-P:4 was renormed on 1,108 children from 16 states. The data were collected from a demographic representative sample of the 2005 school-age population. Geographic region, gender, ethnicity, Hispanic status, family income level, and parental education were stratified by age. Studies report an absence of gender and ethnic bias.

Scores: (1) Standard scores; (2) Percentiles; and (3) Age equivalents.

Link: www.proedinc.com/customer/productView.aspx?ID=4233.

Test of Language Development—Intermediate, Fourth Edition (TOLD-I:4)

Authors: Phyllis L. Newcomer and Donald D. Hammill.

Publisher: Pro-Ed.

Year: 2008.

Age range: Intermediate: 8.0 to 17.11 years.

Administration time: 30–60 minutes.

Computerized scoring: Yes.

Description: The TOLD-I:4 is an individually administered assessment designed to identify children with language disorders and isolate areas of deficit in language development. The TOLD-I:4 comprises six subtests that measure semantics (i.e., meaning and thought) or grammar (i.e., syntax and morphology) skills. Two subtests measure listening abilities; two measure organizing abilities; and two measure speaking abilities. The combination of all six subtests represents overall Spoken Language.

Primary use: Screening, identification, progress monitoring assessments.

Standardization: The TOLD-I:4 was renormed in 2008 on 1,097 children from 14 states. Normative data were collected from a demographic representative sample of the 2005 school-age population. Geographic region, gender, ethnicity, Hispanic status, family income level, and parental education were stratified by age.

Scores: (1) Standard scores; (2) Percentiles; and (3) Age equivalents.

Link: *www.proedinc.com/customer/productView.aspx?ID=4229*.

Clinical Evaluation of Language Fundamentals—Fourth Edition (CELF-4)

Authors: Eleanor Semel, Elisabeth H. Wiig, and Wayne A. Secord.

Publisher: Harcourt Assessment.

Year: 2003.

Age range: 5 through 21 years.

Administration time: 30–60 minutes.

Computerized scoring: Yes (optional).

Description: The CELF-4 is an individually administered, norm-referenced assessment designed to screen the strengths and weaknesses in expressive and receptive language skills. Expressive and Receptive language scores are derived, as well as composite scores in the areas of Language Structure, Language Content, Language Content and Memory, and Working Memory.

Scales: Receptive Language, Expressive Language, Semantic Skills, Grammar.

Primary use: Screening assessments.

Standardization: The CELF-4 was standardized on a sample of 2,650 students representative of the 2000 U.S. population in terms of socioeconomic status, age, gender, geographic region, race, ethnicity, and special populations.

Scores: (1) Standard scores; (2) Percentiles; and (3) Age equivalents.

Link: www.pearsonassessments.com/HAIWEB/Cultures/en-us/Productdetail.htm?Pid=015-8037-200.

Clinical Evaluation of Language Fundamentals—Preschool, Second Edition (CELF-P2)

Authors: Eleanor Semel, Elisabeth H. Wiig, and Wayne A. Secord.

Publisher: Harcourt Assessment.

Year: 2004.

Age range: 3 through 6 years.

Administration time: 30–45 minutes.

Computerized scoring: No.

Description: The CELF-P2 is an individually administered, norm-referenced assessment designed to test comprehensively the language skills of preschool-age children who will be in an academic-oriented setting. The CELF-P2 incorporates 11 subtests (Sentence Structure, Word Structure, Expressive Vocabulary, Concepts and Following Directions, Recalling Sentences, Basic Concepts, Word Classes, Recalling Sentences in Context, Phonological Awareness, Pre-Literacy Rating Scale, Descriptive Pragmatics Profile), and five composites (Core Language, Receptive Language, Expressive Language, Language Content, Language Structure). The CELF-P2 also includes a preliteracy scale and phonological awareness subtest.

Scales: Receptive Language, Expressive Language, Semantic Skills, Grammar.

Primary use: Identification, diagnosis, follow-up assessments.

Standardization: The CELF-P2 was standardized on a sample of 800 children, with 100 children in each of the eight 6-month age groups. The manual provides evidence that the standardization sample was representative of the U.S. population in terms of gender, racial, and ethnic background; geographic region; and the primary caregiver's education. In addition, the sample included appropriate representation of students with special needs (i.e., children receiving special education services).

Scores: (1) Standard scores; (2) Percentile ranks; (3) Scaled scores; and (4) Criterion-referenced scores.

Link: *www.pearsonassessments.com/HAIWEB/Cultures/en-us/Productdetail.htm?Pid= 015-8034-945&Mode=summary.*

Test of Narrative Language (TNL)

Authors: Ronald B. Gillam and Nils A. Pearson.

Publisher: Pro-Ed.

Year: 2004.

Age range: 5.0 through 11.11 years.

Administration time: 15–20 minutes.

Computerized scoring: No.

Description: The TNL is an individually administered assessment designed to measure children's ability to listen to, understand, and tell stories. The TNL identifies language impairments, measures the ability to answer literal and inferential comprehension questions, and measures how well children use language in narrative discourse. There are two subtests in the TNL; Narrative Comprehension and Oral Narration. The TNL also provides a Narrative Language Ability Index. An audio taping of every task is required for scoring purposes.

Primary use: Identification assessments.

Standardization: The norming sample for the TNL included 1,059 children between the ages of 5 and 11 years who lived in 20 states during 2001–2002, stratified by geographic area, gender, race, ethnicity (Hispanic vs. non-Hispanic), family income, exceptionality status, and age. The TNL sample was similar to the U.S. population in terms of geographic area, gender, and race. The age groups were not equally represented in the norm group. Upper-income groups ($35,000/year and above) were slightly overrepresented in the norm group. Children with disabilities were included, but many appear to have disabilities that would specifically impact narrative language. The manual states that children with hearing impairments and unintelligible speech should not be tested with the TNL; however, the norm group had such children.

Scores: (1) Standard scores; (2) Age equivalents; and (3) Percentile ranks.

Link: *www.proedinc.com/customer/ProductView.aspx?ID=3316.*

Psycholinguistic Skills

Bankson Language Test—Second Edition (BLT-2)

Author: Nicholas W. Bankson.

Publisher: Pro-Ed.

Year: 1990.

Age range: 3.0 through 6.11 years.

Administration time: varies.

Computerized scoring: No.

Description: The BLT-2 is an individually administered, norm-referenced test used to measure the psycholinguistic skills of children and to establish the presence of a language disorder and identify areas in need of further testing. BLT-2 provides three general areas of information: Semantic Knowledge (body parts, nouns, verbs, categories, functions, prepositions, opposites); Morphological/Syntactical Rules (pronouns, verb usage/verb tense, verb plurals, comparatives/superlatives, negation, questions); and Pragmatics (ritualizing, informing, controlling, and imagining). A 20-item short form is also available to screen children for language problems.

Scales: Psycholinguistic skills.

Primary use: Screening, identification assessments.

Standardization: The normative sample consisted of 1,108 children living in 18 states. The demographic features of the sample are representative of the U.S. population as a whole on a variety of variables.

Scores: (1) Standard scores; and (2) Percentile ranks.

Link: *www.proedinc.com/customer/productView.aspx?ID=614*.

Comprehensive Achievement Measures That Include Vocabulary Subtest(s)

Woodcock Reading Mastery Tests—Revised—Normative Update (WRMT-R/NU)

Author: Richard W. Woodcock.

Publisher: Pearson.

Year: 1998.

Age range: 5.0 through 75+ years.

Administration time: 10–30 minutes for each cluster of tests.

Computerized scoring: Yes.

Description: The WRMT-R/NU assesses reading ability in students in grades K–12, undergraduate college students, and adults. The tests evaluate basic reading skills, reading comprehension, and reading readiness. Tests include: Visual-Auditory Learning; Letter Identification; Word Identification; Word Attack; Word Comprehension (Antonyms, Synonyms, Analogies); and Passage Comprehension.

Scales: Reading ability.

Primary use: Diagnostic.

Standardization: The WRMT-R/NU was normed on 6,089 individuals from 60 geographically diverse communities in the United States. Subjects were randomly selected and represented the U.S. population. The school-aged sample consisted of 4,201 children from kindergarten through 12th grade. School-aged data were collected over two full school years (1983 through 1985).

Scores: (1) Standard scores; (2) Age- and grade-based percentile ranks; (3) Normal Curve Equivalents (NCEs); and (4) Age and grade equivalents.

Link: www.pearsonassessments.com/HAIWEB/Cultures/en-us/Productdetail.htm?Pid= PAa16640&Mode=summary.

Emerging Technology-Based Vocabulary Screening and Progress Monitoring Measures

As noted above, the current availability of pragmatic and feasible vocabulary and progress monitoring measures is limited at this time. However, there are two technology-based approaches being developed and tested at this time: eMeasures of Root Word and Academic Vocabulary Growth (*www.soprislwest.com*) and easyCBM Vocabulary (*www.easycbm.com*). It is important to note that the psychometric characteristics of these two technology-based approaches are currently being tested. Additionally, a review of proposals funded by the Institute of Education Sciences (IES) reveals that a number of research teams are working on vocabulary measurement systems (*www.ies.ed.gov*). Thus, as noted above, we anticipate that the availability of practical vocabulary screening and progress monitoring measures for use in multi-tiered and RTI models will increase substantially in the near future.

eMeasures includes 20 equivalent forms for measuring students' growth in high-frequency root (Biemiller, 2009) and academic learning words (Coxhead, 2000) (see Chapter 3 for a description). The eMeasures root word and academic learning word versions are typically administered to K–2 and third-grade or older students, respectively. Students respond to 20 multiple-choice items that require the student to match a given meaning by choosing one of three words (one target and two distractors). The distractors are designed to (1) have the same syntactic form as the correct response (e.g., if the target word is a noun, all alternatives are nouns); (2) be separated semantically from the meaning of the target word; and (3) be mutually exclusive from each other (i.e., no two distractors can have the same meaning). The student reads the meaning and then points-and-clicks on one of the three possible responses. eMeasures provides a full complement of individual, classroom, school, and district reports.

The easyCBM Vocabulary measure includes three equivalent forms of high-frequency words from third through ninth grade. The words for the vocabulary measure were derived from the *World Book Encyclopedia* (2001 edition). Each of the three equivalent forms includes 25 items for each grade level. The forms can be downloaded and administered to students. Each item stem consists of a vocabulary word; below it are three possible answer choices: a correct synonym, a word that reflects a near-synonym, and a word not even close to reflecting a synonym. Students select their response by filling in a bubble to the left of the answer choice they believed to be the best definition of the alternatives listed for the vocabulary word.

SUMMARY

Assessing the vocabulary knowledge and language skills of students to guide instruction is challenging, for three primary reasons. First, there are differences among scholars and others regarding what it means to know a word and what kind of knowledge this represents. Inspection of the test descriptions provided above clearly reveal these differences. Not only are there differences in the types of items students are asked to respond to, but also the areas assessed vary widely.

Second, differences in conceptions of what it means to know a word and what kind of knowledge this represents make it difficult for educators to select vocabulary measures among those available for use. We highlighted three dimensions that teachers can use to design and evaluate assessments, including (1) discrete (which treats the student's knowledge of a word as an independent construction) versus embedded (which treats the student's knowledge of a word as embedded within a larger construct such as comprehension); (2) selective (which assesses a small sample of words) versus comprehensive (which assesses a large sample of words drawn from a general corpus of words); and (3) context-independent (which presents the word as an isolated element) versus context-dependent (which presents the word in context). Additionally, both the administration and interpretation of many vocabulary and language skills measures are complex undertakings—especially for educators determined to develop relevant vocabulary and language instruction for students experiencing learning difficulties. For example, the CELF-4 requires the integration of four levels of interpretation: Level 1—core language level; Level 2—assessment of language modalities and content; Level 3—clinical behavior; and Level 4—assessment of language and communication in context.

Finally, most available vocabulary measures are designed to be used as diagnostic measures. Although the developers report that these may be used to screen students for potential vocabulary knowledge and language skills difficulties, we argue that few of them are feasible for universal screening. These norm-referenced measures are unlikely to be used as a part of regular school practices because they are resource intensive with respect to personnel, time, materials, and money. There appears to be only one CBM measure designed specifically to screen and monitor progress of the vocabulary knowledge of K–3 students, namely, WUF. Additionally, we noted that schools might consider using the available CBM Maze measures as a proxy for vocabulary. The general lack of available psychometrically sound and feasible screening and progress monitoring measures represents a significant gap in vocabulary assessment and, in turn, instruction. The limited availability of screening and progress monitoring measures is unfortunate, given schools' increasing use of RTI service delivery models to both prevent and ameliorate student learning and behavior difficulties.

CHAPTER 8

Teaching Vocabulary to English Language Learners

CHAPTER VOCABULARY

Cognates Words in two different languages that derive from the same parent word or share similarities in meaning and spelling (e.g., *immigrate* in English and *immigrar* in Spanish).

Concordance A searchable database created from a specific word *corpus* that consists of a list of sentence fragments from texts in which the target word appears.

Corpus A large database of written or spoken discourse that is used for language analyses that may include word frequencies and *concordances*.

Gloss An annotation to help clarify the meaning of a word in a text; a collection of glosses is a glossary. Glosses may provide information on word meanings, synonyms, word origins, pronunciation, translation, or grammar. Consisting of text, pictures, and/or video, they may also combine hypertext and multimedia and be found on the Web and in e-books.

INTRODUCTION

Many language-minority students enter school with only a limited English vocabulary, which therefore presents an obstacle to learning across content areas. They are less likely to know and are slower to acquire the lower-frequency words typically encountered in written rather than spoken English. Therefore, language-minority students encounter a high proportion of unfamiliar words in their reading, making it much more difficult for them to comprehend the meaning of the text. Limited vocabulary knowledge creates an obstacle for language-minority students for vocabulary growth and reading comprehension as well as writing performance (Burgoyne, Kelly, Whiteley, & Spooner, 2009; Stuart, 2004). Vocabulary knowledge appears to have a greater impact on reading comprehension for language-minority students than for native English-speaking students (Verhoeven, 2000). Although the early course of word reading skills development for language-minority students is similar to that for native English-speaking students (Chiappe & Siegel, 1999; Lesaux & Siegel, 2003), as text demands increase, language-minority students gradually fall behind in reading comprehension (see Lesaux, 2006). Social background variables including socioeconomic status and second-language family background are associated with variations in vocabulary knowledge, and language-minority students may have vocabulary levels one-quarter to one-third of their native English-speaking peers (Vermeer, 2001). Even middle school language-minority students who have been enrolled in English-speaking classrooms since the first grade continue to lag behind their native English-speaking peers on grade-level vocabulary (Jean & Geva, 2009). The limited English language input that results in restricted vocabulary knowledge for language-minority students calls for effective classroom instruction to accelerate their vocabulary acquisition. Helping them develop vocabulary is particularly important because an insufficient vocabulary contributes to limited reading comprehension (Burgoyne et al., 2009; Stuart, 2004) and may also contribute to overidentification for special education (Klingner, Sorrells, & Barrera, 2007).

All of us have experienced the challenge of reading texts that include many unfamiliar words or even several unknown words that are critical to properly comprehending the text. Not surprisingly, students with limited vocabulary skills read less, have fewer opportunities to encounter and learn these new words (especially Tier Two and academic words), and eventually lose motivation for reading. The average number of words that students typically acquire during their school years—some 2,000–3000 words per year—suggests that many words are learned incidentally through reading and that therefore students need effective strategies to learn words independently. Many language-minority students need to learn strategies for rapidly building their vocabulary to keep up with the demands of school. For example, language-minority students often lag behind their native English-speaking classmates in the number of words they know (breadth) as well as in their *depth* of knowledge, which includes phonological and orthographic representation, polysemy, syntactic role/class, collocations and idioms, derivations, and the social register (e.g., colloquial or formal, American or British useage). Depth of word knowledge also includes the knowledge of underlying networks of concepts that develop as students learn more words, and this semantic depth also contributes to reading comprehension (Nation & Snowling, 2004; Oulette, 2006), particularly in the upper grades when school texts become more complex in terms of vocabulary, syntax, and concepts.

Research is emerging on how to help language-minority students draw upon their native language skills for English word learning. For example, depth of word knowledge for their native-language words in some of the dimensions noted above (e.g., word relations) transfers to English, and students who can express superordinate relations in their first language (e.g., a *hammer* is a tool; *zinc* is a mineral) are better able to acquire and know equivalent English superordinate terms (i.e., tool, mineral; Ordonez et al., 2002). Researchers continue to study cross-language relationships to understand which original-language skills transfer and how instruction can promote this transfer.

> **Semantic Depth and Language-Minority Students**
>
> Semantic depth . . .
> - Allows students to understand the relations among words and concepts in reading school texts.
> - Encourages language-minority students to activate their prior knowledge when introducing new words and concepts.
> - Builds on students' knowledge of related L1 and L2 words, including synonyms, antonyms, and related word forms.
> - Encourages language-minority students to relate new English words to words in the students' L1 and to L1 cognates.
> - Contributes to reading comprehension beginning in the early grades and becomes even more important at the secondary level.

In previous chapters, we pointed out the immense challenge of enabling students with limited vocabularies to catch up with their peers solely by directly teaching them new word meanings. The task may be greater for language-minority students with even more limited vocabulary and general English proficiency. Planning instruction is further complicated by the difficulty of identifying language-minority students at the lower level of the English proficiency distribution who may also have learning disabilities.

A growing body of research suggests that language-minority students benefit from explicit vocabulary instruction to develop adequate vocabulary size *and* learning strategies to maximize independent vocabulary learning from context. In its review of the subject, the National Literacy Panel on Language-Minority Children and Youth (August & Shanahan, 2006) found that the recommendations for effective vocabulary instruction for non-language-minority students also hold for language-minority students; namely, that all students benefit from explicit instruction in word meanings, repeated exposures to new words, opportunities for productive use, and active processing of words in varied contexts (see also Genesee, Lindholm-Leary, Saunders, & Christian, 2006). Reading instruction for language-minority students remains an area of active research.

EFFECTIVE VOCABULARY INSTRUCTION FOR PRESCHOOL LANGUAGE-MINORITY LEARNERS

Prior to school entry, the greatest influences on a child's vocabulary development are the home environment in general, including L1 and English language experiences, and book reading practices—in particular, at home. Hart and Risley's (1995) research, for example, revealed the large social class differences in the amount of language experience that parents normally provide to children during their first 3 years of life. The more language and the greater complexity of language that children experience, the faster their vocabulary grows. Limited research on ELL children indicates that these social class differences also influence the early home literacy practices for children from Spanish-speaking homes (Reese, Garnier, Gallimore, & Goldenberg, 2000). Differences in patterns in home language input in minority-language groups may influence language-minority students' L1 and English language and vocabulary development (Scheele, Leseman, & Mayo, 2010). For example, some immigrant groups may have stronger ties to their native language and greater access to books and newspapers that support use of L1 in the home and that may influence the development of English vocabulary (Verhoeven, 2007). Clearly, the spoken language that children hear in the home and at school helps them to increase their vocabulary through a process known as *fast mapping*, that is, instantly reserving a location in their brains for the pronunciation and meaning of a new word. When hearing and learning words in their first language, children internalize meanings they can build upon when they later are told the English labels for these words. L1 receptive vocabulary skills also contribute to the development of phonological awareness skills that readily transfer between languages (Atwill, Blanchard, Christie, Gorin, & Garcia, 2010).

First-Language Vocabulary Skills

- L1 vocabulary knowledge influences the development of L2 vocabulary.
- L1 vocabulary skills *also* influence the development of L2 phonological awareness skills that are a prerequisite for reading achievement.
- Teachers should support and encourage home reading in the child's native language.

The more vocabulary that a child knows, the easier it is for him or her to learn new vocabulary. This means that explicit vocabulary instruction should begin as soon as possible during the preschool years. Roberts (2009) estimates that a reasonable goal for preschool vocabulary instruction, based on vocabulary acquisition research for both non-ELL and ELL children, is 12–15 new vocabulary words per week. Roberts emphasizes the importance of generating large amounts of talk using many different words to properly address the capacity of preschoolers to learn new words.

As outlined in Chapter 4, a strong body of research indicates that storybook reading enhances language development (van Kleeck, Stahl, & Bauer, 2003), including vocabulary development (Robbins & Ehri, 1994). Storybook interventions that include direct vocabulary instruction produce the learning of taught words as well as their transfer to general vocabulary knowledge (Coyne et al., 2010). Storybook reading procedures like dialogic reading, both in the classroom and in the home, have positive benefits for the expressive language and vocabulary skills of preschool children from low-income backgrounds (Bus et al., 1995; Whitehurst, Arnold, et al., 1994).

Research on Storybook Reading

Three recent reviews of research studies by the What Works Clearinghouse (2006–2007) reported positive and mixed effects for oral language outcomes for *shared* and *interactive shared* book reading and *dialogic* reading approaches. Although most of this research has been conducted with English-only children, a small and growing body of research shows that storybook reading in English also enhances vocabulary development for preschool English learners.

In a study by Roberts and Neal (2003), preschool English language learners benefitted from instruction that featured interactive storybook reading and explicit vocabulary instruction regardless of their English proficiency. In a second study, Roberts (2008) examined the benefits of having parents read their preschool English language learners storybooks in their native language prior to having teachers read the storybooks in English during classroom instruction. In this study, children and parents whose native language was Spanish and Hmong were assigned to one of two groups (determined by language group). For the first 6 weeks of the study, one group took home storybooks in their primary language, and the other group took home storybooks in English. For the last 6 weeks of the study, the groups switched languages (i.e., the group that initially read the books in their primary language during the first 6 weeks read the books in English during the last 6 weeks). One week after the parents read the books at home, the teacher provided two classroom lessons on the same storybook in English. At the end of the home reading and classroom vocabulary instruction in English, children in both groups showed similar rates of vocabulary learning. Children who received primary-language storybooks showed the highest rates of vocabulary learning following classroom instruction in English, possibly reflecting their development of primary-language vocabulary and concept knowledge.

Parents of language-minority students provide important support for their children's English vocabulary development through storybook interactions in the family's native language. Vocabulary development is closely linked to world knowledge and knowledge of concepts that are supported through interactions in either the child's native language or English. Characteristics of effective storybook-based vocabulary instruction for young non-language-minority students also benefit young ELL children. These features include the following:

Multicomponent Approach

Multicomponent approaches include introducing vocabulary in a storybook context, explicit instruction in word meanings, child-friendly definitions, active student engagement in word analyses, the use of storybook vocabulary in other meaningful contexts, and clear phonological and orthographic word models (i.e., hearing the word pronounced and seeing the word spelled). In a study of a vocabulary instruction that included these features, both ELL and non-ELL children learned target words and were able to achieve faster growth in overall vocabulary knowledge (Silverman, 2007b; Silverman & Crandell, 2010). Systematic review of taught words appears to boost the vocabulary learning that occurs in well-designed storybook instruction (Zipoli, Coyne, & McCoach, 2011).

Use of Visual Aids

Effective vocabulary interventions often include pictures of noun words (i.e., Rosenthal & Ehri, 2008; Wasik & Bond, 2001), and still pictures and videos have been used to enhance instruction for ELL learners. Multimedia materials that include video clips related to taught vocabulary and story topics may effectively augment vocabulary learning for ELL children (Silverman & Hines, 2009). The use of video images has been studied in a digital picture storybook intervention for 5-year-old low-income immigrant children (Verhallen & Bus, 2010): vocabulary words were represented in either a video or still-picture format. While both formats resulted in receptive vocabulary learning, the video format resulted in greater expressive learning. Researchers suggested that independent use of video storybooks may be an effective and motivating means of helping young prereading language-minority students to expand their vocabulary.

Pictures and images are often useful to establish the association between the verbal label for a concrete concept, like the word *bridge*, and its meaning. However, it is important that pictures not prevent students from building a link between the spoken word and its printed form (Sadoski, 2005). When students see the spellings of words they are being taught, they form connections between the letters and sounds in the words that help them remember how the words are pronounced and what the words mean (Ehri & Rosenthal, 2007; Rosenthal & Ehri, 2008).

Storybook Reading in the Home Language

In many families, parents may not have adequate English proficiency to read English language storybooks to their preschool EL children. However, as the research by Roberts (2008) suggests, interactive storybook reading in the home language has benefits for English vocabulary learning. Parents should be encouraged to engage in basic interactive story reading (and rereading) in their home language. Home storybook reading may be most effective when the stories are introduced at home in the native language, followed by teacher instruction in the classroom in the English vocabulary and story content, or when book reading topics at home and school are coordinated.

EFFECTIVE VOCABULARY INSTRUCTION FOR SCHOOL-AGE LANGUAGE-MINORITY STUDENTS

Morphological Word-Learning Strategies

As we noted earlier, the majority of the words that students learn between grades 3 and 5 are derived words, and typically the development of morphological awareness accelerates during this time (Anglin, 1993). Knowledge of morphemes enables students to read longer words, to read them more efficiently by piecing together familiar parts of the words, and thereby to infer their meanings. Morphological awareness instruction benefits word reading, spelling, and vocabulary (Lyster, 2002; Nunes et al., 2003). This instruction can be effectively integrated with instruction in other reading skills and provided in the context of content-area Tier 1 instruction (Reed, 2008) or used to supplement vocabulary development in Tier 2 or 3 instruction.

Explicit instruction in morphological analysis has been an important feature of second-language instruction and has been more recently studied in classroom-based vocabulary interventions for middle school language-minority students (see August, Branum-Martin, Cardenas-Hagan, & Francis, 2009; Nation, 1990; Snow, Lawrence, & White, 2009). Knowledge of derivational morphology plays an important role in reading comprehension for middle school Spanish-speaking language-minority students, similar to native English speakers (Kieffer & Lesaux, 2008). This knowledge is reflected in a task that requires the student to extract a root word from a derived word to complete a sentence (e.g., "*Availability*: The video will soon be _____"). Explicit morphology instruction includes teaching the meaning of word parts (e.g., *available* as the root word, *-ity* as a suffix) and teaching a strategy to independently analyze the structure of a complex word to infer its meaning.

Instruction in Root Words and Affixes

High-frequency root words warrant explicit instruction because they represent such a large proportion of written texts (see Chapter 3), and these basic words may not be known by language-minority students. Instruction in the most commonly occurring affixes is also recommended to support students' use of morphological analysis in both word reading and deriving word meaning. As noted in Chapter 2, the majority of affixed words feature 20 prefixes, making these high-frequency morphemes prime targets for instruction (White et al., 1989).

Strategy Instruction in Morphological Analysis

Strategy instruction in morphological analysis teaches students skills in decomposition, or how to break a complex word into smaller meaningful parts. For example, Stahl and Nagy (2006) suggest teaching a word-learning strategy that uses word parts to determine the meaning of unfamiliar words. Students may need to be taught how to:

- Look for the root word (e.g., in *introspective*, the root is *spec*, "to look or see").
- Look for a prefix, and see if they know the meaning (*intro*, "within").
- Look for a suffix, and see if they know what it means (*-ive*, "condition").
- Put the meanings of the root word, prefix, and/or suffix together, and see if they can construct the meaning of the word (Baumann, Edwards, et al., 2003).

Use of Cognates

A *cognate* is a word that resembles (to varying degrees) a word in another language and that has a common origin. Cognates are often derived from Romance languages (French, Spanish, Italian) that have their origins in Latin, although some are derived from other language families (e.g., Germanic). Students who are fluent in their native language and L1 vocabulary will be better able to recognize and translate L1–English cognates. For language-minority students whose native language is Spanish and who have a knowledge of written Spanish, it can often be useful to point out spelling similarities in cognates in Spanish and English (e.g., *decide–decidir*; *marvel–maravilla*). Older language-minority students are better able to recognize morphological similarities between cognates, and, as noted earlier, this morphological awareness instruction may be most useful, beginning in middle school. As noted earlier, helping language-minority students to develop lexical networks through the use of cognates further deepens their vocabulary knowledge (Nagy & Herman, 1987; Vermeer, 2001).

Research Support

In two studies of sustained vocabulary strategy instruction, Carlo, August, and Snow (2005) included cognate instruction as one strategy to teach word learning and develop in-depth word knowledge. Fifth-grade language-minority students were taught about word roots, affixes, and multiple meanings as well as cognates for content-area words with Spanish/English cognates. In another Internet-based vocabulary intervention for fifth-grade English–Spanish bilingual students, instruction targeted Tier Two academic words that were Spanish/English cognates (Proctor et al., 2009). One of the digital prereading activities presented Spanish cognates for the target English vocabulary words as well as morphological and semantic information. Although the specific effects of cognate instruction have not been carefully studied, it appears to be a worthwhile component of vocabulary instruction for middle school and older students in Tier 1 classroom applications. First, it fosters a curiosity and interest in words and their origins that encourage a habit of long-term independent vocabulary learning for native English speakers as well as English learners. Second, cognate instruction extends the focus on morphological strategies, learning to use word parts effectively to learn new word meanings.

Several cautions are advised on cognate instruction. Some English words resemble their Spanish cognates more (e.g., *grand–grande*) or less (e.g., *primate–primero*) closely in spelling or morphology. Explicit instruction is therefore often needed to help students notice how an English word is similar in form to a Spanish word the student already knows. Further, many Spanish/English cognates are words that characterize content area and more advanced vocabulary, and students may not already know the meaning of the Spanish cognate. Finally, there are "false cognates"—words that appear similar in spelling and may appear to have a similar word origin but do not (e.g., *bizarro* means "brave" and not *bizarre* in the sense of "strange").

RESEARCH INFORMING VOCABULARY INSTRUCTION FOR SCHOOL-AGE ENGLISH LANGUAGE LEARNERS

Two areas of research inform instruction for school-age language-minority students. The first is the research on second-language instruction, which often has been conducted with secondary school, college-age, and adult English learners. The second body of research includes the more recently accumulating studies on classroom and supplemental interventions for elementary and secondary-school language-minority students.

Research on Second-Language Vocabulary Learning

Individuals who are learning any second language face a daunting vocabulary learning challenge. We can describe it in terms of the number of words required for understanding spoken or written English. Experts estimate that learners must understand about 98% of the words in conversation or in written passages to achieve a reasonable level of comprehension (Nation, 2006; Read, 2004). This criterion seems to require knowledge of 6,000–7,000 word families to understand *spoken* English (Schmitt, 2008) and 8,000–9,000 word families to understand *written* texts (Nation, 2006). It is important to note that these numbers describe word *families*, not individual word *forms*. For example, the word family *constitute* includes the word forms *constituency, constituent, constitutes, constitution, constitutional*, and *constitutive*. Many students who know the base words in these word families may nonetheless continue to have difficulty in understanding the derived and inflected forms (Schmitt & Zimmerman, 2002). The numbers above are therefore underestimates of the number of word *forms* that learners must actually know to truly "know" these word families.

The large number of words that English learners must learn requires prioritizing which words are most important to teach. The initial focus for second-language instruction is typically high-frequency words for comprehension of conversation and general written texts. The next priority is often *academic* words (Coxhead, 2000) to support reading a broad range of school texts. Chapter 3 describes widely used word frequency list resources that include the *General Service List* (West, 1953) and lists based upon the British National Corpus (Leech, Rayson, & Wilson, 2001) often used for second-language instruction. The importance of teaching English learners academic words is suggested by research on ELL student performance on large-scale math and science assessments (Kieffer, Lesaux, Rivera, & Francis, 2009). Researchers found that the use of testing accommodations (e.g., the unregulated use of English dictionaries) had only a small impact on the performance of language-minority students on these tests, and they subsequently hypothesized that the *academic language demands* of large-scale assessments play a significant role in achievement differences between ELL and non-ELL students on these achievement tests. As the researchers noted, academic language skills are central to a full understanding of advanced math, science, and social science content.

As we noted earlier, learning academic vocabulary well entails the deep and rich processing of words that often refer to cognitive phenomena and have multiple meanings. Because language-minority students may take longer than non-language-minority students to develop their academic English (Hakuta, Butler, & Witt, 2000), they likely especially benefit from explicit instruction aimed at speeding up this process as part of either Tier 1 or Tier 2 instruction. Townsend and Collins (2009) examined the benefits of a multicomponent research-based after-school vocabulary intervention for middle school language-minority students. Students received 20 sessions, each about 75 minutes, of instruction based on grade-level standards-based history and science topics. The intervention featured Tier Two academic words. Each week, the instructional regimen featured 12 academic words that were taught through definitions, use of the words in sentences, cloze sentences requiring students to use the target words, pictures that supported the words, matching games, reading texts that featured the words, listening to novels, and using the words in writing activities. Students who demonstrated the greatest growth in academic vocabulary during the intervention were those who had been less successful in learning academic vocabulary in their independent reading and schoolwork. The findings suggest that academic vocabulary can be successfully taught to language-minority students by using evidence-based principles of vocabulary instruction.

One group of academic words that may be particularly valuable to teach both English language learners and students with limited language skills are words that connect clauses and mark relations within text. These connecting and signaling words provide important clues to the meaning of more complex school texts. Students with only a limited understanding of these words are less likely to understand important relationships between segments of academic texts (Crosson, Lesaux, & Martiniello, 2008; Degand & Sanders, 2002). These connective words may signal such semantic relationships as addition (e.g., *in addition*), cause–consequence (e.g., *because*), contrast (e.g., *while*), or temporality (e.g., *before, then*).

The scope of the task of teaching vocabulary to English language learners recommends a balance between breadth and depth (Schmitt, 2008). Learners need to quickly acquire knowledge of high-frequency words that are the foundation for learning more words and developing *breadth* of word knowledge. At the same time, instruction should help the student develop the *depth* of knowledge about words that allows him or her to form rich semantic networks and to use the words fluently and correctly in spoken and written contexts. This latter objective of *deep* and *productive* knowledge requires a long-term approach to vocabulary instruction with multiple opportunities for students to interact with words and with preplanned periodic review of words already taught. Another feature of depth of word knowledge is the ability to retrieve words from memory quickly for use in speech and writing. Students may develop this fluency through training on computer-assisted exercises (e.g., filling in the missing word in short sentences, making judgments about correct word use in a context and substituting correct words, filling in a correct word translation in a meaningful context) in which students are instructed to build up speed in their responses (Snellings, van Gelderen, & de Glopper, 2002). Breadth and depth appear to be useful measures of vocabulary for both L1 and L2 students (Vermeer, 2001). However, depth measures that require students to define words may disadvantage L2 students, as these tasks call upon the student to construct definitions by using abstract and hierarchical academic language.

The size and scope of the immense vocabulary learning task faced by English language learners suggest the wisdom of seeking a balance between incidental and intentional learning (Schmitt, 2008). The following summarizes findings on incidental and intentional vocabulary learning for second-language learning.

Incidental Word Learning for Language-Minority Students

Like their native English-speaking peers, language-minority students acquire most of their English vocabulary through incidental word exposures. The challenge for teachers is to help these students become as successful as possible in increasing their rate of English vocabulary growth. This incidental instruction can begin as early as the primary grades. For example, conspicuous vocabulary instruction can be effectively infused into beginning reading instruction for these students (e.g., in a phonemic segmenting task, first pronounce the word, spell it, and then provide a student-friendly definition of the word, also using it in a sentence: "*bat*: /b//a//t/ —A bat is a wooden stick we use to hit a baseball"; Pollard-Durodola & Simmons, 2009). Research (Hill & Laufer, 2003; Hulstijn, Hollander, & Greidanus, 1996; Mondria, 2003; Nation, 2001; Schmitt, 2008) provides these guidelines to boosting language-minority students' incidental learning.

1. *Second-language learners acquire vocabulary through incidental exposures in reading, but at a very low rate.* Research suggests that these incidental exposures result in better learning of word *forms*—in particular, spelling—and less learning of full meaning (or multiple meanings) or productive knowledge (i.e., being able to translate the word or to recall the word meaning at follow-up). It appears that students' encounters with unfamiliar words during their independent reading lead to partial word knowledge and to short-term word recognition rather than longer-term word recall (Schmitt, 2008).

> Research suggests that incidental exposures are important but not sufficient for deep word learning—in particular, for language-minority students.

2. *The number of reading exposures to a word significantly influences incidental word learning* (Pigada & Schmitt, 2006; Saragi, Nation, & Meister, 1987). It appears that 8–10 encounters with the word are needed to develop initial receptive word knowledge

(Schmitt, 2008). Teachers cannot normally control how many times a word is repeated in a school text. Repeated word exposures in varied contexts in Tier 1 and 2 interventions are also likely to benefit word learning for language-minority students with learning disabilities.

> Text-based instruction should highlight and review important vocabulary. Teacher-developed texts should feature many repetitions of the target vocabulary words.

3. *Extensive reading contributes to vocabulary learning* (see Renandya, Rajan, & Jacob, 1999). However, incidental learning through reading most often results in increased receptive knowledge and partial word knowledge. These repeated encounters with words in text are useful in building incremental word knowledge—but, again, this is a long-term and uncertain learning process that depends on the volume and type of reading the student engages in as well as the student's verbal abilities and inferencing skills.

> Build students' engagement with texts by matching texts to the students' reading levels, background knowledge, and interests whenever possible.

4. *Incidental vocabulary learning is enhanced by the use of dictionaries and glosses* (annotations in text that clarify meanings). Glossing dates back to the Middle Ages, when scripts were routinely annotated with interpretations, comments, and other details. Second-language learners often create their own glosses by notating word translations for unfamiliar words in their L2 texts. Teachers likewise often create glosses for second-language learners. One type of gloss is a "priming" gloss that provides important vocabulary information *before* the student reads a text.

As we noted earlier, dictionaries are effective tools when used to look up or verify the meaning of a word in a reading context. Students who use dictionaries when they are reading demonstrate higher rates of incidental vocabulary learning (Knight, 1994; Luppescu & Cay, 1993). There is one big

> Research suggests that students are more likely to use computer glosses than to use a dictionary. Students can be taught to create glosses—either notes on printed texts or notes in electronic texts. Research indicates that glosses and dictionary look-up practices have greater benefits for vocabulary learning than overall comprehension. Learning how to properly create and use glosses may be particularly useful for language-minority students with learning disabilities.

problem, however, in practice. Dictionaries are useful only when students use them, and many students are more likely to ignore unknown or unfamiliar words than to look them up in the dictionary. Students must closely monitor their understanding in order to know when to use a dictionary. Stopping to look up a word in the dictionary interrupts their reading and thus may interfere with their comprehension. These findings have two implications. First, students need to develop both the motivation to learn unfamiliar words and the habit of using the dictionary as a tool in their independent reading. Second, as an alternative to dictionaries, electronic text glosses can be used to support incidental vocabulary learning. Nation (2001) notes that the advantages of glossing include allowing students to access more difficult texts, ensuring that students have the correct meanings for difficult words they might either ignore or misconstrue, and minimizing reading disruptions. Hulstijn et al. (1996) compared the use of marginal glosses and dictionary use by second-language university students and found that the use of glosses resulted in better word learning than in the control group. However, when students did use the dictionary, vocabulary learning was similar for both the dictionary and the glossing group. Moreover, words that appeared more frequently were learned more comprehensively when meanings were provided, either through glosses or a dictionary.

The types of glosses used to annotate vocabulary words in an electronic text include:

- Definition of the word in the margin.
- Audio pronunciation of the word in English.
- Translation of the word into the student's L1.
- Use of the word in a sample sentence in the student's L1.
- A still picture or video link to illustrate the word.
- A hypertext link to external content.

5. *Incidental learning is reinforced and deepened through the periodic review of previously taught words.* Vocabulary exercises specifically for consolidating and deepening word knowledge include:

- Having students develop their personal list of words important to remember and reviewing and expanding upon these lists on a regular basis.
- Including activities after reading that focus on specific vocabulary words as well as on comprehension.
- Having students practice inferring the meaning of unfamiliar words and then confirming the meaning through a dictionary. One should add words to a list and then practice memorizing them once their meaning is confirmed.
- Reviewing and recycling taught vocabulary words to support long-term vocabulary learning. Memory research suggests that it is most important to repeat exposure and recycle instruction soon after the words are first introduced (Baddeley, 1990)—particularly with students experiencing learning difficulties.

Intentional Word Learning for Language-Minority Students

The large number of lexical items that English learners must acquire supports the wisdom of combining both incidental *and* intentional word learning (Read, 2004). Explicit vocabulary instruction ideally includes providing a dictionary definition and contextual definition (preferably student-friendly), presenting the written version to ensure spelling accuracy, saying the word aloud to model correct pronunciation, and completing comprehension exercises that require writing the word and using the word as many times as possible in a composition. In a series of experiments with university and high school ELL students, Laufer (2003) found that word-focused tasks, compared to reading texts, were more likely to result in the students' remembering the meaning of the word at posttest and at 2-week follow-up. The tasks included writing sample sentences with the target words, incorporating the target words into a student writing composition, and completing sentences with the target words after looking up their meaning. These productive tasks required students to decide how to use the word in a sentence context and involved more intentional learning than might be required through incidental word encounters while reading. Carlo et al. (2004) provided direct word instruction to ELL fifth graders by using tasks that actively engaged the students in word analysis, spelling, and writing. Students gained in their knowledge of taught words, including depth of word knowledge, knowledge of multiple meanings, and reading comprehension.

Word Selection

Second-language instruction often concentrates on the most frequently encountered words, as the 2,000 most common words account for some 80% of the running words in typical text (Nation, 2001). Root words are an important instructional target. Biemiller and Slonim (2001) in their research on root word knowledge, based on Dale and O'Rourke's *Living Word Vocabulary* (1981), found that language-minority students learn vocabulary in a similar sequence to L1 students, providing a guideline for systematic vocabulary instruction that begins in the primary grades. The *University Word List* (Xue & Nation, 1984) and the *Academic Word List* (Coxhead, 2000) are useful for intentional instruction beginning in middle school grades. Because language-minority students may be less likely to learn academic English vocabulary at home, explicit instruction in these challenging and nonconcrete words is especially important. Certain words that characterize school texts pose particular challenges to language-minority students. These include *connectives*, words or phrases that express relationships between clauses in texts such as *therefore, nonetheless, in contrast, despite that,* and *moreover.* Understanding these connectives fully depends upon students' relative language skills, and knowledge of these connectives importantly affects students' reading comprehension levels. Some connectives are more challenging because they signal more complex semantic relationships. For example, connectives indicating additive relations (e.g., *in addition*) are less difficult than those signifying causal relationships (e.g., *because, owing to*) or relationships in opposition or contrast (e.g., *even though*) (Crosson et al., 2008). These important words warrant explicit instruction for all students and may be particularly critical to EL learners. In a study of fifth-grade language-minority students, knowledge of text connection vocabulary (e.g., *although, because, in spite of*) played an important role in their reading comprehension (Rydland, Aukrust, & Fulland, 2010).

Features of Effective Intentional Vocabulary Instruction for Language-Minority Students

A recent review of vocabulary instruction for second-language learning identifies principles to guide vocabulary learning tasks for language-minority students:

1. *Maximize activities emphasizing student engagement with word items*, including:
   - Seeing the words in isolation, reading (pronouncing), and spelling the words.
   - Seeing the words in text and using the words in a retelling or a discussion in sentence contexts.
   - Providing students with a translation of the word and sample use of the word in a sentence in their native language.
   - Having students record new words in a notebook in which they can add information on the words' features.
2. *Provide repeated exposures to word items.* Five to 20 repetitions are needed to fully learn a new vocabulary word. Repetitions should be recycled over time, with early repetitions provided soon after a word is introduced. Students with learning difficulties require even more opportunities to see and practice new vocabulary.
3. *Provide a focus on four learning strands* (Nation, 2001; Nation & Gu, 2007) *that reflect various aspects of word learning*:
   - Meaning-focused input—which provides exposure to vocabulary in reading and listening activities (receptive).
   - Meaning-focused output—which provides opportunities to use words in speech and writing activities (productive). Specific learning activities may include using the target words in sentences, filling in the blanks in sentences by choosing the correct word, and using the target words in writing.
   - Language-focused learning—which includes explicit instruction in key content and academic vocabulary as well as explicit strategy instruction.
   - Fluency development—which includes activities that provide repeated exposures to words (through reading, speaking, listening, and writing) to build word recognition speed (Schmitt, 2008).
4. *Teach academic vocabulary explicitly.* Teach academic English words in small increments across the grades and across content, ESL, and core reading instruction (see "Teaching Literacy in English to K–5 ELs" at the Doing What Works website, *dww.ed.gov*).

Tools for Language-Minority Vocabulary Learning

Because language-minority students in the middle and secondary grades may lag behind their native English-speaking peers in word knowledge, they benefit from sustained efforts to build receptive and productive vocabulary skills. In addition to the intentional and incidental routes to vocabulary learning described above, a growing number of online tools are available to support ongoing and independent vocabulary study. Features of these online tools include:

- *Multimedia sound features.* These allow the student to hear the correct word pronunciation. Students are more likely to use a word in conversation if they are confident about how to pronounce it correctly. Correct models of pronunciation are key considerations for students with speech and language difficulties.
- *Concordances.* These are lists of sentence contexts in which the word is used and that provide semantic, syntactic, and collocational information on the word. (See Figure 8.1 for an example of concordance.) Many online resources for English language learners include links to concordances.
- *Other learning exercises.* These may include self-administered quizzes and cloze-building features that enable students to generate cloze passages from a specific group of words. Students can then use these cloze passages to practice correct word use. Other online vocabulary sites provide crossword puzzles and word games.

Although there is limited research on the usefulness of these resources for ELL vocabulary and language learning (see Horst, Cobb, & Nicolae, 2005), they offer a means to increase word exposures and engage in deeper word processing. Their value is in helping to maintain engagement with vocabulary learning among older language-minority students who need to increase both their vocabulary size and depth of word knowledge.

Classroom Studies: Interventions for Older Language-Minority Students

Findings from a cluster of studies describe classroom- and school-based interventions for middle school language-minority students. In one study, the Word Generation program was used to teach academic vocabulary to students in grades 6–8 (Snow, Lawrence, & White, 2009). As described in Chapter 5, this school-based intervention engages students in discussion and writing on high-interest current topics. Each week's topic is introduced in a brief passage containing five target vocabulary words. Activities prescribed for each day of the week (15 minutes per day) are implemented by the English language arts, math, social studies, and science teachers. Treatment effect sizes for vocabulary improvement were moderate to large (effect sizes ranged from 0.33 to 0.65).

In two studies, a similar multicomponent vocabulary intervention was implemented in the context of content-area instruction for middle school students. In the first study (Vaughn et al., 2009), vocabulary was taught in social studies lessons for seventh-grade students. In the second study (August et al., 2009), vocabulary was taught in the context of science instruction for sixth-grade students. Both

1. e significant conclusions. Part /3, discusses the	**EMPIRICAL**	relevance and policy implications of the
2. ories have been explored to find out about these	**EMPIRICAL**	probabilities" against which to measure
3. cts in his worldly fortunes. Basing action on the	**EMPIRICAL**	determination of cause and effect provid
4. approach to the question of alienation. Almost	**EMPIRICAL**	work has been done on the problem of ali
5. form as something soaring above and embracing the	**EMPIRICAL**	and mathematical sciences. But contrary
6. ew basic lists, items whose forms show as high an	**EMPIRICAL**	retention rate as possible. There would
7. ns, and which rests on certain ethical absolutes,	**EMPIRICAL**	data can be used to support whatever pro
8. rms of philosophy, this very division between the	**EMPIRICAL**	and the rational becomes a sign of the m
9. also permits Fromm to do some dubious things with	**EMPIRICAL**	findings. When alienation is used as an
10. e, where sociology is essentially descriptive and	**EMPIRICAL**	Such a position entails the negation of
1. he eleventh and twelfth years. _10._ Many studies	**INDICATE**	that elementary-school children's interes
2. ailed to you. If you file a Form 1040, you should	**INDICATE**	in the place provided that there is an ov
3. t membership now is only 9,910,741. These figures	**INDICATE**	that we are losing almost as many as we a
4. ust the maid there", he replied, waving a hand to	**INDICATE**	how completely unimportant she was. Kirby
5. otify the Department of Economic Affairs and will	**INDICATE**	the interest rate and the repayment perio
6. discoid shapes of sun and moon were also felt to	**INDICATE**	the shape of celestial things. In light o
7. as Nagel (1957:247-83) and Hempel (1959:271-307	**INDICATE**	that the concept of function in sociolog
8. alignment of the "dots" and "tips", respectively,	**INDICATE**	individual variability of the 21 growth c
9. ilding, aircraft procurement, and weapon programs	**INDICATE**	that there will not be enough of anything
10. eet 11 inches long. What data there are on growth	**INDICATE**	considerable variation in rate; unfortuna

FIGURE 8.1. First 10 lines of concordance output for the words *empirical* and *indicate* drawn from the *Brown Corpus* (Francis & Kucera, 1982) and *The Compleat Lexical Tutor* (Cobb, 1997); *www.lextutor.ca/concordances/multi/*.

interventions were intensive, with instruction extending for 9–12 weeks, 5 days a week, for 40–50 minutes per day. Features of instruction in these studies included:

- Explicit vocabulary instruction within the context of "big ideas" in the subject content.
- Student-friendly definitions and the use of visual and video supports to generate student discussion.
- Peer pairing (ELL and non-ELL students) to foster discussion.
- Strategy instruction (e.g., cognates, morphology).
- Writing with graphic organizers.

Both interventions had benefits for language-minority and non-language-minority students, and treatment effects for comprehension and vocabulary (researcher-developed measures based on the lesson content) ranged from small to moderate for the science-based program and moderate to large for the social science program. Both studies support the view that intensive research-based multicomponent vocabulary instruction has similar benefits for both ELL and non-ELL students. This vocabulary instruction was effectively integrated by classroom teachers with coaching and support within their content-area instruction.

In one of the studies reviewed by the National Literacy Panel on Language-Minority Children and Youth (August & Shanahan, 2006), a bilingual component was added to a multicomponent vocabulary intervention. Carlo et al. (2004) described a study of language-minority fifth graders' experience with an intensive vocabulary intervention. Classroom teachers provided them with 30–45 minutes of instruction, 4 days a week, for 15 weeks. Between 10–15 words a week were taught in the context of readings on the topic of immigration. On Mondays, students previewed the weekly texts in their native language before English texts were introduced on Tuesday. Activities included practice in deriving word meanings from context, small-group practice including cloze activities and semantic features analysis, discussions to develop depth of word knowledge, practice in identifying cognates, and homework assignments that reinforced the daily lessons. When this study was later reviewed by the What Works Clearinghouse (2006), it found that the language-minority students made "substantively important" improvement in reading achievement on a cloze test and also detected "potentially positive effects" for English language development on measures of multiple word meanings and word association. Students gained knowledge of the target words that were explicitly taught. They also improved in their knowledge of polysemy and morphological structure, skills that the authors noted may support students' independent incidental vocabulary learning.

Writing Benefits of Vocabulary Instruction

Because fluent and productive use of vocabulary is the ultimate goal of vocabulary learning, teachers hope to see vocabulary learning reflected in students' writing. As we noted earlier, depth of vocabulary knowledge includes knowledge of meaning as well as word relations and syntactic features that allow students to use words correctly and fluently in speech and in their writing. Effective word-focused instruction for English learners includes practice in using target vocabulary in various writing tasks, from sentence completion to student writing compositions. Recall that activating the spelling of a word also influences knowledge of its meaning (Rosenthal & Ehri, 2008), and the benefits appear to be mutual (Hilte & Reitsma, 2010). In studies of second-language learners, explicit vocabulary instruction has writing as well as reading benefits and enables students to use words correctly in their writing compositions (Lee, 2003). Features of this explicit instruction included visually presenting the printed word, modeling correct pronunciation, providing the definition, explaining the use of the word in context and in relation to other words, practice in using the word in writing, and repeated practice. Although receptive exposure to vocabulary alone may not result in productive mastery of writing skills (Lee & Muncie, 2006), the use of a writing *frame* (an outline to help students organize their writing) that includes the vocabulary words as well as teacher encouragement to use the taught words in their writing both promote the use of taught word items in student writing.

> **Sample Writing Frames to Support Vocabulary Usage**
>
> - "What are the benefits of *immigration*?" Include the words *assimilate* and *culture* in your writing.
> - "Discuss two reasons for *immigration*." Include the words *economic*, *employment*, *persecution*, and *refugee* in your writing.
> - "Discuss one viewpoint on *immigration* policy." Include the words *amnesty*, *citizenship*, and *illegal* in your writing.

For example, a unit on the topic of *immigration* may target instruction on the following vocabulary words: *amnesty, assimilate, citizenship, culture, employment, illegal, migration, persecution*, and *refugee*. After the words have been introduced, defined, used in class discussion, and reviewed, the teacher presents a writing assignment on the topic. Secondary-level writing frames on immigration might include a list of the target vocabulary words that students should incorporate into their writing. Students with learning disabilities may benefit from explicitly linking the meaning and spelling of words prior to independent writing.

Considerations for Assessing the Vocabulary Knowledge of Language-Minority Students

Vocabulary assessment for language-minority students may be used to determine *breadth* or *depth* of word knowledge and may assess *receptive* versus *productive* knowledge.

Breadth of Knowledge

Most assessments target vocabulary breadth or size—the number of words that students know. Depending upon the assessment format, breadth measures may overestimate vocabulary knowledge because they may not indicate how well the student knows the word (i.e., being able to recognize and point to it versus defining it and providing word associations). Because the most common vocabulary assessments measure receptive knowledge and vocabulary breadth, it is useful to know that breadth and depth measures are highly correlated for both L1 and L2 students (Vermeer, 2001). Because words are acquired in a similar sequence in both L1 and L2 children (Biemiller & Slonim, 2001), assessments for language-minority students should include test items from various domains and frequency levels.

Depth of Knowledge

Depth is a measure of the density of the word network and relations and thus may include pronunciation, spelling, morphology, polysemy, usage, sociolinguistic register (i.e., the formal language in a speech, or a casual vernacular dialect), and collocations (Nation, 1990). Test items that require students to supply a definition for a word are often used to measure depth of knowledge, although breadth of word knowledge is also needed to construct a response. In particular, formal definitions require the use of abstract and academic language that language-minority students take longer to acquire (Cummins, 1981). Because depth of vocabulary knowledge includes many dimensions, it is not easily assessed. Teachers may obtain informal information on depth of knowledge from the student's speech and writing.

Progress Monitoring the Vocabulary Acquisition of English Language Learners

Classroom teachers may monitor vocabulary growth in language-minority students in order to adjust their instruction and to maintain student motivation for vocabulary study. A simple assessment might test students' knowledge of words that have been targeted for explicit classroom instruction. One type of recognition assessment format has the student match a list of words with a list that includes extra definitions (so that the student cannot use the process of elimination). Definitions should be short, clear, and simple and not include difficult words or syntax. The following (from Read, 2000) shows a format for a simple matching test that requires the student to match words with a short definition or synonym. The word items are taken from the *Academic Word List* (Coxhead, 2006).

Write the number of the meaning next to each word:

Income _____	1. Something in between
Region _____	2. A magazine
Layer _____	3. A part of a country
Text _____	4. Money earned
Journal _____	5. The smallest part
_____	6. An important group
_____	7. Something written

CONCLUSION

English learners must expand their vocabulary while they are developing their English language proficiency and while they are learning academic content. The size of the task warrants early intervention in vocabulary instruction and continued and sustained instruction in evidence-based strategies. Most of the recommendations for English learners must currently be drawn from research on monolingual English speakers and second-language instruction for older learners, although research on vocabulary instruction for language-minority students is also burgeoning. Many of the interventions described earlier in this book may be adapted for Tier 2 or Tier 3 instructional programs for language-minority students, in particular students with learning difficulties. The following instructional recommendations are suggested by the research we summarize in this chapter:

1. *For preschool and primary school language-minority students*, home language input in both the family's native language and English contributes to language and vocabulary development. This home input includes conversations, storytelling, singing, and book reading. In the preschool and primary school setting, the interactive storybook reading approach often used in Tier 1 instruction is an effective means to build English vocabulary and language skills. The most effective book reading approaches combine explicit vocabulary instruction with storybook reading. Repeated readings provide the multiple word exposures and opportunities for extended word interactions that are needed for in-depth word learning. Systematic review of previously taught words in the storybook instructional program enhances vocabulary learning. High-frequency root words are one useful target for early instruction, as well as introducing appropriate academic vocabulary to prepare students for the language encountered in their textbooks. Research suggests that early classroom reading instruction for language-minority students should focus strongly on vocabulary and reading for meaning.

2. *School-age language-minority students*, like their monolingual peers, benefit from vocabulary instruction that provides explicit instruction in word meaning as well as multiple opportunities to interact with words in oral, reading, and writing contexts. Explicit instruction in word learning strategies equips language-minority students to be more effective in learning vocabulary through incidental reading encounters. Added supports for language-minority students include the use of visual supports and access to audio links for pronunciation models. Hyperlinks to vocabulary words in electronic texts are effective when students learn and remember to access them. Academic vocabulary is an important content component for school-age language-minority students to master in order to be successful in reading and comprehending academic texts.

References

Adams, M. J., & Huggins, A. W. F. (1985). The growth of children's sight vocabulary: A quick test with educational and theoretical implications. *Reading Research Quarterly, 20,* 262–281.

Allington, R. L. (1984). Content coverage and contextual reading in reading groups. *Journal of Reading Behavior, 16,* 85–96.

American Association of School Administrators. (2009). *Response to Intervention (RtI) adoption survey.* Retrieved from *www.spectrumk12.com//uploads/file/RTI%202009%20Adoption%20Survey%20Final%20Report.pdf.*

American Heritage Dictionary (2nd college ed.). (1985). Boston: Houghton Mifflin.

Anderson, A., Anderson, J., & Shapiro, J. (2004). Mathematical discourse in shared storybook reading. *Journal of Research in Mathematics Education, 35,* 5–33.

Anderson, R. C., & Freebody, P. (1981). Vocabulary knowledge. In J. Guthrie (Ed.), *Comprehension and teaching: Research reviews* (pp. 77–117). Newark, DE: International Reading Association.

Anderson, R. C., Reynolds, R. E., Schallert, D. L., & Goetz, E. T. (1977). Frameworks for comprehending discourse. *American Educational Research Journal, 14,* 367–381.

Anderson, R. C., Spiro, R. J., & Anderson, M. C. (1978). Schemata as scaffolding for the representation of information in connected discourse. *American Educational Research Journal, 15,* 433–440.

Anglin, J. M. (1993). Vocabulary development: A morphological analysis. *Monographs of the Society for Research in Child Development, 58* (Serial No. 238).

Arnbak, E., & Elbro, C. (2000). The effects of morphological awareness training on the reading and spelling skills of young dyslexics. *Scandinavian Journal of Educational Research, 44,* 229–251.

Atwill, K., Blanchard, J., Christie, J., Gorin, J., & Garcia, H. (2010). English-language learners: Implications of limited vocabulary for cross-language transfer of phonemic awareness with kindergarteners. *Journal of Hispanic Higher Education, 9,* 104–129.

August, D., Branum-Martin, L., Cardenas-Hagan, E., & Francis, D. (2009). The impact of an instructional intervention on the science and language learning of middle grade English language learners. *Journal of Research on Educational Effectiveness, 2,* 345–376.

August, D., & Shanahan, T. (Eds.). (2006). *Developing literacy in second-language learners: Report of the National Literacy Panel on Language-Minority Children and Youth.* Mahwah, NJ: Erlbaum.

Baddeley, A. (1990). *Human memory: Theory and practice.* Needham Heights, MA: Allyn & Bacon.

Bankson, N. W. (1990). *Bankson Language Test—Second Edition.* Austin, TX: Pro-Ed.

Barnhart, C. L. (1970). *The world book encyclopedia dictionary.* Chicago: Field Enterprises Educational Corporation.

Bauer, L., & Nation, P. (1993). Word families. *International Journal of Lexicography, 6,* 253–279.

Baumann, J. F., Edwards, E. C., Boland, E. M., Olejnik, S., & Kame'enui, E. J. (2003). Vocabulary tricks: Effects of instruction in morphology and context on fifth-grade students' ability to derive and infer word meanings. *American Educational Research Journal, 40,* 447–494.

Baumann, J. F., Edwards, E. C., Font, G., Tereshinski, C. A., Kame'enui, E. J., & Olejnik, S. (2002). Teaching morphemic and contextual analysis to fifth-grade students. *Reading Research Quarterly, 37,* 150–176.

Baumann, J. F., Kame'enui, E. J., & Ash, G. E. (2003). Research on vocabulary instruction: Voltaire redux. In J. Flood, J. Jensen, D. Lapp, & J. R. Squire (Eds.), *Handbook of research on teaching the English language arts* (pp. 752–785). New York: Macmillan.

Beck, I. L., & McKeown, M. G. (1985). Teaching vocabulary: Making the instruction fit the goal. *Educational Perspectives, 23,* 11–15.

Beck, I. L., & McKeown, M. G. (2007). Increasing young low-income children's oral vocabulary repertoires through rich and focused instruction. *Elementary School Journal, 107,* 251–271.

Beck, I. L., McKeown, M. G., & Kucan, L. (2002). *Bringing words to life: Robust vocabulary instruction.* New York, NY: Guilford Press.

Beck, I. L., McKeown, M. G., & Kucan, L. (2008). *Creating robust vocabulary: Frequently asked questions and extended examples.* New York: Guilford Press.

Beck, I. L., McKeown, M. G., & Omanson, R. C. (1987). The effects and use of diverse vocabulary instructional techniques. In M. G. McKeown & M. E. Curtis (Eds.), *The nature of vocabulary acquisition* (pp. 147–163). Hillsdale, NJ: Erlbaum.

Beck, I. L., Perfetti, C. A., & McKeown, M. G. (1982). Effects of long-term vocabulary instruction on lexical access and reading comprehension. *Journal of Educational Psychology, 74,* 506–521.

Bensoussan, M., & Laufer, B. (1984). Lexical guessing in context in EFL reading comprehension. *Journal of Research in Reading, 7,* 15–32.

Biber, D. (1990). A typology of English texts. *Linguistics, 27,* 3–43.

Biber, D. (1993). *Manual of information to accompany the Wellington Corpus of Written New Zealand English.* Wellington, New Zealand: Victoria University of Wellington.

Biemiller, A. (2003). Vocabulary: Needed if more children are to read well. *Reading Psychology, 24,* 323–335.

Biemiller, A. (2005). Size and sequence in vocabulary development: Implications for choosing words for primary grade vocabulary instruction. In E. Hiebert & M. Kamil (Eds.), *Teaching and learning vocabulary: Bringing research to practice* (pp. 223–242). Mahwah, NJ: Erlbaum.

Biemiller, A. (2009). *Words worth teaching*. Columbus, OH: SRA/McGraw-Hill.

Biemiller, A., & Boote, C. (2006). An effective method for building meaning vocabulary in primary grades. *Journal of Educational Psychology, 98*, 44–62.

Biemiller, A., & Slonim, N. (2001). Estimating root word vocabulary growth in normative and advantaged populations: Evidence for a common sequence of vocabulary acquisition. *Journal of Educational Psychology, 93*, 498–520.

Bos, C. S., Allen, A. A., & Scanlon, D. J. (1989). Vocabulary instruction and reading comprehension with bilingual learning disabled students. *National Reading Conference Yearbook, 38*, 173–179.

Bos, C. S., & Anders, P. L. (1990). Effects of interactive vocabulary instruction on the vocabulary learning and reading comprehension of junior-high learning disabled students. *Learning Disability Quarterly, 13*, 31–42.

Bos, C. S., & Anders, P. L. (1992). Using interactive teaching and learning strategies to promote text comprehension and content learning for students with learning disabilities. *International Journal of Disability, Development, and Education, 39*, 225–238.

Bos, C. S., Anders, P. L., Filip, D., & Jaffe, I. E. (1989). The effects of an interactive instructional strategy for enhancing reading comprehension and content area learning for students with learning disabilities. *Journal of Learning Disabilities, 22*, 384–390.

Brabham, E. G., & Lynch-Brown, C. (2002). Effects of teachers' reading-aloud styles on vocabulary acquisition and comprehension of students in the early elementary grades. *Journal of Educational Psychology, 94*, 465–473.

Brownell, R. (2000a). *Expressive One-Word Picture Vocabulary Test manual*. Novato, CA: Academic Therapy Publications.

Brownell, R. (Ed.). (2000b). *Receptive One-Word Picture Vocabulary Test—2000 edition*. Novato, CA: Academic Therapy Publications.

Buckingham, B. R., & Dolch, E. W. (1936). *A combined word list*. Boston: Ginn.

Burgoyne, K., Kelly, J. M., Whiteley, H. E., & Spooner, A. (2009). The comprehension skills of children learning English as an additional language. *British Journal of Educational Psychology, 79*, 735–747.

Bus, A. G., van IJzendoorn, M. H., & Pellegrini, A. D. (1995). Joint book reading makes for success in learning to read: A meta-analysis on intergenerational transmission of literacy. *Review of Educational Research, 65*, 1–21.

Campion, M. E., & Elley, W. B. (1971). *An academic vocabulary list*. Wellington: New Zealand Council for Educational Research.

Carey, S. (1978). The child as a word-learner. In M. Hale, J. Bresnan, & G. A. Miller (Eds.), *Linguistic theory and psychological theory* (pp. 264–293). Cambridge, MA: MIT Press.

Carlisle, J. F. (1995). Morphological awareness and early reading achievement. In L. B. Feldman (Ed.), *Morphological aspects of language processing* (pp. 189–209). Hillsdale, NJ: Erlbaum.

Carlisle, J. F. (2000). Awareness of the structure and meaning of morphologically complex words: Impact on reading. *Reading and Writing: An Interdisciplinary Journal, 12*, 169–190.

Carlisle, J. F., Beeman, M., Davis, L. H., & Spharim, G. (1999). Relationship of metalinguistic capabilities and reading achievement for children who are becoming bilingual. *Applied Psycholinguistics, 20*, 459–478.

Carlisle, J. F., & Fleming, J. (2003). Lexical processing of morphologically complex words in the elementary years. *Scientific Studies of Reading, 7*, 239–253.

Carlisle, J. F., Fleming, J. E., & Gudbrandsen, B. (2000). Incidental word learning in science classes. *Contemporary Educational Psychology, 25*, 184–211.

Carlo, M. S., August, D., McLaughlin, B., Snow, C. E., Dressler, C., Lippman, D. N., et al. (2004). Closing the gap: Addressing the vocabulary needs of English-language learners in bilingual and mainstream classrooms. *Reading Research Quarterly, 39*, 188–215.

Carlo, M. S., August, D., & Snow, C. E. (2005). Sustained vocabulary-learning strategy instruction for English-language learners. In E. H. Hiebert & M. L. Kamil (Eds.), *Teaching and learning vocabulary: Bringing research to practice* (pp. 137–154). Mahwah, NJ: Erlbaum.

Carnine, D., Kame'enui, E. J., & Coyle, G. (1984). Utilization of contextual information in determining the meaning of unfamiliar words. *Reading Research Quarterly, 19*, 188–204.

Carroll, J. B., Davies, P., & Richman, B. (1971). *The American heritage word frequency book*. Boston: Houghton Mifflin.

Carrow-Woolfolk, E. (1995). *Oral and Written Language Scales*. Circle Pines, MN: American Guidance Service.

Carrow-Woolfolk, E. (1999). *Comprehensive Assessment of Spoken Language* (CASL). Circle Pines, MN: American Guidance Service.

Chall, J. S., & Dale, E. (1995). *Readability revisited: The new Dale–Chall readability formula*. Cambridge, MA: Brookline Books.

Chall, J. S., Jacobs, V. A., & Baldwin, L. E. (1990). *The reading crisis: Why poor children fall behind*. Cambridge, MA: Harvard University Press.

Chiappe, P., & Siegel, L. S. (1999). Phonological awareness and reading acquisition in English- and Punjabi-speaking Canadian children. *Journal of Educational Psychology, 91*, 20–28.

Cobb, T. (1997). Is there any measurable learning from hands-on concordancing? *System, 25*, 301–315.

Collins Birmingham University. (2003). *Collins COBUILD learner's dictionary* (concise ed.). Glasgow, UK: HarperCollins.

Cornell, E. H., Sénéchal, M., & Broda, L. S. (1988). Recall of picture books by 3-year-old children: Testing and repetition effect in joint reading activities. *Journal of Educational Psychology, 80*, 537–542.

Coxhead, A. (2000). A new Academic Word List. *TESOL Quarterly, 34*, 213–238.

Coxhead, A. (2006). *Essentials of teaching academic vocabulary: English for academic success*. Boston: Thomson Heinle.

Coyne, M. D., McCoach, D. B., & Kapp, S. (2007). Vocabulary intervention for kindergarten students: Comparing extended instruction to embedded instruction and incidental exposure. *Learning Disability Quarterly, 30*, 74–88.

Coyne, M. D., McCoach, D. B., Loftus, S., Zipoli, R., Ruby, M., Crevecoeur, Y. C., et al. (2010). Direct and extended vocabulary instruction in kindergarten: Investigating transfer effects. *Journal of Research on Educational Effectiveness, 3*, 93–120.

Craik, F., & Lockhart, R. (1972a). Levels of processing: A framework for memory research. *Journal of Verbal Learning and Verbal Behavior, 11*, 671–684.

Craik, F., & Lockhart, R. (1972b). Levels of processing and the retention of words in episodic memory. *Journal of Experimental Psychology, 104*, 268–284.

Craik, F., & Tulving, E. (1975). Depth of processing and the retention of words in episodic memory. *Journal of Experimental Psychology, 104*, 268–284.

Crain-Thoreson, C., & Dale, P. S. (1992). Do early talkers become early readers?: Linquistic precocity, preschool language, and emergent literacy. *Developmental Psychology, 28*, 421–429.

Crain-Thoreson, C., & Dale, P. S. (1999). Enhancing linguistic performance: Parents and teachers as book reading partners for children with language delays. *Topics in Early Childhood Special Education, 19*, 28–39.

Cronbach, L. J. (1942). An analysis of techniques for systematic vocabulary testing. *Journal of Educational Research, 36,* 206–217.

Crosson, A. C., Lesaux, N. K., & Martiniello, M. (2008). Factors that influence comprehension of connectives among language minority children from Spanish-speaking backgrounds. *Applied Psycholinguistics, 29,* 603–625.

Cummins, J. (1979). Cognitive/academic language proficiency, linguistic interdependence, the optimum age question. *Working Papers on Bilingualism, 9,* 1–43.

Cummins, J. (1981). Age on arrival and immigrant second language learning in Canada: A reassessment. *Applied Linguistics, 2,* 132–149.

Cunningham, A. E., & Stanovich, K. E. (1998). What reading does for the mind. *American Educator, 22,* 8–15.

Dale, E. (1965). Vocabulary measurement: Techniques and major findings. *Elementary English, 42,* 895–901, 948.

Dale, E., & O'Rourke, J. (1981). *The living word vocabulary.* Chicago: World Book/Childcraft International.

Dale, E., & O'Rourke, J. (1986). *Vocabulary building.* Columbus, OH: Zaner-Bloser.

Degand, L., & Sanders, T. (2002). The impact of relational markers on expository text comprehension in L1 and L2. *Reading and Writing: An Interdisciplinary Journal, 15,* 739–757.

Dickinson, D. K., McCabe, A., Anastasopoulos, L., Peisner-Feinberg, E. S., & Poe, M. D. (2003). The comprehensive language approach to early literacy: The interrelationships among vocabulary, phonological sensitivity, and print knowledge among preschool-aged children. *Journal of Educational Psychology, 95,* 465–481.

Dunn, L. M., & Dunn, D. M. (2007). *Peabody Picture Vocabulary Test, fourth edition.* Bloomington, MN: NCS Pearson.

Edwards, E. C., Font, G., Baumann, J. F., & Boland, E. (2004). Unlocking word meanings: Strategies and guidelines for teaching morphemic and contextual analysis. In J. F. Baumann & E. J. Kame'enui (Eds.), *Vocabulary instruction: Research to practice* (pp. 159–176). New York: Guilford Press.

Ehri, L. C. (1992). Reconceptualizing the development of sight word reading and its relationship to recoding. In P. Gough, L. Ehri, & R. Treiman (Eds.), *Reading acquisition* (pp. 107–143). Hillsdale, NJ: Erlbaum.

Ehri, L. C. (1998). Grapheme–phoneme knowledge is essential for learning to read words. In J. Metsala & L. Ehri (Eds.), *Word recognition in beginning literacy* (pp. 3–40). Mahwah, NJ: Erlbaum.

Ehri, L. C. (2005). Development of sight word reading: Phases and findings. In M. Snowling & C. Hulme (Eds.), *The science of reading: A handbook* (pp. 135–154). Oxford, UK: Blackwell.

Ehri, L. C., & Rosenthal, J. (2007). Spellings of words: A neglected facilitator of vocabulary learning. *Journal of Literacy Research, 39,* 389–409.

Elleman, A. M., Lindo, E. J., Morphy, P., & Compton, D. L. (2009). The impact of vocabulary instruction on passage-level comprehension of school-age children: A meta-analysis. *Journal of Research on Educational Effectiveness, 2,* 1–44.

Elley, W. B. (1989). Vocabulary acquisition from listening to stories. *Reading Research Quarterly, 24,* 174–187.

Ellis, N. C. (1997). Vocabulary acquisition: Word structure, collocation, word-class, and meaning. In N. Schmitt & M. McCarthy (Eds.), *Vocabulary: Description, acquisition and pedagogy* (pp. 122–139). New York: Cambridge University Press.

Ellis, N. C., & Beaton, A. (1993). Factors affecting the learning of foreign-language vocabulary:

Imagery keyword mediators and phonological short-term memory. *Quarterly Journal of Experimental Psychology, 46A,* 533–558.

Espin, C. A., Busch, T., Shin, J., & Kruschwitz, R. (2001). Curriculum-based measures in the content areas: Validity of vocabulary matching measures as indicators of performance in social studies. *Learning Disabilities Research and Practice, 16,* 142–151.

Fielding, L., Wilson, P., & Anderson, R. (1986). A new focus on free reading: The role of trade books in reading instruction. In T. Raphael & R. Reynolds (Eds.), *The contexts of school-based literacy* (pp. 149–160). New York: Longman.

Fischer, U. (1994). Learning words from context and dictionaries: An experimental comparison. *Applied Psycholinguistics, 15,* 551–574.

Forness, S. R., Kavale, K. A., Blum, B. M., & Lloyd, J. (1997). Mega-analysis of meta-analyses: What works in special education and related services. *Teaching Exceptional Children, 29,* 4–9.

Fowler, A. E. (1991). How early phonological development might set the stage for phonological awareness. In S. Brady & D. Shankweiler (Eds.), *Phonological processes in literacy: A tribute to Isabelle Y. Liberman* (pp. 97–117). Hillsdale, NJ: Erlbaum.

Francis, W. N., & Kucera, H. (1982). *Frequency analysis of English usage: Lexicon and grammar.* Boston: Houghton Mifflin.

Fry, E. B., Kress, J. E., & Fountoukidis, D. L. (1993). *The reading teacher's book of lists* (3rd ed.). Engelwood Cliffs, NJ: Prentice-Hall.

Fuchs, D., Mock, D., Morgan, P., & Young, C. (2003). Responsiveness-to-intervention: Definitions, evidence, and implications for the learning disabilities construct. *Learning Disabilities Research and Practice, 18,* 157–171.

Fuchs, L. S. (2003). Assessing intervention responsiveness: Conceptual and technical issues. *Learning Disabilities: Research and Practice, 18,* 172–186.

Fukkink, R. G., & de Glopper, K. (1998). Effects of instruction in deriving word meanings from context: A meta-analysis. *Review of Educational Research, 68,* 450–468.

Galdone, P. (1984). *Henny Penny.* New York: Clarion Books.

Genesee, F., Lindholm-Leary, K., Saunders, W., & Christian, D. (2006). *Educating English language learners.* New York: Cambridge University Press.

Gershkoff-Stowe, L., & Hahn, E. R. (2007). Fast mapping skills in the developing lexicon. *Journal of Speech, Language and Hearing Research, 50,* 682–697.

Ghadessy, M. (1979). Frequency counts, word lists and materials preparation: A new approach. *English Teaching Forum, 17,* 24–27.

Gillam, R. B., & Pearson, N. A. (2004). *Test of Narrative Language.* Austin, TX: Pro-Ed.

Good, R., & Kaminski, R. (2003). *Dynamic Indicators of Basic Early Literacy Skills, Word Use Fluency* (DIBELS WUF; 6th ed.). Boston: Sopris West Educational Services.

Goswami, U. (1999). Causal connections in beginning reading: The importance of rhyme. *Journal of Research in Reading, 22,* 217–240.

Gough, P. B., & Tunmer, W. E. (1986). Decoding, reading, and reading disability. *Remedial and Special Education, 7,* 6–10.

Goulden, R., Nation, P., & Read, J. (1990). How large can a receptive vocabulary be? *Applied Linguistics, 11,* 341–363.

Graham, S., Harris, K. R., & Chorzempa, B. (2002). Contribution of spelling instruction to the spelling, writing, and reading of poor spellers. *Journal of Educational Psychology, 94,* 669–686.

Graves, M. F. (2006). *The vocabulary book: Learning and instruction.* New York: Teachers College Press.

Graves, M. F., Boettcher, J. A., Peacock, J. L., & Ryder, R. J. (1980). Word frequency as a predictor of students' reading vocabularies. *Journal of Reading Behavior, 12,* 117–127.

Graves, M. F., & Hammond, H. K. (1980). A validated procedure for teaching prefixes and its effect on students' ability to assign meaning to novel words. In M. L. Kamil & A. J. Moe (Eds.), *Perspectives on reading research and instruction* (pp. 184–188). Washington, DC: National Reading Conference.

Graves, M. F., Ryder, R. J., Slater, W. H., & Calfee, R. C. (1987). The relationship between word frequency and reading vocabulary using six metrics of frequency. *Journal of Educational Research, 81,* 81–91.

Hakuta, K., Butler, Y. G., & Witt, D. (2000). *How long does it take English learners to attain proficiency?* Santa Barbara: The University of California Linguistic Minority Research Institute.

Hargrave, A. C., & Sénéchal, M. (2000). A book reading intervention with preschool children who have limited vocabularies: The benefits of regular reading and dialogic reading. *Early Childhood Research Quarterly, 15,* 75–90.

Hart, B., & Risley, T. R. (1995). *Meaningful differences in the everyday experience of young American children.* Baltimore, MD: Brookes.

Hart, B., & Risley, T. R. (2003). The early catastrophe: The 30 million word gap by age 3. *American Educator, 27,* 4–9.

Hayes, D. P., & Ahrens, M. G. (1988). Vocabulary simplification for children: A special case of "motherese"? *Journal of Child Language, 15,* 395–410.

Herman, P., Anderson, R. C., Pearson, P. D., & Nagy, W. E. (1987). Incidental acquisition of word meanings from expositions with varied text features. *Reading Research Quarterly, 22,* 263–284.

Hiebert, E. H. (2005). In pursuit of an effective, efficient vocabulary curriculum for elementary students. In E. H. Hiebert & M. L. Kamil (Eds.), *Teaching and learning vocabulary: Bringing research to practice* (pp. 243–263). Mahwah: Erlbaum.

Hill, M., & Laufer, B. (2003). Type of task, time-on-task, and electronic dictionaries in incidental vocabulary acquisition. *International Review of Applied Linguistics in Language Teaching, 41,* 87–106.

Hilte, M., & Reitsma, P. (2010). Activating the meaning of a word facilitates the integration of orthography: Evidence from spelling exercises in beginning spellers. *Journal of Research in Reading, 11,* 1–14.

Holbrook, H. T. (1983). Oral language: A neglected language art? *Language Arts, 60,* 181–187.

Hoover, W. A., & Gough, P. B. (1990). The simple view of reading. *Reading and Writing: An Interdisciplinary Journal, 2,* 127–160.

Horst, M., Cobb, T., & Nicolae, I. (2005). Expanding academic vocabulary with an interactive on-line database. *Language Learning and Technology, 9,* 90–110.

Hulstijn, J. H., Hollander, M., & Greidanus, T. (1996). Incidental vocabulary learning by advanced foreign language students: The influence of marginal glosses, dictionary use, and reoccurrence of unknown words. *The Modern Language Journal, 80,* 327–339.

Individuals with Disabilities Education Improvement Act of 2004, Public Law No. 108–446. (2004). Retrieved from *www.idea.ed.gov/explore/view/p/%2Croot%2Cstatute%2C*.

Jean, M., & Geva, E. (2009). The development of vocabulary in English as a second language in children and its role in predicting word recognition ability. *Applied Psycholinguistics, 30,* 153–185.

Jenkins, J. R., Matlock, B., & Slocum, T. A. (1989). Two approaches to vocabulary instruction:

The teaching of individual word meanings and practice in deriving word meaning from context. *Reading Research Quarterly, 24,* 215–235.

Jenkins, J. R., Stein, M., & Wysocki, K. (1984). Learning vocabulary through reading. *American Educational Research Journal, 21,* 767–787.

Jitendra, A. K., Edwards, L. L., Sacks, G., & Jacobson, L. A. (2004). What research says about vocabulary instruction for students with learning disabilities. *Exceptional Children, 70,* 299–322.

Joe, A. (1995). Text-based tasks and incidental vocabulary learning. *Second Language Research, 11,* 95–111.

Justice, L. M., & Ezell, H. K. (2002). Use of storybook reading to increase print awareness in at-risk children. *American Journal of Speech–Language Pathology, 11,* 17–29.

Justice, L. M., & Ezell, H. K. (2004). Print referencing: An emergent literacy enhancement strategy and its clinical applications. *Language, Speech, and Hearing Services in Schools, 35,* 185–193.

Justice, L. M., Kaderavek, J. N., Fan, X., Sofka, A., & Hunt, A. (2009). Accelerating preschoolers' early literacy development through classroom-based teacher–child storybook reading and explicit print referencing. *Language, Speech, and Hearing Services in Schools, 40,* 67–85.

Kame'enui, E. J., Carnine, D. W., & Freschi, R. (1982). Effects of text construction and instructional procedures for teaching word meaning on comprehension and recall. *Reading Research Quarterly, 17,* 367–388.

Kamil, M. L., & Hiebert, E. H. (2005). Teaching and learning vocabulary: Perspectives and persistent issues. In E. H. Hiebert & M. L. Kamil (Eds.), *Teaching and learning vocabulary: Bringing research to practice* (pp. 1–26). Mahwah, NJ: Erlbaum.

Kieffer, M. J., & Lesaux, N. K. (2007). Breaking down words to build meaning: Morphology, vocabulary, and reading comprehension in the urban classroom. *The Reading Teacher, 61,* 134–144.

Kieffer, M. J., & Lesaux, N. K. (2008). The role of derivational morphology in the reading comprehension of Spanish-speaking English language learners. *Reading and Writing: An Interdisciplinary Journal, 21,* 783–804.

Kieffer, M. J., Lesaux, N. K., Rivera, M., & Francis, D. J. (2009). Accommodations for English language learners taking large-scale assessments: A meta-analysis on effectiveness and validity. *Review of Educational Research, 79,* 1168–1201.

Klingner, J., Sorrells, A., & Barrera, M. (2007). Considerations when implementing response to intervention with culturally and linguistically diverse students. In D. Haager, J. K. Klingner, & S. Vaughn (Eds.), *Evidence-based reading practices for response to intervention* (pp. 223–244). Baltimore, MD: Brookes.

Knight, S. (1994). Dictionary: The tool of last resort in foreign language reading?: A new perspective. *Modern Language Journal, 78,* 285–299.

Kucera, H., & Francis, W. N. (1967). *Computational analysis of present-day American English.* Providence, RI: Brown University Press.

Kuhn, M. R., & Stahl, S. A. (1998). Teaching children to learn word meanings from context: A synthesis and some questions. *Journal of Literacy Research, 30,* 19–38.

Laufer, B. (1988). What percentage of text-lexis is essential for comprehension? In C. Lauren & M. Nordman (Eds.), *Special language: From humans thinking to thinking machines.* Clevedon, UK: Multilingual Matters.

Laufer, B. (1997). What's in a word that makes it hard or easy: Some intralexical factors that affect the learning of words. In N. Schmitt & M. McCarthy (Eds.), *Vocabulary: Description, acquisition, and pedagogy* (pp. 140–155). New York: Cambridge University Press.

Laufer, B. (2003). Vocabulary acquisition in a second language: Do learners really acquire most vocabulary by reading? Some empirical evidence. *The Canadian Modern Language Review, 59,* 567–587.

Lee, J. (2011). Size matters: Early vocabulary as a predictor of language and literacy competence. *Applied Psycholinguistics, 32,* 69–92.

Lee, S. H. (2003). ESL learners' vocabulary use in writing and the effects of explicit vocabulary instruction. *System, 31,* 537–561.

Lee, S. H., & Muncie, J. (2006). From receptive to productive: Improving ESL learners' use of vocabulary in a postreading composition task. *TESOL Quarterly, 40,* 295–320.

Leech, G., Rayson, P., & Wilson, A. (2001). *Word frequencies in written and spoken English.* London: Longman.

Lesaux, N. K. (2006). Building consensus: Future directions for research on English language learners at-risk for learning difficulties. *Teachers College Record, 108,* 2406–2434.

Lesaux, N. K., & Siegel, L. S. (2003). The development of reading in children who speak English as a second language. *Developmental Psychology, 38,* 1005–1019.

Leung, C. B., & Pikulski, J. J. (1990). Incidental learning of word meanings by kindergarten and first-grade children. *Journal of Consulting and Clinical Psychology, 43,* 601–607.

Lindsey, K. A., Manis, F. R., & Bailey, C. E. (2003). Prediction of first-grade reading in Spanish-speaking English-language learners. *Journal of Educational Psychology, 95,* 482–494.

Liu, N., & Nation, I. S. P. (1985). Factors affecting guessing vocabulary in context. *RELC Journal, 16,* 33–42.

Longman Dictionary of Contemporary English (3rd ed.). (1995). London: Longman.

Lorge, I. (1949). *The semantic count of the 570 commonest English words.* New York: Columbia University, Institute of Psychological Research.

Lorge, I., & Thorndike, E. L. (1938). *A semantic count of English words.* New York: Columbia University, Institute of Educational Research.

Lorge, I., & Thorndike, E. L. (1944). *The teacher's word book of 30,000 words.* New York: Columbia University, Teachers College.

Luppescu, S., & Day, R. R. (1993). Reading, dictionaries, and vocabulary learning. *Language Learning, 43,* 263–287.

Lyster, S. H. (2002). The effects of morphological versus phonological awareness training in kindergarten on reading development. *Reading and Writing, 15,* 261–294.

Marulis, L. M., & Neuman, S. B. (2010). The effects of vocabulary intervention on young children's word learning: A meta-analysis. *Review of Educational Research, 80,* 300–335.

Marzano, R. J. (2004). *Building background knowledge for academic achievement.* Alexandria, VA: Association for Supervision and Curriculum Development.

Mastropieri, M. A. (1988). Using the keyword method. *Teaching Exceptional Children, 20,* 4–8.

Mastropieri, M. A., Scruggs, T. E., Bakken, J., & Brigham, F. J. (1992). A complex mnemonic strategy for teaching states and capitals: Comparing forward and backward associations. *Learning Disabilities Research and Practice, 7,* 96–103.

Mastropieri, M. A., Scruggs, T. E., & Fulk, B. J. (1990). Teaching abstract vocabulary with the keyword method: Effects on recall and comprehension. *Journal of Learning Disabilities, 23,* 92–107.

Maynard, K. L., Pullen, P. C., & Coyne, M. D. (2010). Teaching vocabulary to first-grade students through repeated shared storybook reading: A comparison of rich and basic instruction to incidental exposure. *Literacy Research and Instruction, 49,* 209–242.

McCarville, K. B. (1993). Keyword mnemonic and vocabulary acquisition for developmental college students. *Journal of Developmental Education, 16,* 2–4, 6.

McGee, L. M., & Schickedanz, J. A. (2007). Repeated interactive read-alouds in preschool and kindergarten. *Reading Teacher, 60,* 742–751.

McKeown, M. G., Beck, I. L., Omanson, R. C., & Perfetti, C. A. (1983). The effects of long-term vocabulary instruction on reading comprehension: A replication. *Journal of Reading Behavior, 15,* 3–18.

McKeown, M. G., Beck, I. L., Omanson, R. C., & Pople, M. T. (1985). Some effects of the nature and frequency of vocabulary instruction on the knowledge and use of words. *Reading Research Quarterly, 20,* 522–535.

McNeill, A. (1996). Vocabulary knowledge profiles: Evidence from Chinese-speaking ESL speakers. *Hong Kong Journal of Applied Linguistics, 1,* 39–63.

Metsala, J. L. (1999). Young children's phonological awareness and non-word repetition as a function of vocabulary development. *Journal of Educational Psychology, 91,* 3–19.

Metsala, J. L., & Walley, A. C. (1998). Spoken vocabulary growth and the segmental restructuring of lexical representations: Precursors to phonemic awareness and early reading ability. In J. L. Metsala & L. C. Ehri (Eds.), *Word recognition in beginning literacy* (pp. 89–120). Mahwah, NJ: Erlbaum.

Mezynski, K. (1983). Issues concerning the acquisition of knowledge: Effects of vocabulary training on reading comprehension. *Review of Educational Research, 53,* 253–279.

Miller, G. A., & Gildea, P. M. (1987). How children learn words. *Scientific American, 257,* 94–99.

Moerk, E. L. (1985). Picture-book reading by mothers and young children and its impact on language development. *Journal of Pragmatics, 9,* 547–566.

Mondria, J. A. (2003). The effects of inferring, verifying and memorizing on the retention of L2 word meanings. *Studies in Second Language Acquisition, 25,* 473–499.

Murison-Bowie, S. (1993). *MicroConcord manual.* Oxford, UK: Oxford University Press.

Muter, V., Hulme, C., Snowling, M., & Stevenson, J. (2004). Phonemes, rimes, vocabulary, and grammatical skills as foundations of early reading development: Evidence from a longitudinal study. *Developmental Psychology, 40,* 665–681.

Nagy, W. E. (1997). On the role of context in first- and second-language vocabulary learning. In N. Schmitt & M. McCarthy (Eds.), *Vocabulary: Description, acquisition and pedagogy* (pp. 64–83). New York: Cambridge University Press.

Nagy, W. E. (2005). Why vocabulary instruction needs to be long-term and comprehensive. In E. H. Hiebert & M. L. Kamil (Eds.), *Teaching and learning vocabulary: Bringing research to practice* (pp. 27–44). Mahwah, NJ: Erlbaum.

Nagy, W. E. (2006). On the role of context in first- and second-language vocabulary learning. In N. Schmitt & M. McCarthy (Eds.), *Vocabulary: Description, acquisition and pedagogy* (pp, 64–83). Cambridge, UK: Cambridge University Press.

Nagy, W. E., & Anderson, R. C. (1984). How many words are there in printed school English? *Reading Research Quarterly, 19,* 304–330.

Nagy, W. E., Anderson, R. C., & Herman, P. A. (1985). Learning words from context. *Reading Research Quarterly, 20,* 233–253.

Nagy, W. E., Anderson, R. C., & Herman, P. A. (1987). Learning word meanings from context during normal reading. *American Educational Research Journal, 24,* 237–270.

Nagy, W. E., Berninger, V. W., & Abbott, R. D. (2006). Contribution of morphology beyond phonology to literacy outcomes of upper elementary and middle-school students. *Journal of Educational Psychology, 98,* 134–147.

Nagy, W. E., Diakidoy, I., & Anderson, R. C. (1993). The acquisition of morphology: Learning the contribution of suffixes to the meanings of derivatives. *Journal of Reading Behavior, 25,* 150–170.

Nagy, W. E., & Herman, P. A. (1987). Breadth and depth of vocabulary knowledge: Implications for acquisition and instruction. In M. G. McKeown & M. Curtis (Eds.), *The nature of vocabulary acquisition* (pp. 19–36). Hillsdale, NJ: Erlbaum.

Nakamoto, J., Lindsey, K. A., & Manis, F. R. (2007). A cross-linguistic investigation of English language learners' reading comprehension in English and Spanish. *Scientific Studies of Reading, 12,* 351–371.

Nation, I. S. P. (1990). *Teaching and learning vocabulary.* Boston: Heinle & Heinle.

Nation, I. S. P. (2001). *Learning vocabulary in another language.* New York: Cambridge University Press.

Nation, I. S. P. (2006). How large a vocabulary is needed for reading and listening? *Canadian Modern Language Review, 63,* 59–82.

Nation, I. S. P. (2008). *Teaching vocabulary: Strategies and techniques.* Boston: Heinle.

Nation, I. S. P. (2009). Reading comprehension and vocabulary: What's the connection? In R. Wagner, C. Schatschneider, & C. Phythian-Sense (Eds.), *Beyond decoding: The behavioral and biological foundations of reading comprehension* (pp. 176–194). New York: Guilford Press.

Nation, I. S. P., & Gu, P. Y. (2007). *Focus on vocabulary.* Sydney, Australia: National Center for English Language Teaching and Research.

Nation, K., & Snowling, M. J. (2004). Beyond phonological skills: Broader language skills contribute to the development of reading. *Journal of Research on Reading, 27,* 342–356.

Nation, P., & Waring, R. (1997). Vocabulary size, text coverage and word lists. In N. Schmitt & M. McCarthy (Eds.), *Vocabulary: Description, acquisition and pedagogy* (pp. 6–19). New York: Cambridge University Press.

National Center on Response to Intervention. (2010). *Essential components of RtI-a closer look at response to intervention for a complete description of the elements of RtI service delivery models.* Retrieved from *www.rti4success.org/images/stories/pdfs/rtiessentialcomponents_051310.pdf.*

National Reading Panel. (2000). *Teaching children to read: An evidence-based assessment of the scientific research literature on reading and its implications for reading instruction.* Washington, DC: National Institute of Child Health and Human Development.

Nelson, J. R., & Marchand-Martella, N. E. (2005). *The multiple meaning vocabulary program: Level I.* Denver, CO: Sopris West.

Nelson, J. R., & Vadasy, P. J. (2007). *Early vocabulary connections: First words to know and decode.* Denver, CO: Sopris West.

Nelson, J. R., Vadasy, P. F., & Sanders, E. A. (2011). Efficacy of a Tier 2 supplemental root word vocabulary and decoding intervention with kindergarten Spanish-speaking English learners. *Journal of Literacy Research, 43,* 2, 184–211.

Newcomer, P. L., & Hammill, D. D. (2008a). *Test of Language Development—Intermediate* (4th ed.). Austin, TX: Pro-Ed.

Newcomer, P. L., & Hammill, D. D. (2008b). *Test of Language Development—Primary* (4th ed.). Austin, TX: Pro-Ed.

No Child Left Behind Act of 2001, Pub. L. 107-110. (2001). Retrieved from *www.ed.gov/policy/elsec/leg/esea02/107-110.pdf.*

Nunes, T., & Bryant, B. (2006). *Improving literacy by teaching morphemes*. London: Routledge.

Nunes, T., & Bryant, P. (2011). Morphemic approaches for teaching words. In R. E. O'Connnor & P. F. Vadasy (Eds.), *Handbook of reading interventions* (pp. 88–112). New York: Guilford Press.

Nunes, T., Bryant, P., & Olsson, J. (2003). Learning morphological and phonological spelling rules: An intervention study. *Scientific Studies of Reading, 7*, 289–307.

Ordonez, C. L., Carlo, M. S., Snow, C. E., & McLaughlin, B. (2002). Depth and breadth of vocabulary in two languages: Which vocabulary skills transfer? *Journal of Educational Psychology, 94*, 719–728.

Oullette, G. P. (2006). What's meaning got to do with it?: The role of vocabulary in word reading and reading comprehension. *Journal of Educational Psychology, 98*, 554–566.

Pany, D., Jenkins, J. R., & Schreck, J. (1982). Vocabulary instruction: Effects on word knowledge and reading comprehension. *Learning Disability Quarterly, 5*, 202–215.

Pellegrini, A. D., & Galda, L. (1982). The effects of thematic-fantasy play training on the development of children's story comprehension. *American Educational Research Journal, 19*, 443–452.

Penno, J. F., Wilkinson, I. A., & Moore, D. W. (2002). Vocabulary acquisition from teacher explanation and repeated listening to stories: Do they overcome the Matthew effect? *Journal of Educational Psychology, 94*, 23–33.

Perfetti, C. A. (1985). *Reading ability*. New York: Oxford University Press.

Phythian-Sence, C., & Wagner, R. K. (2007). Vocabulary acquisition: A primer. In R. Wagner, A. Muse, & K. Tannenbaum (Eds.), *Vocabulary acquisition: Implications for reading comprehension* (pp. 1–14). New York: Guilford Press.

Pigada, M., & Schmitt, N. (2006). Vocabulary acquisition from extensive reading: A case study. *Reading in a Foreign Language, 18*, 1–28.

Pinker, S. (1994). *The language instinct: How the mind creates language*. New York: Morrow.

Pollard-Durodola, S. D., & Simmons, D. C. (2009). The role of explicit instruction and instructional design in promoting phonemic awareness development and transfer from Spanish to English. *Reading and Writing Quarterly, 25*, 139–161.

Praninskas, J. (1972). *American University Word List*. London: Longman.

Pressley, M., Disney, L., & Anderson, K. (2007). Landmark vocabulary instructional research and the vocabulary instructional research that makes sense now. In R. K. Wagner, A. E. Muse, & K. R. Tannenbaum (Eds.), *Vocabulary acquisition: Implications for reading comprehension* (pp. 205–232). New York: Guilford Press.

Pressley, M., Levin, J. R., Kuiper, N. A., Bryant, S. L., & Michener, S. (1982). Mnemonic versus nonmnemonic vocabulary learning strategies: Additional comparisons. *Journal of Educational Psychology, 74*, 693–707.

Pressley, M., Levin, J. R., & McDaniel, M. A. (1987). Remembering versus inferring what a word means: Mnemonic and contextual approaches. In M. G. McKeown & M. E. Curtis (Eds.), *The nature of vocabulary acquisition* (pp. 107–127). Hillsdale, NJ: Erlbaum.

Proctor, C. P., Dalton, B., Uccelli, P., Mo, E., Snow, C. E., & Neugebauer, S. (2009). Improving comprehension online: Effects of deep vocabulary instruction with bilingual and monolingual fifth graders. *Reading and Writing: An Interdisciplinary Journal, 22*, 10.

Read, J. (2000). *Assessing vocabulary*. Cambridge, UK: Cambridge University Press.

Read, J. (2004). Research in teaching vocabulary. *Annual Review of Applied Linguistics, 24*, 146–161.

Reed, D. K. (2008). A synthesis of morphology interventions and effects on reading outcomes for students in grades K–12. *Learning Disabilities Research and Practice, 23*, 36–49.

Reese, L., Garnier, H., Gallimore, R., & Goldenberg, C. (2000). Longitudinal analysis of the antecedents of emergent Spanish literacy and middle-school English reading achievement of Spanish-speaking students. *American Educational Research Journal, 37*, 633–662.

Renandya, W. A., Rajan, B. R. S., & Jacob, G. M. (1999). Extensive reading with adult learners of English as a second language. *RELC Journal, 30*, 39–60.

Resnick, L. B. (1989). *Knowing, learning, and instruction*. Hillsdale, NJ: Erlbaum.

Richards, J. C. (1976). The role of vocabulary teaching. *TESOL Quarterly, 10*, 77–89.

Robbins, C., & Ehri, L. C. (1994). Reading storybooks to kindergartners helps them learn new vocabulary words. *Journal of Educational Psychology, 86*, 54–64.

Roberts, T. A. (2008). Home storybook reading in primary or second language with preschool children: Evidence of equal effectiveness for second-language vocabulary acquisition. *Reading Research Quarterly, 43*, 103–130.

Roberts, T. A. (2009). *No limits to literacy for preschool English learners*. Thousand Oaks, CA: Corwin.

Roberts, T. A., & Neal, H. (2003). Relationships among preschool English language learner's oral proficiency in English, instructional experience and literacy development. *Contemporary Educational Psychology, 29*, 283–311.

Rosenthal, J., & Ehri, L. C. (2008). The mnemonic value of orthography for vocabulary learning. *Journal of Educational Psychology, 100*, 175–191.

Rosenthal, J., & Ehri, L. C. (2011). Pronouncing new words aloud during the silent reading of text enhances fifth graders' memory for vocabulary words and their spellings. *Reading and Writing: An Interdisciplinary Journal, 24*, 921–950.

Russell, D. H., & Saadeh, I. Q. (1962). Qualitative levels in children's vocabularies. *Journal of Educational Psychology, 53*, 170–174.

Ryan, A. (1997). Learning the orthographical form of L2 vocabulary—a receptive and a productive process. In N. Schmitt & M. McCarthy (Eds.), *Vocabulary: Description, acquisition and pedagogy* (pp. 181–198). Cambridge, UK: Cambridge University Press.

Rydland, V., Aukrust, V. G., & Fulland, H. (2010). How word decoding, vocabulary, and prior topic knowledge predict reading comprehension: A study of language-minority students in Norwegian fifth grade classrooms. *Reading and Writing: An Interdisciplinary Journal*. doi 10.1007/s11145-010-9279-2

Sadoski, M. (2005). A dual coding view of vocabulary learning. *Reading and Writing Quarterly, 21*, 221–238.

Saragi, T., Nation, I. S. P., & Meister, G. F. (1987). Vocabulary learning and reading. *System, 6*, 72–78.

Scarborough, H. (2001). Connecting early language and literacy to later reading (dis)abilities: Evidence, theory, and practice. In S. B. Neuman & D. Dickinson (Eds.), *Handbook of early literacy research* (pp. 97–110). New York: Guilford Press.

Scarcella, R. (2003). *Academic English: A conceptual framework*. Los Angeles: University of California Language Minority Research Institute.

Scarcella, R., & Zimmerman, C. (1998). ESL student performance on a text of academic lexicon. *Studies in Second Language Acquisition, 9*, 201–220.

Scheele, A. F., Leseman, P. P. M., & Mayo, A. Y. (2010). The home language environment of monolingual and bilingual children and their language proficiency. *Applied Psycholinguistics, 31*, 117–140.

Scherer, N. J., & Olswang, L. B. (1984). Role of mothers' expansions in stimulating children's language production. *Journal of Speech and Hearing Research, 27*, 387–396.

Schmitt, N. (2008). Review article: Instructed second language vocabulary learning. *Language Teaching Research, 12*, 329–363.

Schmitt, N., & Zimmerman, C. B. (2002). Derivative word forms: What do learners know? *TESOL Quarterly, 36*, 145–171.

Scholfield, P. (2006). Vocabulary reference works in foreign language learning. In N. Schmitt & M. McCarthy (Eds.), *Vocabulary: Description, acquisition and pedagogy* (pp. 279–302). Cambridge, UK: Cambridge University Press.

Schwanenflugel, P. J., Stahl, S. A., & McFalls, E. L. (1997). Partial word knowledge and vocabulary growth during reading comprehension. *Journal of Literacy Research, 29*, 531–553.

Scruggs, T. E., & Mastropieri, M. A. (2000). The effectiveness of mnemonic instruction for students with learning and behavior problems: An update and research synthesis. *Journal of Behavioral Education, 10*, 163–173.

Scruggs, T. E., Mastropieri, M. A., Levin, J. R., & Gaffney, J. (1985). Facilitating the acquisition of science facts in disabled students. *American Educational Research Journal, 22*, 575–586.

Semel, E. M., Wiig, E. H., & Secord, W. A. (2003). *Clinical Evaluation of Language Fundamentals 4—Screening Test* (CELF-4). San Antonio, TX: Harcourt Assessment.

Semel, E., Wiig, E., & Secord, W. (2004). *Clinical Evaluation of Language Fundamentals—Preschool, 2nd edition*. San Antonio, TX: Harcourt Assessment.

Sénéchal, M. (1997). The differential effect of storybook reading on preschoolers' acquisition of expressive and receptive vocabulary. *Journal of Child Language, 24*, 123–138.

Sénéchal, M., & Cornell, E. H. (1993). Vocabulary acquisition through shared reading experiences. *Reading Research Quarterly, 28*, 360–374.

Shanahan, T., & Beck, I. L. (2006). Effective literacy teaching for English-language learners. In D. August & T. Shanahan (Eds.), *Developing literacy in second-language learners: Report of the National Literacy Panel on language-minority children and youth* (pp. 415–488). Mahwah, NJ: Erlbaum.

Shu, H., Anderson, R. C., & Zhang, H. (1995). Incidental learning of word meanings while reading: A Chinese and American cross-cultural study. *Reading Research Quarterly, 30*, 76–95.

Silverman, R. (2007a). A comparison of three methods of vocabulary instruction during read-alouds in kindergarten. *The Elementary School Journal, 108*, 97–113.

Silverman, R. (2007b). Vocabulary development of English-language and English-only learners in kindergarten. *The Elementary School Journal, 107*, 365–383.

Silverman, R., & Crandell, J. D. (2010). Vocabulary practices in prekindergarten and kindergarten classrooms. *Reading Research Quarterly, 45*, 318–340.

Silverman, R., & Hines, S. (2009). The effects of multimedia-enhanced instruction on the vocabulary of English-language learners and non-English-language learners in prekindergarten through second grade. *Journal of Educational Psychology, 101*, 305–314.

Snellings, P., van Gelderen, A., & de Glopper, K. (2002). Lexical retrieval: An aspect of fluent second language production that can be enhanced. *Language Learning, 52*, 723–754.

Snow, C. E. (2010). Academic language and the challenge of reading for learning about science. *Science, 328*, 450–452.

Snow, C. E., Lawrence, J. F., & White, C. (2009). Generating knowledge of academic language among urban middle school students. *Journal of Research on Educational Effectiveness, 2*, 325–344.

Snow, C. E., Tabors, P. O., Nicholson, P. E., & Kurland, B. F. (1995). SHELL: Oral language and early literacy in kindergarten and first grade children. *Journal of Research in Childhood Education, 10,* 37–47.

Sokmen, A. (1997). Current trends in teaching second language vocabulary. In N. Schmitt & M. McCarthy (Eds.), *Vocabulary: Description, acquisition, and pedagogy* (pp. 237–257). New York: Cambridge University Press.

Solso, R. L., & Juel, C. L. (1980). Positional frequency and versatility of bigrams for two- through nine-letter English words. *Behavior Research Methods and Instrumentation, 12,* 297–343.

Sparks, R., Ganschow, L., Patton, J., Artzer, M., Siebenhar, D., & Plageman, M. (1997). Prediction of proficiency in a foreign language. *Journal of Educational Psychology, 89,* 549–561.

Stahl, S. A. (1986). Three principles of effective vocabulary instruction. *Journal of Reading, 29,* 662–668.

Stahl, S. A. (2005). Four problems with teaching word meanings (and what to do to make vocabulary an integral part of instruction). In E. H. Hiebert & M. L. Kamil (Eds.), *Teaching and learning vocabulary: Bringing research to practice* (pp. 95–114). Mahwah, NJ: Erlbaum.

Stahl, S. A., & Fairbanks, M. M. (1986). The effects of vocabulary instruction: A model-based meta-analysis. *Review of Educational Research, 56,* 72–110.

Stahl, S. A., & Nagy, W. E. (2006). *Teaching word meanings.* Mahwah, NJ: Erlbaum.

Stanovich, K. E. (1986). Matthew effects in reading: Some consequences of individual differences in the acquisition of literacy. *Reading Research Quarterly, 21,* 360–407.

Stanovich, K. E., West, R. F., Cunningham, A. E., Cipielski, J., & Siddiqui, S. (1996). The role of inadequate print exposure as a determinant of reading comprehension problems. In C. Cornoldi & J. Oakhill (Eds.), *Reading comprehension disabilities* (pp. 15–32). Hillsdale, NJ: Erlbaum.

Sternberg, R. J. (1985). *Beyond IQ: A triarchic theory of human intelligence.* Cambridge, UK: Cambridge University Press.

Sticht, T. G., Beck, L. J., Hauke, R. N., Kleiman, G. M., & James, J. H. (1974). *Auding and reading: A developmental model.* Alexandria, VA: Human Resources Research Organization.

Storch, S. A., & Whitehurst, G. J. (2002). Oral language and code-related precursors to reading: Evidence from a longitudinal structural model. *Developmental Psychology, 38,* 934–947.

Stuart, M. (2004). Getting ready for reading: A follow-up study of inner city second language learners at the end of Key Stage 1. *British Journal of Educational Psychology, 74,* 15–36.

Swanborn, M. S. L., & de Glopper, K. (1999). Incidental word learning while reading: A meta-analysis. *Review of Educational Research, 69,* 261–285.

Tabors, P. O., Roach, K. A., & Snow, C. E. (2001). Home language and literacy environment final results. In D. K. Dickinson & P. O. Tabors (Eds.), *Beginning literacy with language* (pp. 111–138). Baltimore, MD: Brookes.

Thorndike, E. L., & Lorge, I. (1944). *The Teacher's Word Book of 30,000 Words.* New York: Columbia University, Teachers College.

Tsesmeli, S. N., & Seymour, P. H. K. (2008). The effects of training of morphological structure on spelling derived words by dyslexic adolescents. *British Journal of Psychology, 100,* 565–592.

Umbel, V. M., Pearson, B. Z., Fernandez, M. C., & Oller, D. K. (1992). Measuring bilingual children's receptive vocabularies. *Child Development, 63,* 1012–1020.

Vadasy, P. F., & Nelson, J. R. (2008). *Early vocabulary connections: Important words to know and spell.* Denver, CO: Sopris West.

Vadasy, P. F., Nelson, J. R., & Sanders, E. A. (2011). Longer-term effects of a Tier 2 kindergarten intervention for English learners. *Remedial and Special Education.* doi.10.1177/0741932511420739

van Kleeck, A., Stahl, S. A., & Bauer, E. B. (Eds.). (2003). *On reading books to children: Parents and teachers.* Mahwah, NJ: Erlbaum.

Vaughn, S., Linan-Thompson, S., & Hickman, P. (2003). Response to instruction as a means of identifying students with reading/learning disabilities. *Exceptional Children, 69,* 391–409.

Vaughn, S., Martinez, L. R., Linan-Thompson, S., Reutebuch, C. K., Carlson, C. D., & Francis, D. J. (2009). Enhancing social studies vocabulary and comprehension for seventh-grade English language learners: Findings from two experimental studies. *Journal of Research on Educational Effectiveness, 2,* 297–324.

Veit, D. T., Scruggs, T. E., & Mastropieri, M. A. (1986). Extended mnemonic instruction with learning disabled students. *Journal of Educational Psychology, 78,* 300–308.

Verhallen, M. J. A. J., & Bus, A. G. (2010). Low-income immigrant pupils learning vocabulary through digital picture storybooks. *Journal of Educational Psychology, 102,* 54–61.

Verhoeven, L. (1990). Acquisition of reading in a second language. *Reading Research Quarterly, 25,* 90–114.

Verhoeven, L. (2000). Components in early second language reading and spelling. *Scientific Studies of Reading, 4,* 313–330.

Verhoeven, L. (2007). Early bilingualism, language transfer, and phonological awareness. *Applied Psycholinguistics, 28,* 425–439.

Verhoeven, L., & Van Leeuwe, J. (2008). Prediction and the development of reading comprehension: A longitudinal study. *Applied Cognitive Psychology, 22,* 407–423.

Vermeer, A. (2001). Breadth and depth of vocabulary in relation to L1/L2 acquisition and frequency of input. *Applied Psycholinguistics, 22,* 217–234.

Walberg, H. J., & Tsai, S. (1983). Matthew effects in education. *American Educational Research Journal, 20,* 359–373.

Walberg, H. J., & Tsai, S. (1984). Reading achievement and diminishing returns to time. *Journal of Educational Psychology, 76,* 442–451.

Wallace, G., & Hammill, D. D. (2002). *Comprehensive Receptive and Expressive Vocabulary Test, second edition* (CREVT-2). Los Angeles: Western Psychological Services.

Wasik, B. A., & Bond, M. A. (2001). Beyond the pages of a book: Interactive book reading and language development in preschool classrooms. *Journal of Educational Psychology, 93,* 243–250.

Wasik, B. A., Bond, M. A., & Hindman, A. (2006). The effects of a language and literacy intervention on Head Start children and teachers. *Journal of Educational Psychology, 98,* 63–74.

Webster's third new international dictionary. (1963). Springfield, MA: Merriam.

Wells, G. (1985). *Language development in the preschool years.* Cambridge, UK: Cambridge University Press.

West, M. (1953). *A general service list of English words.* London: Longman, Green.

What Works Clearinghouse. (2006). *Vocabulary improvement program for English language learners and their classmates.* Washington, DC: U.S. Department of Education, Institute of Education Sciences. (Revised October 30, 2006). Retrieved from *ies.ed.gov/ncee/wwc/reports/english_lang/vip/.*

Wheeler, P. (1983). Context-related age characteristics in mothers' speech: Joint book reading. *Journal of Child Language, 10,* 259–263.

White, T. G., Graves, M. F., & Slater, W. H. (1990). Growth of reading vocabulary in diverse elementary schools: Decoding and word meaning. *Journal of Educational Psychology, 82,* 281–290.

White, T. G., Power, M. A., & White, S. (1989). Morphological analysis: Implications for teaching and understanding vocabulary growth. *Reading Research Quarterly, 24,* 283–304.

White, T. G., Sowell, J., & Yanagihara, A. (1989). Teaching elementary students to use word-part clues. *The Reading Teacher, 42,* 302–308.

Whitehurst, G. J. (2002). *Research on teacher preparation and professional development.* White House Conference on Preparing Tomorrow's Teachers, March 5. Washington, DC. Retrieved from *www.ed.gov/admins/tchrqual/learn/preparingteachersconference/whitehurst.html.*

Whitehurst, G. J., Arnold, D. S., Epstein, J. N., Angell, A. L., Smith, M., & Fischel, J. E. (1994a). A picture book reading intervention in day care and home for children from low-income families. *Developmental Psychology, 30,* 697–699.

Whitehurst, G. J., Epstein, J. N., Angell, A. L., Payne, A. C., Crone, D. A. & Fishcel, J. E. (1994b). Outcomes of an emergent literacy intervention in Head Start. *Journal of Educational Psychology, 86,* 542–555.

Whitehurst, G. J., Falco, F., Lonigan, C. J., Fischel, J. E., Valdez-Menchaca, M. C., & Caulfield, M. (1988). Accelerating language development through picture-book reading. *Developmental Psychology, 24,* 552–558.

Williams, K. T. (2007). *Expressive Vocabulary Test, second edition.* Circle Pines, MN: AGS.

Woodcock, R. W., McGrew, K. S., & Werder, J. K. (1994). *Woodcock–McGrew–Werder Mini-Battery of Achievement.* Chicago: Riverside.

Woodcock, R. W. (1998). *Woodcock Reading Mastery Tests—Revised—Normative Update: Examiners manual.* Circle Pines, MN: American Guidance Service.

Wysocki, K., & Jenkins, J. R. (1987). Deriving word meanings through morphological generalization. *Reading Research Quarterly, 22,* 66–81.

Xue, G., & Nation, I. S. P. (1984). A university word list. *Language Learning and Communication, 3,* 215–229.

Zeno, S. M., Ivens, S. H., Millard, R. T., & Duvvuri, R. (1995). *The Educator's Word Frequency Guide.* Brewster, NY: Touchstone Applied Science.

Zipoli, R. P., Coyne, M. D., & McCoach, D. B. (2011). Enhancing vocabulary intervention for kindergarten students: Strategic integration of semantically related and embedded word review. *Remedial and Special Education, 32,* 131–143.

Index

An *f* following a page number indicates a figure; a *t* following a page number indicates a table. Page numbers in bold refer to chapter vocabulary words.

Academic vocabulary
   decisions regarding teaching and learning vocabulary and, 43
   instructional implications and, 36, 101
   language-minority students and, 154–155, 160
   overview, 32–33, 94
   Word Generation program and, 94–100
   word lists and, 53–56, 54*t*, 56*t*
Academic Word List, 32–33, 55–56, 56*t*, 61*f*, 159, 165
Academic words, **38**, **86**
   instructional implications and, 101
   semantic mapping and, 105
   Word Generation program and, 94–100
Affix, **16**
   derivations and, 21–23
   language-minority students and, 152
   list of common affixes and their meanings, 22*t*
   overview, 20
The American Heritage Word Frequency Book (Carroll, Davies, & Richman, 1971), 49–50
Analytical questions, 70. *see also* Questioning
Articulation problems, 19
Assessment, **120**
   conceptions of vocabulary knowledge and, 123–130, 123*t*, 125*f*, 126*f*, 127*f*, 129*f*
   dimensions of, 125–127, 126*f*
   examples of vocabulary and language skills measures, 131–144
   language-minority students and, 155, 164–165
   overview, 121–122, 144–145
   technology-based measures, 143–144
Associations, word. *see* Word associations
At-risk students, 17

B

Background knowledge, 6
Bankson Language Test—Second Edition (BLT-2), 142
Basal reading series, 39–40
Base word, **38**
Benchmark, **120**
Breadth, **121**
   assessment and, 124–125, 125*f*, 164–165
   language-minority students and, 147, 155–156, 164–165
Bringing Words to Life (Beck et al., 2002), 91–92
The Brown Corpus of Standard American English (Kucera & Francis, 1967), 52
Building Background Knowledge for Academic Achievement (Marzano, 2004), 58–59, 59*t*, 61*f*

C

CBM Maze, 129–130, 145
Clinical Evaluation of Language Fundamentals—Fourth Edition (CELF-4), 139–140
Clinical Evaluation of Language Fundamentals—Preschool, Second Edition (CELF-P2), 140–141
COBUILD (Collins Birmingham University International Language Database) dictionaries, 33–34, 91, 114–115
Cognates, **146**, 153–154
Collocation, **16**
   conceptions of vocabulary knowledge and, 123*t*
   instructional principles and, 36
   overview, 9–10, 29–31

Comprehension
  overview, 4–5
  rich and robust vocabulary instruction and, 89–90, 101
  vocabulary development and, 2–3
  vocabulary knowledge and, 6–7
Comprehensive Assessment of Spoken Language (CASL), 137–138
Comprehensive Receptive and Expressive Vocabulary Test—Second Edition (CREVT02), 135–136
Computer-based assessment measures, 143–144, 155–156
Concordance, **16**, **146**, 161, 162*f*
Construct, **120**
Context, **102**
Context independence–context dependence assessment measures, 126–127, 127*f*, 144
Context use approaches
  dictionary entries and, 115–116
  overview, 104, 107–113
  research on, 112–113
  sources of vocabulary growth and, 10–11
  vocabulary development and, 4
Contexts and situations for target words, 90–91
Contextual analysis strategies, 104, 111–112
Corpus, **38**, 44–60, 44*f*, 48*t*, 51*t*, 54*t*, 56*t*, 58*t*, 59*t*, **146**
Corpus of Contemporary American English, 60
Coverage, **38**
  decisions regarding teaching and learning vocabulary and, 41–43, 42*f*, 43*t*
  word lists and, 47–52, 48*t*, 51*t*
Creating Robust Vocabulary (Beck et al., 2008), 91–93
Criterion-referenced, **120**
Curriculum-based measurement (CBM), 128–130, 129*f*, 145

D

Decisions regarding teaching and learning vocabulary. *see* Words for teaching and learning vocabulary
Decoding skills, 2
Deep processing, 13
Definitions. *see also* Dictionaries
  overview, 114
  rich and robust vocabulary instruction and, 90
  Word Generation program and, 96–97
  word meanings and, 27
Depth, **121**
  assessment and, 124–125, 125*f*, 165
  of instruction, 13
  instructional principles and, 15
  language-minority students and, 147, 155–156, 165
  overview, 6, 29
Depth of processing hypothesis, 13
Derivations, **16**, 20, 21–23, 22*t*, 33
Diagnostic, **120**, 122. *see also* Assessment

Diagnostic measures, 130, 130–131, 144–145
Dialogic reading. *see also* Reading aloud
  Early Vocabulary Connections (EVC) intervention, 76–82
  interactive book reading, 66–68
  overview, 64–66, 84*t*
  repeated interactive read-alouds, 68–71
DIBELS WUF measure. *see* Dynamic Indicators of Basic Early Literacy Skills, Word Use Fluency (DIBELS WUF)
Dictionaries. *see also* Definitions
  decisions regarding teaching and learning vocabulary and, 40
  instructional principles and, 36
  language-minority students and, 157–158
  overview, 33–35, 113–116, 114*t*
Dictionary definitions/entries, 27, 115–116. *see also* Definitions
Direct instruction, 12–14, 15. *see also* Explicit instruction
Discrete–embedded assessment measures, 126, 126*f*, 144
Distal vocabulary knowledge, 89–90. *see also* Vocabulary knowledge
Dolch list, 31
Dynamic Indicators of Basic Early Literacy Skills, Word Use Fluency (DIBELS WUF), 128–129, 145

E

Early Vocabulary Connections (EVC) intervention
  enhancing student success and, 81–82
  overview, 82–85, 83*t*–84*t*, 84*t*
  reading aloud and, 76–82, 77*f*
EasyCBM Vocabulary, 143–144
The Educator's Word Frequency Guide (Zeno, Ivens, Millard, & Duvvuri, 1995), 47–49, 48*t*, 61*f*
Electronic dictionaries, 35. *see also* Dictionaries
eMeasures of Root Word and Academic Vocabulary Growth, 143–144
Embedded vocabulary assessment measures, 126, 126*f*
English language learners. *see* Language-minority; Second-language learners
Evaluation, 66. *see also* Assessment
Evocative instructional techniques, 63, 64, 82
Explicit instruction. *see also* Direct instruction
  language-minority students and, 148, 158–161
  overview, 12–14
  word meanings and, 27
Expressive One-Word Picture Vocabulary Test— Revised (EOWPVT-R), 135
Expressive vocabulary
  examples of vocabulary and language skills measures, 131–132, 134–137
  vocabulary development and, 3
Expressive Vocabulary Test—Second Edition (EVT-2), 134–135
Extended instruction, 71–73. *see also* Reading aloud

F

Fast mapping, 8, 149
Figures of speech, 37
Form, **39**
    conceptions of vocabulary knowledge and, 123*t*
    receptive and productive functions of word usage and, 9
Frequency, **39**. *see also* High-frequency words
    conceptions of vocabulary knowledge and, 123*t*
    decisions regarding teaching and learning vocabulary and, 41–43, 42*f*, 43*t*
    instructional principles and, 36
    language-minority students and, 37
    overview, 31–32
    word lists and, 47–52, 48*t*, 51*t*

G

General Service List (GSL) of English words, 46
A General Service List of English Words (West, 1953), 51–52
Gloss, **146**, 157–158
Gradient models of word knowledge, 124–125
Grammar, **16**
    conceptions of vocabulary knowledge and, 123*t*
    dictionaries and, 33
    language-minority students and, 36–37
    word grammar, 24–25, 35, 36–37

H

Headword, **39**
High-frequency words. *see also* Frequency
    academic vocabulary, 32–33
    explicit instruction and, 13
    idioms as, 30–31
    language-minority students and, 37
    morphological analysis and, 108
    overview, 31–32
    rich and robust vocabulary instruction and, 89
    word lists and, 44–60, 44*f*, 48*t*, 51*t*, 54*t*, 56*t*, 58*t*, 59*t*, 60
    word meanings and, 26
Homograph, 28
Homonym, **16**, 37

I

Idiom, **16**
    instructional principles and, 36
    language-minority students and, 37
    overview, 29–31
Imagery, 117–118
Incidental learning
    instructional principles and, 15
    language-minority students and, 156–158
    overview, 17–18
    vocabulary knowledge and, 6–7, 10–11
Incremental learning, 6–7
Individuals with Disabilities Education Improvement Act of 2004 (IDEA), 122
Inflections, **17**, 20, 23–24
Instruction. *see also* Direct instruction; Explicit instruction; Supplementary instruction; Vocabulary instruction
    decisions regarding, 40–43, 42*f*, 43*t*, 60–61, 61*f*
    instructional principles, 14–15
    overview, 17–18
    word lists and, 56–59, 58*t*, 59*t*, 60–61, 61*f*
    word properties and, 35–37
Instrumentalist hypothesis, 89
Intentional word learning, 158–161. *see also* Explicit instruction
Interactive book reading. *see also* Reading aloud
    Early Vocabulary Connections (EVC) intervention, 76–82
    overview, 66–68, 84*t*
    repeated interactive read-alouds, 68–71
Interventions. *see* Early Vocabulary Connections (EVC) intervention; Reading aloud; Response to intervention
Irregular word features, 37

K

Keyword methods, **102**, 104, 117–119
Knowledge hypothesis, 104

L

Language comprehension, 4. *see also* Comprehension
Language-minority, **1**. *see also* Second-language learners
    assessment and, 164–165
    dictionary use and, 115–116
    direct instruction and, 14
    intentional word learning, 158–161
    keyword methods and, 117–118
    morphology and, 110
    overview, 146–148, 166
    preschool instruction and, 148–151
    research and, 154–155, 161*f*
    school-age instruction, 151–165, 161*f*
    sequence in which words are acquired, 44
    spelling and, 20
    vocabulary development and, 3
    word features and, 36–37
Learner dictionaries, 114–115, 114*t*. *see also* Dictionaries
Learning disabilities
    mnemonic techniques for remembering word meanings and, 118–119
    morphology and, 110
    overview, 17

Lexical, **39**
Lexical restructuring hypothesis, 3–4
Lexicon, **1**, 6, **17**
Listening comprehension, 4. *see also* Comprehension
Living Word Vocabulary (LWV), 159
The Living Word Vocabulary (Dale & O'Rourke, 1981), 31, 53, 61*f*

M

Matthew effect, 7
Meaning. *see also* Word meanings
    collocation instruction and, 29–30
    conceptions of vocabulary knowledge and, 123*t*
    receptive and productive functions of word usage and, 9
    rich and robust vocabulary instruction and, 91
Memory, 116–119
Mental Measurement Yearbook series, 131
Metalinguistic awareness, **1**
Mnemonic, **102**
Mnemonic techniques
    overview, 104, 116–119
    research on, 118–119
    SCANR mnemonic, 112
Morpheme, **17**, 20, 21, **102**
Morphological, **102**
Morphological analysis, 108–110, 151–152
Morphology, 20–21, 151–152
Most Common 100 Words in English, 31
Multicomponent approaches
    language-minority students and, 161, 163
    preschool language-minority students and, 150–151
Multiple Meaning Vocabulary Program, 125*f*
Multiple meanings, 28. *see also* Word meanings

N

No Child Left Behind Act of 2001, 122

O

Open-ended question prompts, 65. *see also* Prompts
Oral and Written Language Scales (OWLS), 136–137
Oral language experiences, 2, 3, 10–11
Orthographic features, 18–20, 147
Outcome, **120**
Outcome measures, 122, 130–131. *see also* Assessment

P

Parts of speech, 21–23, 24–25. *see also* Grammar
Peabody Picture Vocabulary Test—Fourth Edition (PPVT-4), 132–133

PEER sequence (Prompts, Evaluates, Expands, and Repeats), 65–66
Phonemes, 4
Phonological awareness, **1**, 2, 18–20, 147
Phonologically transparent and opaque derived words, 108
Picture book read-aloud interventions. *see* Reading aloud
Polyseme, **17**, 37, 147
Prefix, **17**
    derivations and, 21–23
    morphological analysis and, 109–110
    overview, 20
Preschool instruction, 148–151, 166
Preteaching, 90–91
Preventive interventions. *see* Tier One intervention
Professional development
    rich and robust vocabulary instruction and, 93–94
    Word Generation program and, 98–99
Progress monitoring, **120**. *see also* Assessment
    language-minority students and, 165
    overview, 122, 127–130, 129*f*
    technology-based measures, 143–144
Prompts. *see also* Questioning
    PEER sequence (Prompts, Evaluates, Expands, and Repeats) and, 65
    repeated interactive read-alouds and, 70
Pronunciation
    dictionaries and, 33
    morphology and, 20–21
    overview, 18–19
Proximal vocabulary knowledge, 89–90. *see also* Vocabulary knowledge

Q

Questioning. *see also* Prompts
    interactive book reading and, 68
    repeated interactive read-alouds and, 70

R

Reading aloud
    dialogic reading, 64–66
    diverse learners and, 74
    extended instruction, 71–73
    integrating picture book and storybook interventions, 73–74
    interactive book reading, 66–68
    overview, 63–64, 82–85, 83*t*–84*t*, 84*t*
    preschool language-minority students and, 149–151
    repeated interactive read-alouds, 68–71
    response to intervention and, 74–82
    sources of vocabulary growth, 11
Reading comprehension. *see also* Comprehension
    instructional principles and, 15
    overview, 4–5
    rich and robust vocabulary instruction and, 89–90

Reading development
　language-minority students and, 157
　overview, 2
　vocabulary development and, 3
Recall question prompts, 65. *see also* Prompts
Receptive functions of word usage, 9
Receptive One-Word Picture Vocabulary Test (ROWPVT), 133–134
Receptive vocabulary, 131–134, 135–137
Reflection, 68. *see also* Prompts
Reliability, **121**
Repeated interactive read-alouds, 68–71, 84*t*
Repetition
　explicit instruction and, 13–14
　PEER sequence (Prompts, Evaluates, Expands, and Repeats) and, 66
Response to intervention, **62**. *see also* Tiers
　assessment and, 144–145
　overview, 74–82
　progress monitoring and, 127–130, 129*f*
　screening and, 121–122, 127–130, 129*f*
Rich and robust vocabulary instruction, 88–94, 100, 101, 103. *see also* Vocabulary instruction
Root word, **1**, **17**, **39**
　language-minority students and, 152, 159
　overview, 20
　word lists and, 60

S

Scaffolding, 25
School-age second-language instruction, 151–165, 161*f*, 166
Screening, **121**, 121–122, 127–130, 129*f*, 143–144. *see also* Assessment
Second-language learners. *see also* Language-minority
　assessment and, 164–165
　collocation instruction and, 29–30
　dictionary use and, 115–116
　keyword methods and, 117–118
　morphology and, 110
　overview, 17, 103, 166
　research and, 154–155, 161*f*
　sequence in which words are acquired, 44
　word features and, 36–37
Selective–comprehensive assessment measures, 126, 144
Semantic, **39**, **102**
Semantic approaches to vocabulary instruction, 104–107
Semantic awareness, **1**
Semantic clues, 111–112
Semantic depth, 148
Semantic feature analysis, **102**, 106–107
Semantic mapping, 97, **102**, 104–105
Sentence Completion activity
　Early Vocabulary Connections (EVC) intervention, 79–80, 83*t*

rich and robust vocabulary instruction and. *see* Word associations
"Simple view" model of reading, 4–5
Small-group instruction, 75
Spelling
　Early Vocabulary Connections (EVC) intervention, 78, 83*t*
　morphology and, 20–21
　overview, 19–20
　pronunciation and, 18–19
　teaching spelling patterns and rules, 23
Standard protocol interventions, **62**, 74–82
Standardized measure, **121**
Storybook read-aloud interventions. *see* Reading aloud
Strategy instruction
　language-minority students and, 152
　Word Generation program and, 96
Suffix, **17**, 20, 21–23
Supplementary instruction, 17. *see also* Instruction
Synonyms, **17**
Syntactic awareness, **2**
Syntactic clues
　contextual analysis and, 111–112
　language-minority students and, 147
Syntax, **17**

T

The Teacher's Word Book of 30,000 Words (Thorndike & Lorge, 1944), 50–51, 51*t*
Technology-based assessment measures, 143–144, 155–156
Test of Language Development—Intermediate, Fourth Edition (TOLD-I:4), 139
Test of Language Development—Primary, Fourth Edition (TOLD-P:4), 138
Test of Narrative Language (TNL), 141
Tests in Print website, 131
Tier One intervention. *see also* Tiers
　dialogic reading, 64–66
　overview, 75
　reading aloud and, 63–64
　rich and robust vocabulary instruction and, 88–94
　semantic approaches to, 104–107
　Word Generation program and, 94–100
Tier One words, 89. *see also* High-frequency words
Tier Two intervention. *see also* Tiers
　Early Vocabulary Connections (EVC) intervention, 76–82, 77*f*
　overview, 75
　screening and, 121–122
Tier Two words, **86**
　instructional implications and, 101
　language-minority students and, 147
　rich and robust vocabulary instruction and, 89–93
Tier Three intervention, 75. *see also* Tiers

Tiers. *see also* Response to intervention; Tier One words; Tier Two words
　decisions regarding teaching and learning vocabulary and, 41–43, 42f, 43t
　instructional principles and, 36
　overview, 32, 75
Tokens, **39**

U

Universal screening, 121–122, 127–130, 129f. *see also* Assessment
University Word List (Xue & Nation, 1984), 53–54, 54t
Usage, 9

V

Validity, **121**
Verbal efficiency theory, 89
Vocabulary breadth, **121**, 124–125, 125f. *see also* Breadth
Vocabulary depth, **121**, 124–125, 125f. *see also* Depth
Vocabulary development, 2, 2–4, 3t, 10–14
Vocabulary instruction. *see also* Instruction
　context use approaches, 107–113
　instructional principles, 14–15
　language-minority students and, 148–165, 162f
　Matthew effect and, 7
　overview, 5–10, 12–14, 87–88, 100
　preschool language-minority students and, 148–151
　rich and robust vocabulary instruction, 88–94
　semantic approaches to, 104–107
　Word Generation program, 94–100
Vocabulary knowledge
　conceptions of, 123–130, 123t, 125f, 126f, 127f, 129f
　overview, 2–3, 5–10, 86–88
　proximal and distal vocabulary knowledge, 89–90
Vocabulary matching, 129–130, 129f

W

<u>Wh</u>-question prompts, 65, 70. *see also* Prompts
Woodcock Reading Mastery Tests—Revised—Normative Update (WRMT-R/NU), 142–143
Word associations
　conceptions of vocabulary knowledge and, 123t
　rich and robust vocabulary instruction and, 90
Word chunks, 29–31. *see also* Collocation; Idiom
Word family, **2**, **39**
　decisions regarding teaching and learning vocabulary and, 40
　overview, 18
　word lists and, 46
Word form, 18–20, 35
Word frequency. *see also* Frequency; High-frequency words
　instructional principles and, 36
　language-minority students and, 37
　overview, 31–32
Word Generation program
　instructional implications and, 101
　language-minority students and, 161
　overview, 94–100, 103
　professional development and, 98–99
　research on, 100
　sample weekly schedule, 99–100
Word grammar. *see also* Grammar
　instructional principles and, 35
　language-minority students and, 36–37
　overview, 24–25
Word knowledge, 7–10
Word lists
　development of, 44–46, 44f
　instructional implications and, 60–61, 61f
　overview, 46–60, 48t, 51t, 54t, 56t, 58t, 59t
Word meanings
　Early Vocabulary Connections (EVC) intervention, 78–79, 83t
　instructional principles and, 35
　mnemonic techniques for remembering, 116–119
　multiple meanings, 28
　overview, 26–27
　pronunciation and, 19
　spelling and, 19–20
　teaching, 12–14
Word origins, 33
Word phrases, 33
Word structure, 20–24, 22t, 35
Word Zones (www.textproject.org), 57–58, 58t, 61f
Word-level context clues, 107–108
Words for teaching and learning vocabulary
　basal reading series and, 39–40
　decisions regarding, 40–43, 42f, 43t
　language-minority students and, 159–160
　rich and robust vocabulary instruction and, 89–93
　sequence in which words are acquired, 43–44, 43t
　word lists, 44–60, 44f, 48t, 51t, 54t, 56t, 58t, 59t
Words Worth Teaching (Biemiller, 2009), 56–57, 61f
Written form
　conceptions of vocabulary knowledge and, 123t
　language-minority students and, 163–164
WUF. *see* Dynamic Indicators of Basic Early Literacy Skills, Word Use Fluency (DIBELS WUF)